The *Poetic Journey* of

SELF-
LEADERSHIP

LEADERSHIP DEVELOPMENT ALONG
STAGES OF PSYCHOLOGICAL GROWTH

Endorsements

There is an African saying that the road is made by walking it. This riveting and timely and appropriate publication, takes us on a journey of self-discovery as we master the art of leadership. I commend the book to all for we are all leaders and we must drink from each other's journeys.

Archbishop Thabo Makgoba, Archbishop of Cape Town and
Chancellor of the University of the Western Cape

This book focuses on the self and acknowledges that leadership is a journey and not a destination. Self-leadership is about knowing who you are, work on your personal growth and become the leader you wish to be. This book gave me a different perspective of leadership by weaving through poetic expressions to bring life and self to the leadership discourse.

Advocate Bience Gawanas, Former UN Under Secretary General
and Special Adviser on Africa

The link between life stages, art as a catalyst of self-discovery and leadership styles is absolutely brilliant. This book will touch the depth of your spirit, will charm with its sensibility and kindness. Opening your soul, will offer the insights able to challenge the hard-coded self, shifting the entrenched perspectives.

The complexity of emotions and the richness of the 'aha moments' perfect the elegance of the reading. It is life-changing through a better life-understanding.

Mihai Bonca, Brand Architects, Marketing & Brand Transformation Professional

This book reflects the place where many of us find ourselves now, in what seems like an endless pandemic, forced to abandon routines and typical social interaction. We are examining our priorities, our relationships and what gives meaning to our lives. Authenticity in leaders is more important than ever, so the investigation of the personal leadership journey through poetry is both apt and timely. Dharani, April and Harvey draw insights from the intuitive – the poetic – to animate psychology-based leadership constructs in ways that will resonate strongly with those seeking to understand the demands and challenges of leadership in a rapidly changing environment.

Roxanne Decyk, Independent Director of Maxar and Sinai Health Systems
and retired Executive Vice President, Royal Dutch Shell

Dharani, April, and Harvey beautifully crafted a book that connects personal reflections and leadership through poetries. This book helps us understand how our life experiences shape our development and growth as leaders.

Eddy Ng, Smith Professor of Equity and Inclusion in Business, Queen's University, Canada

The Poetic Journey into Self-leadership is a courageous dive into the unusual combination of leadership, psychology, and poetry. For generations, writers and poets have used their words as expressions of self-discovery and as a means to interpret their world and lived experiences. The universality of those thoughts created a link from the past to the present and will undoubtedly take us into the future. These links remain resilient to change, allowing us to agree with John Donne that "no man is an island."

Dharani, April, and Harvey have walked a new path, cutting through the thicket of clinical research. Together they have found open spaces and invited readers to go on a journey of self-discovery using poetry and words as a map. This map navigates our thoughts to forgotten places while inspiring us to overcome life's obstacles and dream about what is yet to come. Be bold, be courageous. Explore every stage of your journey, a journey that may encourage others to leave the shores of self acceptance and move to a new place of self-leadership that is life-giving for self and others.

Graham Power, Chairman: Power Group, Founder of the
Global Day of Prayer and Unashamedly Ethical

The attributes of the highest form of authentic leadership, as servant leader, would resonate with many poets. Indeed, the late Seamus Heaney once said that "the aim of the poet and poetry is finally to be of service," that we write for others, that the poet is in the service of the poem. As in business, it is a journey of vulnerability, and Dharani, April and Harvey, have shown us theirs in this fascinating book.

After a career as a business executive, Dr Lew Watts is now a widely-recognized poet.
His most recent collections are Lessons for Tangueros, *and* Tick-Tock.

Professor Kurt April is an academic par excellence and sought after thought leader in diversity and business leadership. It's been my greatest pleasure to collaborate with him as he unearths excellence in those around him.

We rise and fall on leadership, and *The Poetic Journey of Self-Leadership* will certainly elevate its readers to raise their leadership prowess!

Candice Watson, AECI, Group Executive: Human Capital

Since the first time Kurt and I met in Rotterdam - more than twenty years ago - I have been following his discoveries' path from self-awareness to self-leadership to serving leader. Now, he and his fellow co-authors propose us to look at this intriguing parallel between self-leadership and leadership styles through the lenses of Poetry. Take it deeper, feel it and appreciate.

Mario Nobre Ghiggino, Consultant in Marketing, Business Development and Trading

The Poetic Journey of Self-Leadership combines two disciplines that are rarely related: psychological development and poetry. These can sound heavy yet are borne lightly in this unusual and insightful book. Reflection and self-development - in the authors' term 'self-leadership' - are key to maturity. Reflection is both triggered and deepened by different perspectives and, in my experience, poetry is a wonderful source of new views. Here we find not a selection of professional poetry but the work of numerous leaders working to deepen their reflection and to express their struggle authentically. Reading through the book, certain phrases caught my eye - I want to remember them, then the comments lead to further insights... This is a book of exploration that supports self-exploration. And that is fundamental to good leadership.

Dr. Nandani Lynton, Global head of Organizational Growth, Siemens Energy

First published in 2021.

ISBN: 978-1-86922-921-4 (Printed)
eISBN: 978-1-86922-922-1 (PDF ebook)

Published by KR Publishing
P O Box 3954
Randburg
2125
Republic of South Africa

Tel: (011) 706-6009
E-mail: orders@knowres.co.za
Website: www.kr.co.za

Printed and bound: HartWood Digital Printing, 243 Alexandra Avenue, Halfway House, Midrand
Typesetting, layout and design: Cia Joubert, cia@knowres.co.za
Cover design: Marlene De Lorme, marlene@knowres.co.za
Editing and Proofreading: Valda Strauss, valda@global.co.za
Project management: Cia Joubert, cia@knowres.co.za

The *Poetic Journey* of SELF-LEADERSHIP

LEADERSHIP DEVELOPMENT ALONG STAGES OF PSYCHOLOGICAL GROWTH

DR. BABAR DHARANI
PROF. KURT APRIL
KATHY HARVEY

kr
publishing

2021

ACKNOWLEDGEMENTS

DR. BABAR DHARANI

My teachers during my formative years, Mrs. Kamal Grewal and Mrs. Nina Rebeiro at The Nairobi Academy, encouraged me into disciplines of English language and literature that previous teachers of these subjects had hesitated in aspiring to jog my interests in due to my aptitude for mathematics and quantitative sciences. In addition to acknowledging their efforts and dedication to their profession, I particularly attribute the publishing of this book to their innovative and flexible teaching methods that seeded and cultivated my interest and appreciation for the arts, when I was naturally not inclined towards them as a youngster. Mrs. Grewal did so by grounding these subjects in realism to better align them with my natural philosophical stance. For example, her approach for teaching punctuation was rule-based rather than leveraging a natural language speaker's narration style. She was also the first to introduce me to poetry through the rules of poetry, such as the number of lines and rhymes in sonnets, and by clinically identifying the poet's use of alliterations, similes, onomatopoeia, etc., rather than attempting to teach me to grasp the holistic impact of the poet's expressions to understand and appreciate classic poetry. Such a tailor-made approach aligned better with my quantitative abilities and gradually stretched my aptitude in the arts. Mrs. Rebeiro read some pieces of literature with exaggerated expressions to introduce a basic understanding of the author or poet's attempt and ability to tap into the reader's emotions through words, which had not resonated with me by reading it. She also recommended thought-provoking movies that worked better for me as a starting point than directly reading the literature. As such, they hand-held me toward a literary and poetic inclination. While I certainly do not claim for it to have led to an ability to flowingly write poetry in a literary way, or naturally grasp classic poetry; nonetheless, they gave me an understanding and appreciation of the use of a poetic medium as an art of expression. It was this understanding which evolved into the novelty of tapping into poetry as a source of more expressive, uninhibited, and free-flowing hermeneutic phenomenological data collection for sociological and psychological research.

In an era where teachers are underappreciated, underpaid, and even abused by students at times, I would like to extend my gratitude to all teachers who are led by their natural desires for nurturing and educating, and assure them that their profession, personal efforts, innovations, and patience are decisive in future accomplishments of their students, and our collective future.

PROF. KURT APRIL

My best friend and wife, Amanda, has been my editor, language coach and life coach for the majority of my life, and encouraged me into areas and disciplines that were not always comfortable for me, given that the first half of my life was spent mostly in the quantitative sciences and in my qualified professions as both an electronic technician initially, and then later as an electrical engineer.

She has encouraged me to give voice to that which has always "lurked" within me, when I did not have the confidence previously to fully show who I was and when I was without the courage to expose the shadow/imperfect sides of myself – this book, which explores both poetry and psychology is a personal 'coming out' and an acknowledgement of the importance of honesty and the transformative role of confronting our own 'existential strivings' through creative means. Thank you for your continued love and encouragement, even though you know my flaws and all. I also want to acknowledge my son, Jordan, who contributed two poems to this book – he never ceases to amaze me: great character, funny, empath, and a balance of technical brilliance with artistic flair (whether that be through his piano renditions, his amazing graphics and artwork, or in exploring his vivid imaginative realms through both storytelling and writing). You continue to show me the hope for our world's future!

KATHY HARVEY

This book, and my own contribution to it, would not have been possible without the many students at Oxford and in South Africa, who have taken time out of their professional lives to reflect on their experience. They created something special, for all of us as well as for themselves as reflective leaders. It has been a privilege to work with so many of our Executive MBA students at Oxford over the years and humbling to realise how much we can learn from each other. I would like to acknowledge and celebrate the friendship and thoughtfulness of my fellow authors, the patience of my husband as I committed so much of my time to this and all my work, and the power of poetry. As a former English Literature student I should also thank Keats, T.S. Eliot and John Donne for accompanying me on my own leadership journey.

We wish to thank Wilhelm Crous, Cia Joubert and Tina van der Westhuizen from Knowledge Resources, in particular, who believed in this book project and skillfully guided us over the finish line. It has been a privilege to, once again, work with such professional colleagues at KR Publishing, and we value their time, effort and professional engagement with us, and the care with which they stewarded the content of our book. We remain deeply thankful for Allan & Gill Gray's generous endowment, which ensures that we can continue to research and publish in the domains of values-based leadership, responsible leadership, inclusive leadership, and work towards helping emerging leaders, alumni, and established leaders stay resilient through purposeful reflection and self-care, in order that they may better and sustainably serve their stakeholders and communities.

CONTENTS

FOREWORD

Leadership is not simply something we do. It emanates from deep within us, our 'being' …
a systemic integration of genetic imprinting and nurtured experience. And leadership is the
process where we understand how to bring that forth in ways that add value to ourselves,
and others. Thus far, there has been little discussion, in traditional media and publications,
relating to the use of poetry to leadership and leadership development. For centuries people in
various strata of societies and communities have used the oral tradition to tell stories through
narratives and poetry to convey ideas, to coalesce around communal visions, to inspire
others, to bring hope, and to convey complex ideas to others. Poetry and story have been
used by leaders to warn, to transfer knowledge, to revisit, to set direction, to elicit emotive
feelings, and to engage others.[1] Additionally, poetry serves as the sensemaking link for leaders
to look into their deep selves, the necessary self-reflection required of leaders in the modern
world – premised on the notion that as we grow, so shall we lead. The figure below shows the
use of stories and narratives, poetry, the language we use (including metaphor), and the uses
of story and poetry:

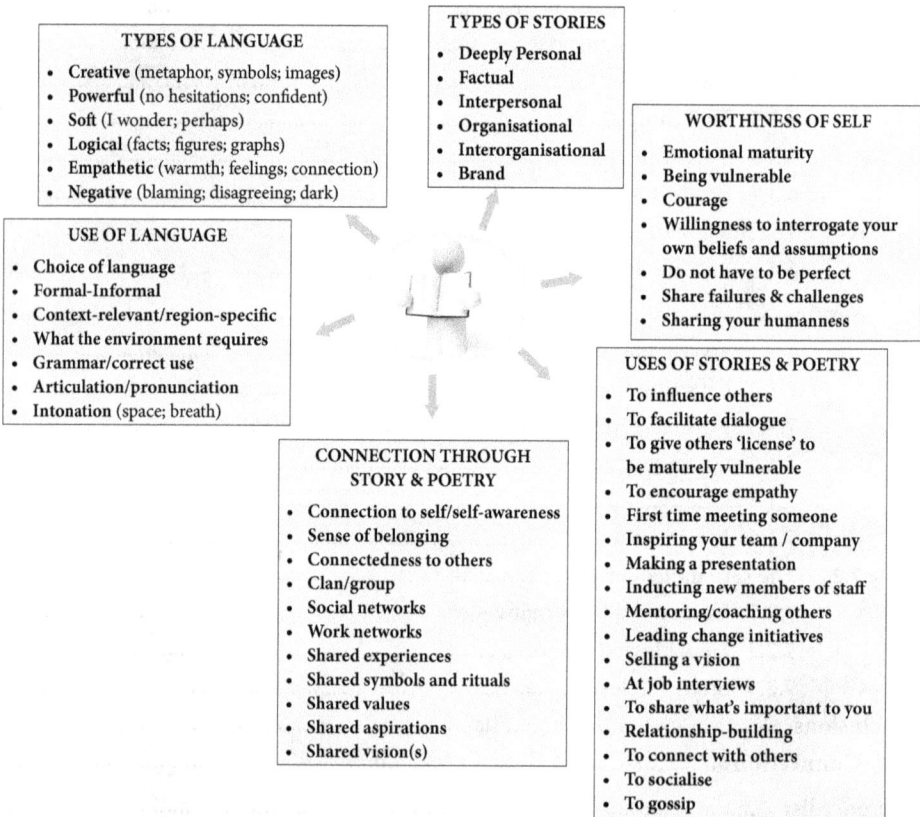

TYPES OF LANGUAGE
- Creative (metaphor, symbols; images)
- Powerful (no hesitations; confident)
- Soft (I wonder; perhaps)
- Logical (facts; figures; graphs)
- Empathetic (warmth; feelings; connection)
- Negative (blaming; disagreeing; dark)

USE OF LANGUAGE
- Choice of language
- Formal-Informal
- Context-relevant/region-specific
- What the environment requires
- Grammar/correct use
- Articulation/pronunciation
- Intonation (space; breath)

TYPES OF STORIES
- Deeply Personal
- Factual
- Interpersonal
- Organisational
- Interorganisational
- Brand

WORTHINESS OF SELF
- Emotional maturity
- Being vulnerable
- Courage
- Willingness to interrogate your own beliefs and assumptions
- Do not have to be perfect
- Share failures & challenges
- Sharing your humanness

CONNECTION THROUGH STORY & POETRY
- Connection to self/self-awareness
- Sense of belonging
- Connectedness to others
- Clan/group
- Social networks
- Work networks
- Shared experiences
- Shared symbols and rituals
- Shared values
- Shared aspirations
- Shared vision(s)

USES OF STORIES & POETRY
- To influence others
- To facilitate dialogue
- To give others 'license' to be maturely vulnerable
- To encourage empathy
- First time meeting someone
- Inspiring your team / company
- Making a presentation
- Inducting new members of staff
- Mentoring/coaching others
- Leading change initiatives
- Selling a vision
- At job interviews
- To share what's important to you
- Relationship-building
- To connect with others
- To socialise
- To gossip

Poetry is the equivalent of looking in, looking up, looking away – a shift in orientation and a necessary growing in perspective. Revealing their innermost motivations, their secrets, their internal battles and struggles, it is all part of emerging and established leaders' journeys to wholeness (*whole-person growth*). It requires dropping into their own abyss, engaging in lots of long gazes into the distance, shifting of their milieu – it is like a mindful journey of walking long distances alone without purpose (*wandering and daydreaming*), stopping (*creating pauses*), observing that which one has not consciously been aware of before (*noticing*), still moving further (*avoiding stagnation*), though it may be among and past people with their humming sounds and noises as they unconsciously go about their business and day-to-day tasks.

Poetry connects the past (*where we come from*), the present (*where we are at*) and the future (*where we think we are going, and what we desire for ourselves and others*), and often challenges our contextualisation (*our perceived temporality and location*) to the edge of our comfortability (*complex adaptation*). It is at this edge, this uncomfortable edge, where creativity exists (*divergence*), and our thoughts and dreams come into real focus (*convergence*). One of the connections between storytelling, poetry, music, literature, and art is the use of metaphor.[2] Jordan April, in *Mindful Journey*, provides a metaphor for us to consider the leader's moving out/shift:

MINDFUL JOURNEY

In the early hours of the morning the hard, creaky anodized metallic floor of the train felt cold and rough. Frost had crept into its crevices. The frozen engine kicked into motion, pushing the sleek, modern train up the beaten old track and into the black abyss. Mist swirled gently across the desolate track, covering it in a wispy blanket. The track was now hidden beneath a mysterious layer, like a secret. All you could hear was the unbroken humming of people conversing with each other in their private cabins. The sound glided through every crevice, presenting itself through the totality of the train.

The raucous, metallic shriek of the wheels subdued, and the mouth of the tunnel gateway opened itself toward the oblivious passengers. The sounds of the train skating on the rails were amplified by the compact shaft. The mist ascended, reaching up into the sky, extinguishing the stars. After the mist receded, the glowing medallion in the sky feebly peered through the mess, warmly embracing us as we abandoned the tunnel. The surroundings came into sharp focus as the sun's rays woke whatever they touched. Lush trees covered the landscape with a flourish of warm colours. Daisy yellow, sunset orange, and apple red swirled together as the wind ruffled the leaves. The soft squeal of the machinery was present but did not affect the sound of nature. Outside you could hear a faint-but-present sound of birds chirping as gusts of wind flew by. Through the window, faint silhouettes 'whirred' by. The small houses were sewn by the seam of the horizon onto the vast fields, casting askew shadows as smoke was vomited from the chimneys.

The inconsistent rattle of the tracks turned into a methodical 'ding' as the train rolled into the station. The sunset was cast over the entire sky, dazzling with the light of liquid amber, flowing through the gaping openings of the locomotive. The hum of the passengers started to increase in volume as they searched for the welcoming arms of relatives. The worn, metallic floor of the train lay warm and rough as the heated engine started to return to rest, pushing the modern train down a beaten old track and into the final destination.

Poetry is the pathway from inside-out and outside-in, simultaneously, within the spaces which we occupy on a day-to-day basis: *structural space* – where we interact with others, *intellectual space* – our willingness to reframe our realities, and *psychological space* – how we interact with others and ourselves. It requires a mix of realism/reality-confronting and aspiration/imagination, simultaneously (*confluence*), in order to choose whether to show up authentically or inauthentically. Like an improvisational actor, one can learn its techniques, but we prefer the authentic, untrained voice of emerging and established leaders, which is so rarely heard – real lived experiences and perspectives, in the true phenomenological and sociological tradition (*voice*). Poetry is a form of therapy – existential therapy, connecting us back – a pathway back from disconnection, separation and loneliness in the "hard metallic world" towards belonging and community (*connection*). It causes us to confront our psychic scars, our challenges, our imperfections, and find the beauty in it, the strength we do possess deep down, and the resilience to purposefully carry on (*Wabi-sabi – beauty from struggle*). Through poetry, we learn to wean ourselves of our resistance to face that which we circumvent through busy-ness, laughter, rationalisation, avoidance and procrastination (*defence mechanisms*).

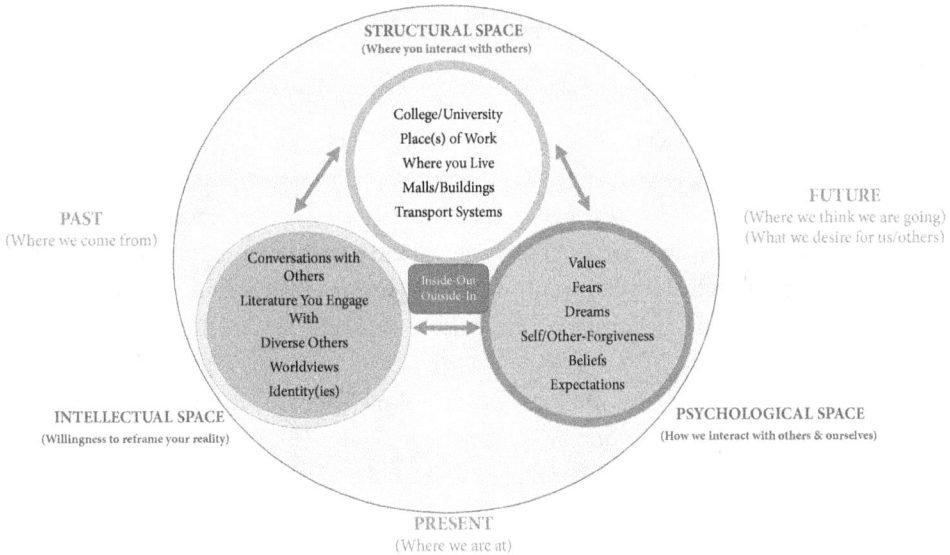

STRUCTURAL SPACE
(Where you interact with others)

College/University
Place(s) of Work
Where you Live
Malls/Buildings
Transport Systems

PAST
(Where we come from)

FUTURE
(Where we think we are going)
(What we desire for us/others)

Conversations with Others
Literature You Engage With
Diverse Others
Worldviews
Identity(ies)

Inside-Out Outside-In

Values
Fears
Dreams
Self/Other-Forgiveness
Beliefs
Expectations

INTELLECTUAL SPACE
(Willingness to reframe your reality)

PSYCHOLOGICAL SPACE
(How we interact with others & ourselves)

PRESENT
(Where we are at)

The act of writing poetry is an act of courage, a reconciliation with our imperfections and with the world. The courage to stop, to show up, to be – the courage to listen to the genuine within you, to dwell in imperfection without abandoning the notion of improvement. Not always obvious the first time around, but we can eventually notice the mosaic, the shifts, the eschewal of people, fears, failures, potential successes and even our real selves (*patterns*). Poetry gives us the courage to venture in, to partake in the first act of having a courageous conversation with ourselves. The second act of courage is to offer it to others and the world – a gift, as Plato would require of us in his urgings in *The Republic*, to re-enter the cave with our gift. The third act of courage is more of an orientation, to suspend ourselves and approach those still chained in the cave with understanding and compassion (*courage*).

Poetry, a purposeful act of reflective-penning and sense-making, exists so that others may learn and grow bigger than us, because of our willingness to be still.

ABOUT THE AUTHORS

DR. BABAR DHARANI

Dr. Babar Dharani is a Senior Lecturer in the Allan Gray Centre for Values-Based Leadership at the Graduate School of Business, University of Cape Town. His research focuses on various facets operating within the umbrella concept of subjective well-being at work, including: personality variables and person-organizational fit for happiness and contentment at work, job satisfaction and affective organizational commitment, work engagement and boredom, as well as diversity, inclusion, and exclusion, focusing on hegemonic masculinity and inclusive leadership.

Outside of academia, Babar is a Business Finance Professional (B.F.P.) and a Fellow of the Institute of Chartered Accountants in England and Wales (F.C.A.). His career started at Deloitte in London (UK), and his consultancy career led him to work in audit and assurance, and corporate tax departments in the area of mergers and acquisitions in some of the largest international accounting firms in London (UK), Port Louis (Mauritius), and Nairobi (Kenya). He moved into industry with FedEx in Dubai (U.A.E.), and his career largely excelled in the Diamond industry, which led him to take the position of C.F.O. for one of the largest and leading global diamond manufacturing businesses in Amsterdam (The Netherlands), and subsequently in Luxembourg, lastly running the investor's family office in Singapore.

His PhD at the Graduate School of Business (GSB) focused on happiness at work. Babar's interest in finance and subjective well-being in organizations may seem like a dichotomy; however, it is founded on the belief that managing any department requires technical knowledge associated with the job, as well as leadership skills. He promotes the concept of leading through well-being in organizations, which require managing employee happiness for optimising success and performance – a strategy that can ensure competitive advantage that is difficult to imitate by competitors. He believes that these complementary interests supported his career, and laid foundations for his personalized approach to research, often taking a quantitative approach to highly subjective concepts.

PROF. KURT APRIL

Prof. Kurt April, a Fellow of the Royal Society for Arts, Manufactures and Commerce (UK), is currently the endowed Allan Gray Chair specialising in Leadership, Diversity & Inclusion and Director of the Allan Gray Centre for Values-Based Leadership at the Graduate School of Business, University of Cape Town (1998-present), is Adjunct Faculty of Saïd Business School (University of Oxford, UK, 2000-present), and is an Orchestrator & Faculty Member of DukeCE (Duke University, USA, 2008-present). Previously, he was a Research Fellow of Hult-Ashridge Business School (UK, 2004-2016), Visiting Professor at London Metropolitan University (UK, 2014-2017), Visiting Professor at Rotterdam School of Management (Erasmus University, Netherlands, 2001-2013), and Visiting Professor in the Faculty of Economics & Econometrics

(University of Amsterdam UvA, Netherlands, 2004-2007). Outside of academia, Kurt is the Managing Partner of LICM Consulting (SA, 2001-present), Managing Director: Leadership, Diversity & Inclusion Practice at Oxford Acuity (Singapore, 2019-present), Shareholder and Director of the Achievement Awards Group (SA, 2007-present), Shareholder of bountiXP (Pty) Ltd (SA, 2019-present), as well as Ambassador of the global Unashamedly Ethical movement (2016-present). He plays a range of roles and consults to many companies and organizations around the globe, having worked in 24 countries. Kurt is an Advisory Board Member and Reviewer to a number of international academic journals, and holds a PhD in Economics & IT Strategy, Certificate in Japanese Production, an MBA, MSc(ElecEng) in Electronic Engineering, Higher Diploma in Education (HDE), BSc(ElecEng) in Electrical Engineering, National N6 Diploma in Electronic Engineering (NDip EE), and National N6 Diploma in Logic Systems (NDip LS) completed at the University of Cape Town (SA), University of Oxford (UK), Wingfield College (SA) and AOTS Nagoya (Japan). He has published 196 peer-reviewed academic articles, book chapters, conference papers, dissertations and op-eds, and written 10 books previously. Author email: kurt.april@uct.ac.za

KATHY HARVEY

Kathy Harvey is Associate Dean for the MBA and Executive Degrees at Saïd Business School, and a Fellow of Keble College, University of Oxford, with responsibility for the success of the School's main degree and postgraduate diploma programmes. Before this she was the Director of the School's Open Enrolment Executive Programmes and went on to be Programme Director for the School's flagship Executive MBA Programme. She continues to lead the Entrepreneurship Project for the EMBA, coaching individuals and teams as they embark on their start-up journeys. Kathy also teaches crisis management, stakeholder management and the leadership of teams and is a visiting lecturer at the Vedica Scholars' Programme in India. She is a founding member of the Saïd Business School Coaching Community and an accredited leadership coach.

Kathy began her career as a journalist, working as a BBC radio reporter, TV political correspondent and commissioning editor before founding her own consulting business, working mainly in investment and financial services. After joining Oxford University, she led the development and growth of the School's executive qualifications and open enrolment programmes.

She is a trustee of the Orwell Foundation, which honours the work of George Orwell, celebrating modern, untold stories and working to expose social evils through writing and public debate.

INTRODUCTION

What is leadership? Can it be taught and developed? What gives us greater insight into our own leadership capacities? Accompanied by an abundance of literature and theories that aim at answering these questions is an array of leadership development courses, training programmes, and coaching engagements. Many such courses, programmes and engagements emphasize the tools for leadership or review mostly historic examples of the heroic actions of iconic leaders with the aim of teaching leadership skills, e.g., showing the 8-steps to be Steve Jobs, the leadership competencies of Maria Ramos, or the pathways to emulate Mary Barra. Ordinary citizens too love reading biographies of heroic leaders. However, does learning about and attempting to emulate other leaders support authentic leadership development? A major critique of such idiosyncratic orientations is that while such approaches to leadership may allow for learning about other leaders and the techniques that they had used to become admired figures, it rarely highlights their daily, personal struggles and can fall short in supporting significant and authentic leadership development in others.

Popular approaches that are frequently employed by leadership courses in Business Schools include teaching through the use of leader case studies, leadership frameworks and the use of 2x2 or 3x3 matrices, which are designed to simplify and analyse the experiences of leaders, and offer previously successful leaders' lenses through which to view their decisions/choices when faced with personal and organizational dilemmas. But, as the leadership landscape becomes increasingly complex, uncertain and fast-changing, particularly when faced with global pandemics and multiple crises such as the climate crisis and inequality crises, the roles and requisite responses of the leader change with it, and the foundational role of the leader as a communicator has become more dominant. Like conductors, who are trained musicians but who no longer play an instrument in an orchestra and are the messengers of the composer(s), leaders of organizations have to lead through communicating – they cannot return to the shop-floor or get embroiled in the technical work required (even if they were previously qualified to do so); they have to influence through communicating (about themselves, about others, about the organization, about the stakeholders, and about the environment in which their organization operates). A novel approach to leadership and communicating as leaders is required in light of the above.

A NOVEL APPROACH

To fulfil the reformed role of a leader, rather than the conventional approach of knowledge about leaders or categorizing of leadership into a matrix, instead, an understanding of one's own personal frameworks and the matrix of experiences, emotions, aspirations, and fears which foundationally form one's personality and character become more important. To develop such a framework for leadership, individuals need to psychologically unpack themselves to become cognisant of the underlying personal experiences that are foundational in the development of their personality attributes to better understand where their thoughts, feelings, and behaviours stem from.

To coach, teach and develop leadership through personal expression requires the provision of containment and a safe space for the participants. Therefore, HR professionals, mentors, coaches, and academics need to ideally give individuals a protected environment and useful tools for documenting their reflections. Simply asking someone to write about formative experiences without any containment of the outcomes from such retrospection could be dangerous. This is particularly true for participants, clients, or students who may be in psychologically transitional states, or those experiencing heightened emotional vulnerability. To avoid such negative repercussions, "wrapping" or "containment" of the learning experience is critical. Additionally, it is important to acknowledge that self-reflection and retrospection may be akin to a short hike amongst the Himalayas. There is likely to be plenty that will remain unaddressed in the short-term. As such, for HR professionals, coaches, academics and employees/clients/students, there is a need to incorporate long-term self-reflection processes and tools for incorporation into their lives, such as a journaling practice lasting over several employee/client/student coaching sessions.

For the above leadership development approach, creative arts, such as poetry, become an important tool for self-mastery, as poetry writing facilitates uncovering of the unspoken self-expressions to better enable the authors to view themselves by reviewing their own creations. Poetic expressions may be unnerving to document; nevertheless, the medium presents an important tool for releasing facets of one's inner self – the subconscious and the unconscious psyche that bears trapped energies which, when not released, can lead to irrational and damaging behaviours, personally and in the workplace, if left untamed. As such, poetry allows individuals the chance to observe their entire self (the conscious and the unconscious alike) from a distance, and reflect on how it expresses itself through the lives they lead and the relationships they interact in. It, simultaneously, allows individuals to acknowledge and celebrate what has passed and to consider how it forms their present in order to better manoeuvre, and make choices, regarding their futures.

In other words, it can be argued that poetry writing permits self-growth and leadership development. And since leadership skills develop along with overall psychological growth throughout an individual's life (a psychological and cognitive maturing), an analysis of poetry writing aims to tap into the lived experiences and narrative inquiry of individuals to support their ongoing psychological growth, hence their mature choices regarding their own leadership journeys. By leveraging on their personal histories and their experiential learnings, such an approach can support individuals' willpower to emerge and develop leadership capabilities from their unique, personal life circumstances. Such a lens of leadership, that leverages self-leadership development, serves as the underlying philosophy for this book.

OPEN QUESTIONS

Similar to psychological growth and maturation, self-leadership is said to develop throughout one's life span. As with physical maturation, which is theorized to occur in stages, the framework of stage theories of personality development is applied to the development of self-leadership to frame the book – as highlighted by Tobelo Lewis Malepe in his poem: *"Self-Care"*. Malepe's poem refers to Shakespeare's *"All the world's a stage"*, which famously poeticized the seven ages of humans between birth and death. He explains this as: *"Birth in this case does not only refer to the actual day a person is born. It encompasses every stage of life that a person goes through"*. His poem below, followed by the explanation, thoroughly supports a staged development of self-leadership through the *"journey of growth"* that ascribes to progressive stages of development of the human psyche.

SELF-CARE

From birth
We are born to lead a life
From fear to courage
We are taught to stand still
We learn, we grow and change

In this life we write our own stories
As Shakespeare once alluded
All the world is a stage
And we are all actors

From the broken man behind the broken mirror
The reflection of our own strength and troubles

A page is turned
A page is burned

Every day is a page filled with memories,
Kept in the libraries of life.

This is who I am
A leader.

Tobelo Lewis Malepe

Malepe's Explanation: Every person exists in a continually changing world of experience in which he or she is the centre. This perpetual field of experiences and perception is their reality – Carl Rogers.

Self-care, as a title, refers to the caution that one has to take when they embark on the journey of growth. It is closely related to stanza 3 of this poem.

This poem speaks about a journey of inception. Birth, in this case, does not only refer to the actual day a person is born. It encompasses every stage of life that a person goes through. Particularly where one has to undertake new responsibilities, or change your life – drawing on lessons from past experiences, both that we are aware of and the ones that are on our subconscious. To live every day without fear, learn from mistakes, allowing yourself to be vulnerable. What matters at the end of the day is living a fulfilled life, and how others will remember you, your legacy.

Such a staged development theory of leadership presents many avenues that remain incompletely explored in leadership literature. Firstly, it requires an evaluation of the extent to which the stage theory of personality development matches self-leadership development. It also demands an examination of stages to evaluate if some are more significant than others from a self-leadership development point of view. Additionally, it raises questions regarding one's progression direction along the stages of development. Malepe states: *"A page is turned, A page is burned"*. Does that entail that self-leadership development is unidirectional, or can certain life experiences pull one back into earlier stages of development? Also, it raises the question as to whether certain life experiences prevent one from self-leadership growth and fixate one to a specific stage of leadership, or does everyone: *"... learn, we grow, we change"*? Similarly, from a practice point of view, there are unanswered questions regarding which 'traps' or 'stumbling blocks' exist within the respective stages that can halt continued progression on the path of self-leadership development. And how can these traps be avoided, using enablers, for continued self-leadership development?

Conceptual Framework

The book aims to answer these questions using Barrett's[3] framework of the seven-stage model of psychological development of: surviving, conforming, differentiating, individuating, self-actualizing, integrating, and serving.[4]

Serving +60

Integrating 50-59

Self-actualizing 40-49

Individuating 25-39

Differentiating 8-24

Conforming 2-7

Surviving 0-2

Left-side boxes:

Use Kintsugi metaphor. Embrace imperfections and share them as gifts to others. Investigate one's values, leverage on personal heroes, integrate with others to achieve a common goal.

Forgive oneself and those that founded the complexes, heal over time, utilize imperfections and traumas as intense experiential learning experiences.

Knowing oneself from external sources: Seek 'out of box' and out of comfort zone experiences, being vulnerable.

Intense belonging: Self-reliance, independence, find support or inner courage to individuate. Balancing belonging and individuality. Leverage intersectionality.

Lack of belonging: Cognition about misalignment of personal and societal aspects, intersectionality, Wabi-sabi.

Personality imbalances: Professional help including therapy, counselling, and coaching.

Abandonment: Professional help including therapy, counselling, and coaching. Identifying trauma inducing patterns. Forgiveness of primary caregivers.

Right-side boxes:

Self-care, self-love, self-empathy, and self-compassion. Support social and religious values. Seek silence and nature to become better attuned to the needs of others. Chemically induced.

Align values with day-to-day living and work and with others, to aim at shared goals derived from purpose in life.

Introspection: Conquering complexes, knowing one's shadow psyche. Experience exhaustion of a persona, live authentically.

Belonging to a marginalized group: Religions that support egalitarianism, education about source of prejudice, intersectionality, seeking individuated people within the social group.

Active listening, un-learning and re-learning, questioning aspects of followership, challenging norms, cultivating a flexible mindset, self-reflection, cognition, meditation, mindfulness, stillness.

Overwhelment: Establishing boundaries with primary caregivers, experiencing 'dread' in interactions with others can balance the skewed experiences with primary caregivers.

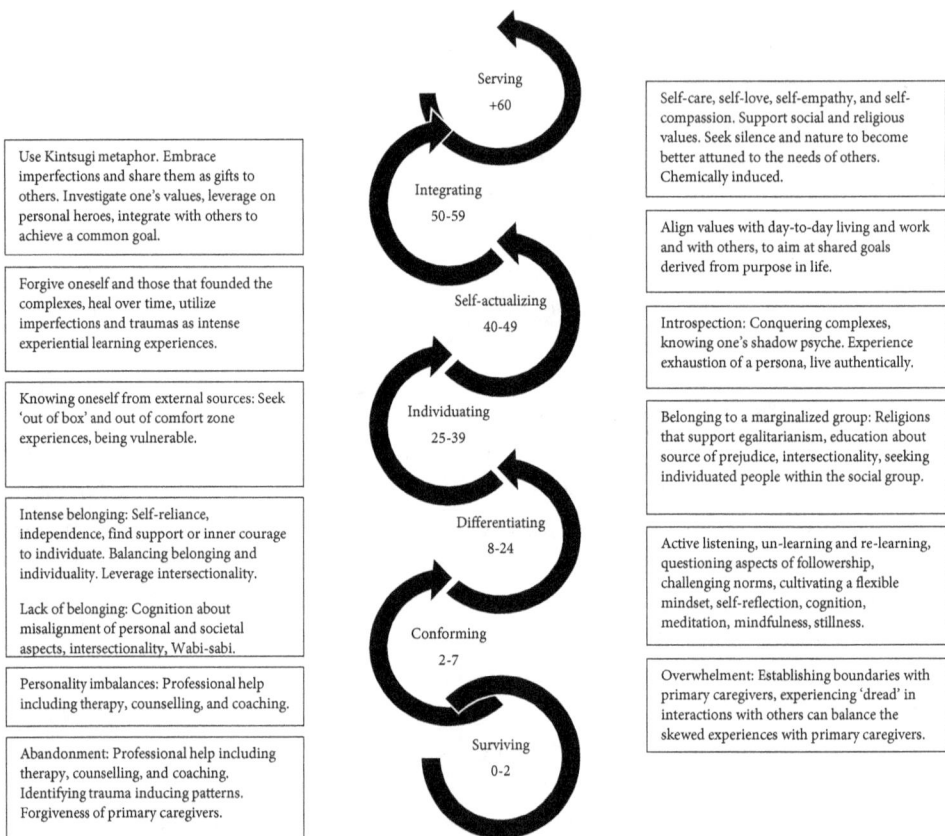

Surviving (<2 years): Our journey starts at birth, where the foundational demand of any infant is to satisfy their physiological needs, such as obtaining nourishment, hydration, and temperature regulation to stay alive and physically healthy. The field of psychology that optimally addresses this stage of psychological development is evolutionary psychology, deemed to represent selfish and spiteful behaviour.[5]

Conforming (3-7 years): Upon satisfying physiological needs, the infant becomes a toddler. This stage of childhood is motivated by love and belonging needs, to feeling safe and protected by staying close to those providing the physiological needs which lead to bonding and development of love and belonging. Major personality traits are seeded during this stage of development.[6]

Differentiating (8-24 years): Towards the end of childhood, there are attempts to progress from seeking physiological, loving, and belonging needs provided by the family to seeking to belong to a group or a gang. The motivation to do so is triggered by a need for respect and recognition, which can only be accomplished by seeking to be different by exhibiting one's superior skills and talents to the community. The field of psychology that optimally addresses this stage of psychological development is social psychology.[7]

Individuating (25-39 years): Satisfying the need for differentiating, individuals move on to target satisfaction of their needs for freedom and autonomy by ensuring a lack of dependence on family for provision of physiological needs, and dispersion of obtaining love and belonging needs from the family to their group, and onto romantic partners and those further afield. In doing so, they embark on a path of true identity[8] by forming relationships with those chosen by them, rather than those whom they found themselves to be around at birth and during early socialization.

Self-actualizing (40-49 years): Satisfying the need to find meaning and purpose. Expressing one's true nature by embracing one's soul's values and purpose.[9]

Integrating (50-59 years): Upon uncovering one's meaning and purpose, the motivation shifts to satisfying the need to make a difference to serve that meaning and purpose. An initial stage to do so requires deeply connecting with others, not merely for the sake of one's belonging and love needs, but for developing unconditional loving relationships.

Serving (>60 years): After having identified a community to integrate into, a secondary stage of satisfying the need to make a difference and serve one's meaning and purpose in life is to actively service that community's needs in a selfless and dedicated manner. This frequently relates to alleviating the suffering of others, who are loved unconditionally, as such demanding little to nothing in return. A frequent target of such love is caring for the well-being of future generations, humanity, and the planet.

While we acknowledge the age-related basis for the changes in personality functioning purported to exist by the stage theorists, in the case of self-leadership, we regard a greater basis of maturation as being more fundamental for the stages of development than age. Nonetheless, the references to the ages that are associated with each stage of psychological development are retained in the book as a point of reference for enhancing understanding for the reader, while acknowledging their potential inaccuracy and limitation when applied to any specific individual.

LIVED EXPERIENCES – THE PHENOMENOLOGICAL TRADITION

To tap into richer aspects of individuals' life histories and lived experiences that supported their personal psychological growth, or hindered it, "… we must use the richer, deeper language of poetry, which engages us in a way that goes beyond the mere exchange of information".[10] We approached a number of emerging and established leaders, as well as coaching clients, many of whom attended post-graduate Masters and PhD courses at Saïd Business School at the University of Oxford (England) and the Graduate School of Business at the University of Cape Town (South Africa), and encouraged them to take a step back, in an open-ended way, and self-reflect through the medium of poetry. We did so in order to encourage them to reimagine their professions, their jobs, their lifestyles and their relationships and, as a result, purposefully negotiate new roles as leaders in this increasingly uncertain and ambiguous world. They had the space and time to construct their own gateways to new understanding.[11] Their heightened curiosity, specifically about the requirements for 'new leadership' and the complexities in trying to live authentic lives, formed the basis for our phenomenological inquiry into an enriched understanding of the modern-day human condition. As a result, our participants represent demographic diversity in respect of age, gender, race, ethnicity, nationality, as well as educational backgrounds, and work disciplines. They generously submitted their reflections and musings through poetry, either anonymously, using pseudonyms, or using their names, as well as their own explanations of their poetic writing for enhanced understanding for the book reader(s).

A number of themes, relating to the stages of personality development, emerged, as well as nuanced sub-themes to the stage theory of self-leadership development. Each of the significant sub-themes is discussed in the respective chapters of the book along with the appropriate poetry. Using the stage theory framework, several key assumptions for the framework are noted, as outlined by Thomas & Segal[12]: (1) that stage-specific functioning rests upon previous stages and is preparatory for the subsequent stage, (2) that the stages are qualitatively different from one another and, consequently, are differentiated by distinct organizing principles, (3) that the organization of the individual's functional structures integrates previous structures that were preparatory, and (4) that the sequence of stages is universal and not subject to substantial individual variability, except to the extent that the tempo/timing of each stage may vary across persons.

A CULTIVATED QUALITY

Based on the above theoretical foundations, frameworks, and assumptions, we approach leadership as a quality to be cultivated using narrative inquiry and lived experiences for it to allow an individual a more responsive cultivation into leading others and, subsequently, teams and organizations. And by exploring the highlights of this journey of our participants, we address the unanswered questions regarding self-leadership development. The analysis of the poems and their respective explanations is used to discuss the questions, and build on the theory that addresses the gaps in leadership literature and practice regarding stage development theories of leadership development.

1   SURVIVING

A quest for survival is embedded in all living creatures. The survival instinct is encapsulated in the genes, and executed (without cognitive thought) as actions and behaviours that support one's survival. It not only ensures the survival of individuals, but of the species as well. In humans, these include and range from biological processes such as regulation of body temperature which exist at birth, to the execution of unconscious impulses such as an instinct to suckle for nourishment that exist during infancy, as well as more conscious yet automated behavioural responses such as the fight, flight, or freeze response when faced with a threat which accompanies everyone throughout their lives. An association of notions regarding survival with the survival instincts and with natural selection entails that it is more frequently associated with the so-called hard-sciences. As such, the link between genetics and biological processes of physical development with self-leadership can appear to be a stretch of the imagination. Nonetheless, evolutionary psychology is founded on this link, and is based on the belief that our behaviour has evolved through natural selection in the same way that physical characteristics are selected by nature over time to ensure that they are best suited to the external environment.[13] For example, similar to biological reflexes, psychological reflexes exist that determine our behaviours to external stimuli. Additionally, theories of socio-biology[14] are underpinned by the belief that human social behaviour is reflective of natural selection and other biological processes. For example, nepotism from such a lens is deemed an expression of a quest for survival of those with the closest genes to ours.

Such a link is also acknowledged by some of our research participants. Tanya Vollenhoven-Brown, in her poem: *"Growth"* (1.1.1), uses an analogy of biological processes to express some aspects of personal self-leadership development. The overlap between the two, biological processes and emotional growth, sketched in her poem is explained as: *"... Our ... organs and our gut do much more than simply process physical stimuli, they are the vessels through which we experience much of our emotional and psychological struggles and strengths"*. While she acknowledges the challenges associated with exercising free-will under such a premise, she equates not doing so to: *"... spitting up of opportunity in favour of starving"*, and *"... rejecting the work of digesting the foreign, the nutritious and the new"*. Thus, she highlights growth to emerge from escaping evolutionary inclinations and behaviourism (psychological reflexes to external stimuli) and by progressing to exercise one's free-will that facilitates self-leadership growth, which she expresses as embracing new flavours that help to develop one's palate.

Vollenhoven-Brown goes on to dismiss cognitive theoretical fundamentals by expressing that observation and understanding of growth in others, though rightly romanticised and admired, falls short as leverage or enablers for personal growth. Again, using the analogy of biological processes, she expresses this as: *"It is impossible to satiate my hunger by watching them eat"*. As such, she regards the journey of personal self-leadership development to be achievable by embarking on the unromantic, experiential journey oneself.

Though Vollenhoven-Brown uses an analogy that supports the ground between biological development and personal psychological growth, it raises the question of whether the self-leadership journey begins at the survival stage of psychological development. It is difficult to imagine how the survival stage of development, that is typically associated with the period from the foetal stage until two years of age, corresponds to the start of a journey of leadership development. Definitions of leadership in its simplest form argue it to be the application of social influence that is said to be observable from early childhood.[15] "The first thing the baby has to learn, as soon as it is born, is to interact with (control) the world around it, so it can get its survival needs met".[16] As such, academic literature supports the theory that the birth of leadership in its simplest form is an exercise of control or influence over others and the environment to favour one's survival. Our research participant's opinion, that is founded on evolutionary psychology and behaviourism and challenge to cognition, supports the premise that the start of the journey of self-leadership begins with this stage of survival.

1.1.1 GROWTH

The beauty of the raw and unfiltered in others,
Superimposed on your distaste of your own.
Your voice wailing through the cacophony
of those whose sounds
You help to find.

Tell yourself the truth about what fear tastes like in your mouth
Of the spitting up of opportunity in favour
of starving in the familiar.

In rejecting the work of digesting the
foreign, the nutritious and the new,

In fasting from the unexpected bursts of unprocessed fuel,
you reinforce an immature palate
A constricted gullet
A body that continues to believe it is unable,
Rather than emerging

Tanya Vollenhoven-Brown

Vollenhoven-Brown's Explanation: I chose to describe the uncomfortable, complex experiences of growth using words connected with sensory and digestive processes in the body. Our sensory organs and our gut do much more than simply process physical stimuli, they are the vessels through which we experience much of our emotional and psychological struggles and strengths.

Working with mental health and supporting people through change allows me a profound privilege in witnessing how they draw from the rough, raw elements of their lives. This poem highlights my personal experience with tussling through change – the circular patterns that come with choosing new thought processes and reflecting on uncomfortable feelings. I hope it highlights the visceral experiences we hold when choosing and then rejecting healthy elements of change because its effects on us feel unfamiliar and difficult.

While it is a privilege to witness the change in others, it means nothing for my own personal growth unless I invite those very processes that I romanticize in them, to do its real, very unromantic work in me. I cannot change by appreciating and championing change in others. I will not grow while I am only identifying how many of their characteristics I am missing in my life. It is impossible to satiate my hunger by watching them eat.

1.2 ABANDONMENT VS. OVERWHELMENT

All living creatures possess the survival instinct and are fully capable of behaviours that ensure survival when encountering threats to its survival. Similar holds true for all mammals, but unlike in other species, in mammals the survival needs are met by the primary caregivers during infancy. As such, the survival instincts have been 'fine-tuned' for dependence upon the caregivers such that if the caregivers are unable to cater to the survival needs, it triggers instinctive behaviours by the offspring to demand support for survival from the caregivers. Should the survival demands remain unanswered, then the chance of survival of the offspring is diminished, ending the journey of growth and life. In humans, if the survival needs are met and the infant grows into a child, any traumatic instances that triggered a fear of survival during infancy can leave scars on the psyche. If the primary caregivers are unable to convey comfortable delivery of survival needs to the infant, survival threats that are experienced during infanthood can fester fears for survival in the psyche throughout life. These unsatisfied needs for survival stem from psychologically significant instances of 'abandonment'[17] experienced during infancy, which can lead to the demands for survival needs to become deep-seated in the psyche, making them linger into adulthood. "When you do not get your safety needs met at a young age, they do not go away; they are imprinted in the subconscious memory of your emotional mind. As an adult, you become subconsciously needy, always searching for love or wanting to be liked. You will blame others for your mistakes because you desperately need the love and adoration of the authority figures in your life."[18] From an evolutionary psychology perspective, such a trap in the survival stage of development is termed as a "fixation of an adaptive solution" to survival.[19] While the survival instinct is universal, a fixation is differentiated from it by the degree of prominence and centrality of the survival quest within the adult's psyche[20] that leads to its prevalence in adults, which is exhibited as more frequent actions that demand satisfying basic survival needs, seen as 'selfish and spiteful behaviour'[21] in everyday life.

Our research participant, Sonja Kotze in her poem: "The girl" (1.2.1), describes this survival threat stemming from childhood experiences as: "... *a lack of love from a primary caregiver*". She describes 'fixation' in the survival stage as the: "... *experience of a little girl that got stuck for 42 years*"; thus, supporting the notion that one can get 'fixated' or 'trapped' in the survival stage of development. She shares the consequences of this abandonment in her life to have resulted in: continually encountering (potentially unconsciously seeking) further traumas in life, wearing a mask or a persona[22] as a defence mechanism, defining herself by the roles she performed, evaluating her self-worth from her achievements, and most importantly, expecting a change in behaviour from her unloving mother to remedy the situation. Kotze shares enablers to self-leadership development through self-reflection in therapy, counselling, and coaching that encouraged an acknowledgement of traumas as opportunities for growth; thus, learning to embrace her traumas that are her imperfections. Through acceptance of her past experiences and using them as tools for learning and development, she shares how she began to incorporate self-empathy, self-love, and self-care in her life to start her self-leadership development journey.

The polar opposite of abandonment, or if the child experiences the opposite of abandonment, is termed 'overwhelment' or 'engulfment'.[23] It refers to development during childhood that was perceived by the child to be so intensely attentive by the caregivers that it leads to a disregard for dangers in the world. Such perceptions are unlikely to develop during infancy, as the dependence on the attention of the primary caregivers to cater to the survival needs of the infant is so great that an infant is unlikely to experience overwhelment. However, such instances are more likely to be felt during childhood rather than during infancy. Our research participant, Nidheesh Sharma in his poem: *"From dented cages to inspiring leader"* (1.2.2), shares his memories of his childhood that was largely devoid of concerns for survival. He generalizes his experiences of childhood and shares his belief that childhood is a time of: "... *living in a bubble where the world is a great place. Where we are safe. Where we can trust everyone*". This overwhelment is shared to have translated into a host of typical behaviours such as lack of discipline, motivation, and an abundance of trust in others. For example, during instances when there is a need to pass judgement regarding the trustworthiness of others, and due to overwhelment, the judgement is skewed in favour of trusting others, bears the risk of experiencing 'dread',[24] which Sharma describes as: *"Breaking of trust is dreadful"*, but it is the rising from its ashes that permits growth. As such, Sharma supports the existential notion of 'dread' or 'angst' that suggests that while one experiences anxiety from what one fears, one also desires what one fears. The concept is frequently associated with the desire and the orientation to sin, but Sharma reveals the hidden growth that lurks in 'dread'. As such, since a prime shortcoming for growth for those having encountered such a childhood development is a continued dependence on support and love by family and friends which leads to challenges to: "... *trust one's own self and your own decisions*", making bad decisions and experiencing 'dread' emerges as an enabler for growth beyond overwhelment.

Similar to Sharma, our research participant, Meena in the poem: *"Dear Orchid"* (1.2.3), shares facets of parental overwhelment. These include: over-attentiveness, alertness, patience, praise, adoration, advice, provision, and protection which she expresses to have been suffocating. She expresses this as: *"... Your sweet protection that robbed me of air"*. The effects on her are shared as emotional dependence, leading to a deep fear of losing parents and extreme proximity which she states as having left little room for a spouse in her life, which she expresses as: *"... they almost fill the role of a spouse in terms of a lifelong support system"*. Physical distancing is shared as an enabler to personal growth for her, which she states as: *"Leaving my parents enabled the questioning and acknowledgement of the life I define for myself"*, adding that: *"it is empowering to take control of your own life and decide on your future"*.

Emerging from the poetries regarding abandonment during infancy and childhood, and overwhelment during childhood are the problems of an imbalance for self-leadership growth that arises from both. While enablers from abandonment are suggested to require professional help in the form of psychotherapy and coaching, and learning to love oneself and practising self-care, our participants who encountered overwhelment suggest balancing of the overprotection with dread, and balancing engulfment with self-empowerment using distance, space, and separation from the caregiver responsible for it to facilitate growth. This enabler may be firstly seen as erecting boundaries between oneself and those who engulf one. The enabler can be extended to be regarded as 'epistemological distance'[25] between oneself and those that infringe upon one's ability to have a perspective about oneself.

1.2.1 THE GIRL

You are not planned
You are a difficult child
You are bossy
You are not smart enough
The girl shrunk away

Your body does not belong to you
Your brain is average
Your heart belongs in a locked box
Your ambition is too big for this world
The girl starts rebelling

You are a teenage mom and wife

You have to be a helpmate
You need to work
You need to study
The girl worked hard and loved hard

You get your degree
You are a success
You don't feel it
You don't value yourself
The girl starts questioning

You bury a child
You bury a marriage
You deal with your baggage
You pick yourself up
The girl walks a journey of self-discovery

You find yourself
You love yourself
You find love again
You own your value
The girl is now a woman

Sonja Kotze

Kotze's Explanation: This poem represents my life journey using words and phrases that I have heard from my mom and other influential people during my journey. Some of those phrases were ones I came up with myself as a narrative to make sense of my inner workings and circumstances. I walked a hard journey to self-discovery and ultimately self-love. Imperfection marred my life, but I can now see the beauty and opportunity it created. I used the analogy of a girl becoming a woman to express the experience of a little girl that got stuck for 42 years. This journey allowed me to nurture her, fill the emotional gaps, and love her as she deserved, and now deserves to be loved.

Lack of love and connection, wearing masks, and assuming roles defined me as a human being. I allowed it to define me. Despite years of therapy and counselling, I still held on to a naive hope and believed that my mom could and should provide me with the love that I deserve. Today I realise that she is incapable of giving that and I have the responsibility to self-actualise and stop looking to her, other people, experiences, and achievements to self-actualise. Through therapy, coaching, encouragement, and love from my husband, my father, and other loved ones I can relook at the little girl inside and admire her for her courage, resilience, big heart, and legacy.

My journey allows me to relate to women in various ways. I have experienced a lack of love from a primary caregiver, sexual abuse, teenage pregnancy, emotional abuse from a husband, the illness and death of a child, divorce, and cancer of my new husband. Despite the pain I also experienced achievement, seeing my two beautiful daughters grow up and be successful at being human, an amazing career that took me all over the world, a legacy of people I mentored and supported and the love of a husband that I did not think was possible. These experiences allow me to have the gift of empathy and love. I was so bogged down by what I believed I did not have or did not get that I missed the beauty of my journey. By reflecting on my now almost 42-year life journey I can value even the pain and imperfections to see that my life with its pain and imperfection is a gift. I can inspire and motivate, and I can love like no other.

1.2.2 FROM DENTED CAGES TO AN INSPIRING LEADER

When life spreads its bounteous hands
Trust is what morning is to night
We step into the world with a leap of faith
The pages are blank, the hopes are bright

But change is persistent
Deceit is in the veins
Seen appears so unseen
Till the day the truth unveils

People come and people go
The impact on us we would only know
When loyalty puts itself to a test
Leaving behind a lesson or the feeling of being blessed

Don't trust, I was warned
Life is not always fair
Still valued honesty and faithfulness
As I always had the people who really care

Surely, there will come a time
When from the ashes of the pages
Rises a story of imperfection
Rescuing others from their dented cages

Nidheesh Sharma

Sharma's Explanation: This poem is based on trust and how people today use others to achieve their own goals.

We start life with an empty book. As children, we are so naive and raw, and end up living in a bubble where the world is a great place. Where we are safe. Where we can trust everyone. But this changes with life experiences as the real faces of others come to the surface.

Deceitfulness and dishonesty are such a common practice in today's world, both in professional and personal life. Going through betrayal really changes one as a person. As a result, it is not only difficult to trust others but it becomes difficult to trust one's own self and your own decisions. Various people come into your life for various learnings. But when their loyalty to you is put on the test, you will either feel betrayed and learn something from it, or you would feel grateful for the loyal people in your life.

These days, everyone easily says: "don't trust anyone", "be careful" and "life is not fair". With such negativity around, it is easy to follow the crowd and perhaps make wrong decisions that are against your values. One can easily go astray after such an experience but what makes the difference is the support of family and friends. The people around us can greatly influence our recovery period from a life event. As long as your family and friends care and love you, you have all the motivation in the world to heal and move on with life.

With the right support, one is definitely able to come out of this pain as a much stronger person with a better view of the world. The soul, as well as the ability to trust, is scarred but one can heal and then carry these scars to support others in their battles. And this can only happen by talking to others. One can only teach others about life's battles once one has gone through the harsh experiences of life and turned those experiences into life learnings. Breaking of trust is dreadful, especially if it was perpetrated by someone you really loved or looked up to. However, it is not impossible to rise above this and make a positive impact on the people around you.

1.2.3 DEAR ORCHID

As he poured a glass of wine,
A sigh full of life,
reminiscent of death,
He contemplated...

Dear Orchid, why is it that your petals
hang
so
heavy?

I was never the confident gardener -
Always attentive, patient.
A slave to your temperament.
Trial and error,
I've done everything I could to give you the life I wanted you to live

With you I have learnt many lessons:
Direct sunlight has burned scars in your leaves;
Protective glass has smothered and suffocated
You;
Waterlogged roots have scared me with your near death, as I was
almost forced to
dispose of your
remains.
Against all odds, with faith and prayer and God's good grace
Once more, I saw your blooming face

You've been with me a lifetime now,
Like soul mates.
I have watered your soul for 31 years
Blossoming
more beautiful each year, extending tall towards the sun – further away
Sublime humidity
Temperature
Kind words of praise
Advice – only for your well being
Loving gaze of adoration each
Night.
And still
Now,
Your petals
Wilt.
Your leaves
Dry.
Your roots
Age.
And the water remains.

Oh, Giver of Life!
It was not Your sun
that wounded me.
It was not Your sweet protection

that robbed me of air.
It was not Your water
that weakened the blood the flows within my veins.

What could You do as
I blossomed with courage into my own?
Growing away from You,
Bittersweet as I lose my
Religion.
The more I live, the more I realise
Only I can save my tortured soul.

Meena

Meena's Explanation: One of my biggest fears is that of losing my parents. I am very close to them and in my mind, they almost fill the role of a spouse in terms of a lifelong support system (I even have their wedding date tattooed on my shoulder). I have been single for a while now, and as I am well into my thirties, the societal pressures of getting married have affected me. I have felt loneliness in terms of not being able to share my journey with a partner and I know that my parents will not be there forever. I see this emotional dependence on my parents as a form of imperfection in my life.

Also, in growing up, I have realised I cannot share as much with my parents as I used to, they are very protective and come from a different generation where life and expectations were very different. Although I have lived away from home and in a different province for over a decade now, moving to Cape Town and completing the MBA this year was the first time I made a move on my own, financially supporting myself and moving across the country alone, with no existing support structures. I was forced to build my own relationships and support structures from scratch. I realised that I have been very dependent on them over my life for emotional support and stability, so it is a difficult journey for both my parents and me to move past this and become more independent. They have also had significant influence over the decisions in my life. I grew up thinking that they knew best, and coming from quite a conservative close-knit community, there was a lot of shaming done. The words that resonate are "what will people think?".

Part of my story is that ten years ago I was involved in a near-death accident because one of my best friends was driving under the influence. I had to have surgery for internal organ repair and it was very traumatic for my parents, which also made them hold on to me much more. It was an extremely shameful experience that was not really ever discussed, but it was also a blessing that brought us so much closer together that I don't think we would have enjoyed the last ten years together as much as we have. This experience is also representative of the close family deaths we have experienced along the way – my grandparents, my mom's best friend being the closest.

To this day, my dad still calls me to ask, "My child how can I make your life easier?" He feels my feelings so deeply; however, he also feels helpless because as I grow older there are things that my parents cannot understand nor fix. In the last year, my dad has taken up a new hobby in raising orchids. Each night he comes home and talks to his orchids over a glass of wine, which formed the backdrop of this poem.

The uneasy tension between growing up and becoming your own person but also losing the joys and safety of youth and the parent-child relationship.

Experiences with dealing with and accepting death.

Pain can be used as a gift – I am made up of all the mistakes I have made, which have enabled me to become stronger.

Leaving my parents enabled the questioning and acknowledgement of the life I define for myself and moving away from the burden of meeting their expectations based on a life they have defined for me.

Take away:

Life is uncertain, cherish and appreciate the people you love.

I find that gratitude is where I find my solace.

Find your own path, you can't follow someone else's expectations.

Strength can be found in looking at the journey you have been on thus far in order to give you hope for the future, and it is empowering to take control of your own life and decide on your future.

1.3 The survival-stage leader

Using the poetry shared by our research participants, a prominent area of psychological scarring concerning abandonment by the caregivers during infancy or early childhood results in fundamental psychological growth stumbling blocks that have the potential to trap or fixate one in the survival stage of leadership development. Our last research participant in this section, Wayne Idas, in his poem: *"Reflections on leadership"* (1.3.1), links the fundamentals of this developmental stage to leadership.

Having been pushed into a leadership role without self-leadership development, beyond the stage of survival, Idas confesses: *"My own need for safety has been a barrier to my team and myself"*. Furthermore, he reflects on a manager whose: *"... own history created this need for safety"*. He goes on to elaborate on some characteristics of leadership stemming from the survival stage of leadership, which include being untrusting, defensive (*"to survive, all's attack"*), intrusively questioning (*"My questions are our snare"*) that curb innovation and enthusiasm, and conforming to such an extent that it stifles creativity.

Such leadership can be challenged to qualify as 'leadership', as it is more representative of people in leadership roles rather than people exhibiting leadership capabilities. Several behaviours emerge as typical of people trapped in the survival stage of self-leadership development, such as heightened cautiousness and vigilance, impatience which leads them to be highly demanding, suppressed anger and projection of the anger onto others, and a lack of trust in others, to name a few. When in leadership positions, such behaviours result in an inability to delegate, intense planning, a tendency to micro-manage, and a general risk-averseness (except for instances where the psyche or cognitive assessment of survival relies on taking the risk).

1.3.1 REFLECTIONS ON LEADERSHIP

You come to me idea in hand
what, when, why, who, how,
All you wanted was for me to understand,
Cross your t's I'll show you now.

You've finished your t's,
Never again to create new,
Innovation on her knees
Another talent gone too soon.

Reflection stares back
Forgotten stories laid bare
To survive all's attack
My questions are our snare

Another recruit – idea on the first day,
You are talent – build it right away.

Wayne Idas

Idas' Explanation: The first 2 stanzas speak to my leadership before the leadership and advanced leadership courses. These get the most lines as the most time was spent here. The third stanza speaks to my experience in advanced leadership module 1 and the exploration of my Enneagram type (6). Very little time has passed since the advanced leadership course and therefore few lines. The poem shows how my own need for safety has been a barrier to my team and myself.

Stanza 1

A direct report approaches a leader with an idea. The leader is not dismissive but needs all of the information upfront, whereas the report is just looking for support and enthusiasm. The line manager insists that the idea is beyond reproach.

Stanza 2

The report has ensured that the idea is beyond reproach but much of the innovation and enthusiasm has been drained from the idea and the report is unlikely to quickly bring another.

Stanza 3

The line manager understands that his own history created this need for safety that he creates through all of the questions. But also, the questions trap the direct report and himself.

Stanza 4

A new recruit joins and the line manager trusts him/her to grow it right away. There is also a much faster movement without all of the questionings.

2   CONFORMING

Emerging out of the first stage of survival, by having satisfied their survival needs, children enter into the age that is popularly known as the 'terrible twos'. The difficulty faced by the child is that unlike the selfish stage of survival, the child begins to understand the needs of the caregivers in addition to his, her or their[26] own needs. To effectively address this novel understanding of the 'other', children around this age are forced to learn to communicate. Communications with their caregivers, at this stage, are a negotiation between self-needs and the needs of the caregiver. The learning that is ideal to emerge from it is for the child to understand that: "life is more pleasant and enjoyable, less threatening, and less difficult, if it can live in a state of harmony with its caregivers and siblings".[27] This teaches the child to compromise some of his, her or their needs, or accept delays by the caregivers in addressing their needs as a means. This helps to ensure that the needs of the caregivers are also being catered for, to a certain extent. To do so, the child learns to obey the rules set by the caregivers, and develops a harmony with them in conforming to the rules.

Although this stage is typically associated with ages from two to seven, the fear of loss of safety, comfort, and love can make one restrict themselves to the behaviours as prescribed by the caregivers, which can ensure the following of the path laid out for them by the family even in later years in life. Either out of demands for respect by the caregivers, demands for love towards them, or stemming from a fear of abandonment, the need to conform may become imprinted in the psyche of the child and incorporated into patterns of behaviour to such an extent that it can fixate them to this stage of development. Our research participant, Nomandlovu Dumse in her poem: *"Purposefully"* (2.1.1), expresses her feelings of how expectations of parents and her aunt, who was a psychologically influential adult figure in her upbringing, are incredibly well-aligned to what she believes is her purpose in life. The naming of her, the way she was raised, the way she was loved, and the path she was directed to follow have led to her success and purpose in life. She expresses it as the: *"... universe [to have] laid my purpose bare for me to live"*; thus, sharing the extent of her devotion to the path laid out for her. This makes her question, in her poem: *"who am I then to not listen, who am I then to not follow"*. As such, the participant highlights some facets of the trap of the conforming stage of psychological growth.

While Dumse regards conforming to embody her purpose in life, most of our research participants challenged the desirability of continued conforming in adulthood. For example, a research participant who decided to stay anonymous, in his/her/their poem *"Perrin's roundabout"* (2.1.2), represents this path as followership; thus, deeming it opposite to leadership. Anonymous expresses the contrast between conforming and non-conforming as the: *"loop that is worn and travelled"*, and the other as the execution out of a personal choice. Through the example of a fictional character and the choices he makes in life, the research participant expresses the clear vision of the choices of either conforming, where *"... the path is smooth"* or questioning the norms and taking the road with: *"... the bush overgrown"*. The research participant highlights the fact that a lack of fixation at this stage, with a choice of conforming to the prescribed path, is felt as the decision to rub one against one's grain. The participant talks about solitary activities and a passion for writing, but the Calvinistic work ethic that is required to be conformed to by the family does not permit him/her/them to see such work as a vocation. Thus, the participant highlights a demand of conforming as sacrificing one's optimal person-job fit,[28] which is proven to be a prominent factor for being happy at work.[29] As such, the participant suggests that conforming may require one to sacrifice one's happiness by being a follower.

Another research participant extends the concept of conforming, from adhering to the prescribed path dictated by the caregivers to one that is ingrained in society. Alun Josias in his poem: *"Ode to be free"* (2.1.3), talks about his: *"... life forced"* out of necessity. He talks about his socio-economic background as: *"Coming from a background where I'm the first generation to gain a tertiary education despite limited financial resources and a household where alcoholism and abuse were common place"*. Lack of privilege made the known-path-to-success his direction in life, that was taken whilst shrouded in: *"... self-doubt, guilt, worry, feelings of inadequacy"*. Yet the obligation to: *"repay the sacrifices made on my behalf"* presented him with sufficient pressure to continue on the path, and achieve success. Retrospectively, he regards this behaviour as an attempt at *"masking my feelings of inadequacy"* due to the socio-economic background he belonged to. Sadly, despite the successes, he considers them to be meaningless. In seeking substance, he dreams of a life of spontaneity, a less forced, and more natural growth. He emotionally expresses how his 15-month-old son is teaching him about naturally growing, and being spontaneous, to let-go and find peace in doing nothing.

One of our research participants, Amanda April in her poem: *"Questionable truths"* (2.1.4), explicitly challenges 'conforming' in the explanation of her poem from a moral stance. She states: *"We have been socialized and conditioned by our caregivers, our culture and society, to accept thoughts and ideas as truths"*. In her poem, she regards this as a: *"... thinly-veiled blanket of security"*, highlighting that the safety in conforming to the collective is one's comfort zone,[30] but challenges it by stating it to be 'thinly-veiled'. She associates this blanket with warmth, but regards it to be: *"mouldy"*; thus, highlighting that not all aspects of conforming can be adopted without a cognitive assessment. She presents an example drawn from Apartheid in South Africa, where following the historic separation of the people based on race represented the status quo, but it needed to be challenged and questioned. She urges for bravery to do so, despite the: *"... fear of losing what I was conditioned to believe"*. As such, she urges others to challenge the knowledge before embarking on: *"well-worn paths"*.

April presents some enablers to avoid the trap at this stage, including: flexibility instances, listening and learning, as well as drawing back on an inquisitive childhood mindset before choosing to conform. Another research participant, Jacques Vogeli, in his poem: *"The squeeze"*

(2.1.5), presents meditation and mindfulness[31] as enablers to relieve oneself from the pressures of conformity. He expresses the relapse into fulfilling the expectations of conforming from childhood that he states in the lines: *"Expectation floods the eye, From the early days at school"*, when the push for performance was so great that he had developed irritable bowel syndrome. He explains how aspects of this stage in life linger to date and interfere in his relationships and productivity, for example, by self-sabotaging workflow and deadlines through procrastination to effectively induce stress in scenarios that may well have been stressful. He attributes this inclination to ensuring that the scenario represents a 'push for performance' so as to psychologically regard it worthwhile to attempt. He suggests that continued meditation can facilitate an escape from this tendency.

While the conforming state of psychological development entails adherence to the boundaries set by the primary caregivers, cultural and societal norms influence these boundaries that may be adhered to by the primary caregivers, and as a result prescribed to the child. As such, challenging these may require non-conformance towards the path prescribed by the parents, but also the path adhered to by the parents.

2.1.1 PURPOSEFULLY

from the day I was born
from the place and the time
from the position and family
to whom I was born
it's as if the universe conspired

my ups and my downs
my successes and my challenges
my quirks and what I stumble upon
my interests and my convictions
all have an unmistakable congruity

who am I then to not listen?
who am I then to not follow my calling?
for there is a purpose for me to fulfil
it is when I have fulfilled it that I will have lived

Nomandlovu Dumse

Dumse's Explanation: When I look at my life journey, where I am today and where I have been, I realise that its always been that there is a reason I was born and there is a clear purpose which I was born to achieve.

I look at my Aunt who named me Nomandlovu, I listen to her speak of her reasons behind giving me the name, her circumstances at the time and hopes (while she tells me these after I had turned 40); I realise that I have been living up to her expectations and hopes without even realizing it. I then understand why she always looked at me the way she did. I see the purpose I was born to fulfil.

My parents' way of raising me (among my many siblings), the way they showed me love, the way they taught me responsibility and care for self or others as well as the messages they drilled into my head seems to have been intended or useful to drive me to a path that will enable me to live my purpose. My siblings, family and friends keep telling me messages (through words or actions) that I have been ignoring, or not making sense of, but when I look back, and taking stock of my journey with them in my life – it all make sense and it's been clear to me that they are all part of this beautiful conspiracy (universe laid my purpose bare for me to live).

I look at my career journey, the choices and mistakes I made, the successes I achieved and the challenges I went through; they all seem to have been teaching me lessons and preparing me to successfully live my purpose. I look at the various people (managers, colleagues, leaders, teams, suppliers, clients etc.) who have had an impact on my career and see how they have in their different ways contributed in my life's purpose.

As I grow or mature through education (life, corporate and academic lessons), I am starting to see a connection and I'm starting to make sense of why I am always pulled to certain things and find peace when doing certain things. When sensing conflict in my life, be it at work and/or socially, I am reminded that these conflict-generating activities/conditions are pulling me away from (or are in contradiction to) my purpose – hence they feel like a conflict. When I see the ease with which I engage in certain spaces or do certain things, I get an affirmation that my purpose is clear.

This poem, purposefully, is a reminder to me of this clarity of purpose and a challenge to me to live my life purposefully, not just for me but for the universe and those who are part of the conspiracy (dad, mom, family, siblings, friends, lecturers, classmates, colleagues, bosses, community, society at large).

2.1.2 PERRIN'S ROUNDABOUT

Two dusty circles side by side; kissing briefly in the middle
The first loop worn and travelled, flanked with spears of ash
The second far smaller, strewn with avenues of beech
Down one a young wolf strides, his footfalls sure and brash

The scent of samara thick and heavy sticks to his furry brow
Meliae steal the light; daggers clenched between their teeth
He hurries down this figure eight, but soon his path is forked
Before him lies two simple arches, which shall he pass beneath?

On the right, the path is smooth and an axe lies in the road
Its handle, long and black, flecked with streaks of white
Sharpened wedge grinning cruelly, with whippets on the sides
The axe sings to him softly; a song of power and of might

To the left, the bush overgrown, a hammer lies forgotten
Handle stained with years of forgeman's soot and embers
Blunt-face hard and worn, hemmed with cranes in flight
Promising to create what lasts as long as anyone remembers

And so he stops and thinks; which path shall be choose?
Shall he choose the left or to right? The hammer or axe?
Does he want to change his loop? Or to build and to develop?
And if he chooses wrongly, how long until he cracks?

Anonymous

Anonymous' Explanation: At the heart of this poem is the young wolf, which is a reference to Perrin Aybara, one of the main characters in Robert Jordan's Wheel of Time series. At the beginning of the series, Perrin is apprenticed to the local blacksmith and has a very kind and gentle disposition. However, as the series progresses it is revealed that he and his two best friends are destined to change the world. Though each of the three are thrust into roles of great prominence by fate, the burden of this responsibility seems to weigh heaviest on Perrin who never seems to reconcile himself to his new life as a general. Frequent references are made throughout the series to Perrin trying to choose between a life defined by the hammer (his life as a blacksmith) and the axe (his weapon of choice in battle).

Perrin would be happiest if he were able to return to his master's forge, but his protective nature means he always chooses, albeit reluctantly, the axe, as this will always help him to protect those that cannot protect themselves. In many ways, Perrin's inability to choose between the life he wants (blacksmith) and his duty (general) mirrors my own inability to do the same.

I am never happier than when I am reading and/or writing. My enjoyment of these activities comes in large part from the fact that they are solitary activities; it's not that I dislike people, but rather without interruptions I am able to exercise my creativity to the full. In a perfect world I would be a fantasy writer. The heron, a symbol of Hephaestus, is a reference to the need to create I feel deep down in my bones as is the beech tree.

But I was raised with a profound sense of duty and a Calvinistic work ethic: that success was not an objective for me, but rather an obligation. I have to succeed. To work myself into positions of authority and from that position to use my authority to do as much good as possible. Though these qualities do come from my family, to some extent, they are largely due to my schooling, referenced by the black and white on the axe's handle and the whippets on its sides. I know that this will/can never make me happy. However, like Perrin, I forsake my own happiness in favour of that of others (symbolised by the ash trees on the one path) leading me to resent my own success which is why the Meliae (usually peaceful wood nymphs that live exclusively in ash trees) are armed to the teeth in the poem.

Perrin never did get back to his forge, at least not for long and not while there were people to protect, though he did find some small measure of happiness along the way. However, I fear that as long as I live this half-life of roundabout servitude then I never will find that same small measure as I will be too busy resenting my life to recognise the good in it. I do realise that, like Perrin, the only person who can decide the path my future will take is me, but even as I write this I can feel the axe's pull; calling me to walk the path I've chosen so many times before when all I want to do is take the one less travelled.

2.1.3 ODE TO BE FREE

To this day, a life forced...
a journey shaped by circumstance and will,
always fighting the current, afraid to let go.
Stop, trust and follow.

Twice before have I relinquished this tendency.
Choosing to forge a life with my partner; creating a legacy.
The gift of my son, my pride, my love, my glee.
Proof that I can let go and be free;
Stop, do less, just be.

Still I keep running this individual race,
motivated by self-doubt, guilt, worry, feelings of inadequacy.
Or perhaps it's just me?
How will I know when the race is won?
Will it be enough or will I come undone?
Stop, accept, try honesty.

Competition for my time:
Month ends, deadlines, meetings, lead and be led,
Sleep, eat well, exercise, be kind to yourself,
Husband, father, provider, family man,
Purpose, courage, self-love, values…
Stop, be still, and breathe.

Alun Josias

Josias' Explanation: This poem represents my journey to date. Coming from a background where I'm the first generation to gain a tertiary education despite limited financial resources and a household where alcoholism and abuse were commonplace, I felt tremendous pressure to succeed. This pressure was largely self-imposed; initially the drive to succeed was to repay the sacrifices made on my behalf. But over the years it has morphed into something more superficial and less meaningful. To this end, all significant decisions in my life have been forced, often foregoing what I would 'like' for what I thought represented the highest payoff. Spontaneity avoided at all costs and efficiency preferred over substance. Too afraid to just let things develop naturally and at its own pace, I'd attempt to impose my will. As a result, the outcome would either be sub-optimal or I'd abandon it prematurely and not see it through to fruition.

I've since come to the realization that this behaviour is an attempt at masking my feelings of inadequacy. Moreover, the two greatest gifts in my life viz. my wife and son, serve as shining beacons in my life, reminding me of when I chose to simply follow. My son is almost 15 months old and is the embodiment of spontaneity. He has taught me to let go and find peace in doing nothing.

Recently, I had the privilege to attend a lecture on the physiological effects of breathing and was amazed at how being deliberate about one's breathing can alter one's behaviour. Now and then when I find myself getting caught in the web of life's transactions, I try to remember these lessons of stopping, keeping still and remembering to breathe… These are my first steps on my journey to being free.

2.1.4 QUESTIONABLE TRUTHS

What is this thinly-veiled blanket of security
Where I hide and seek comfort under –
the solace of my own unquestioned ignorance

The well-worn paths that never encounter diversity
The sophisticated lies shrouded in believable truths
of unscientific concepts of race, gender and religion

21

– the opioids of compliant masses
that gave birth to slavery of the mind and heart

Hold tightly to its feeble thread
Resist the notion of 'other'
Resist the mantle of truth
that transforms and opens gaping wounds

The weight of it ties me to fear
of losing what I was conditioned to believe
It locks me inside, where it is warm and mouldy
comfortable and imprisoned

Others dictate my thinking
because I have forgotten to question
because I choose to remain trapped
under the blanket of my demise

Amanda April

April's Explanation: To do otherwise would force me to confront the truths that I have been taught to fear the unknown, change, growth, enlightenment and transformation. We have been socialized and conditioned by our caregivers, our culture and society, to accept thoughts and ideas as truths.

As infants and children, our inquisitive minds propel us to learn and grow, to adapt and remain flexible in an ever-changing world around us.

As adults, we choose to enshrine ourselves in the familiar (all the things we already know). We fear the experience of a different 'me' – someone who, instead of judging and dismissing, is open to listen and learn. We often stubbornly refuse to shift our stance – preferring to die in the comfort of the old familiar 'truths' rather than grow in newness and hope.

2.1.5 THE SQUEEZE

Breathe in, breathe out.
Cold air in, warm air out.
Her voice warms my ears.
"Focus on here and now."
She guides me deeper into the present moment.
Breathe in, breathe out.

Breathe in,
My jaw unclenches and my frown dissolves.
The anxious tension slowly escapes.
Physically, my shoulders relax and settle.
Slowly, I break away from its grasp.
Breathe out.

Breathe in,
Where does this feeling come from?
Why has it always been here?
Expectation floods the eye,
From the early days at school
Don't go there!
Back to the now!
Breathe out.

Breathe in,
I've wondered again, lost in the past.
It isn't fair, why me?
Why do I have to carry them?
Why am I the responsible one?
"You can't end up like your brothers."
"You can't fail."
"You can do better."
Breathe out.

Breathe in,
But it is how you've always managed.
Your *modus operandi*,
Procrastination and pressure squeeze the best from you.
Look how far you've come.
"Return to the now,
Don't let the frustration claim you."
Breathe out.

Breathe in, breathe out.
Cold air in, warm air out.
"Clear your mind, and let the tranquillity wash over you."
(And equalise the highs and lows)
"For you cannot change the past,
But only the now."
Breathe in, breathe out.

Jacques Vogeli

Vogeli's Explanation: From an early age, a tremendous amount of pressure was placed on me to perform well at school. My two older half-brothers had not done particularly well at school and are struggling financially today. My parents thought I had a chance at living a financially successful life, so they pushed me to do well at school. Living with the constant fear of "financial failure" over my life, I was pushed in many ways to perform well at school. I was often placed in the top 10 of my grades; however, it was never good enough according to my stepfather. The pressure was so great in Grade 11 and 12 to perform academically, that I had developed Irritable Bowel Syndrome (IBS), a physical manifestation of this stress.

As a result of this pressure, I had become accustomed to performing under stress, where I would only work efficiently under pressure. Only once the cortisol was flowing through my veins and I had my back against the wall, was I capable of performing above what was expected of me. I sabotaged myself by procrastinating and creating some self-inflicted pressure. I still carry this habit of procrastination today, and it negatively impacts my relationship with my fiancée and my productivity at work.

I wish that I could accept this flaw of mine, something that I had developed in the pursuit of "perfection" and running away from failure. It prevents me from discovering what really interests me, as I'm perpetually caught in a state of catching-up on work. This results in unnecessary stress and anxiety in my life, which manifests itself physically. I can physically feel the anxiety leave my body at the start of a meditation session. It is notable and quite concerning to observe how we actually carry stress in our everyday lives. I've tried to justify my MO to myself by arguing that it has made me successful. I'm hoping to build a future of constructive stress management, while creating healthy working habits.

2.2 INTERNALITY VS. EXTERNALITY

"The first thing the baby has to learn, as soon as it is born, is to interact with (control) the world around it, so it can get its survival needs met".[32] This suggests that the strive to control others and the environment is initiated during infancy. Should positive outcomes emerge out of these attempts, i.e., the environment and others respond by catering to the needs of the infant, such behaviours are encouraged. The contrary occurs should the response from the external environment fail to support desired outcomes for the infant.

In research, the prominence of this positive or negative reinforcement[33] to control has been validated during childhood. These reinforcements have been found to lay the foundations for beliefs regarding control, which forms a core self-evaluation personality trait, one's locus of control,[34] that has implications for one's perceptions of control throughout life. An inclination to exercise personal control over the environment and others is known as an internal locus of control. The contrary leads to the development of a perception that control exists outside of personal control, known as an external locus of control.

While several aspects of childhood development contribute to the development of one's locus of control, parental care that is accompanied with autonomy and freedom to exercise control by the child is the essential first element of it. Additionally, such actions by the child require positive reinforcements to encourage them to control their surroundings. This supports the development of a perception of a link between one's actions and outcomes, which are foundational for an internal locus of control.

Research that aims at creating associations between personality traits with leadership inclinations regard internality, or an internal locus of control, to be associated with leadership,[35] with limited research opposing this relationship.[36] However, our research participant, with the pseudonym Iceberg in the poem: *"The waves of worry"* (2.2.1), explicitly challenges this link between internal locus of control and leadership. Iceberg states in the line: *"A lack of control is not lack of leadership, But rather too much control may indicate the exact opposite"*. Iceberg expresses how he/she/they has struggled to overcome this need for exercising personal control. He/she/they highlights shortcomings of internality, stating that it leads to deeply embedded fears.

So, how is it that such a personality trait can be largely viewed as conducive to leadership? *"… autonomy orientation was found to be positively associated with ego development, self-actualization, self-esteem, and other indicators of well-being, the control orientation was found to be associated with public self-consciousness, anxiety, and the coronary-prone behaviour pattern".*[37] The expectation of a positive response to one's actions leads to clarity of goals, direction, objectives, and vision, which can draw followers. However, the internal environment of such a leader is unquestioned by such research referred to earlier. Our research participants shed some much-needed light on this aspect. Iceberg refers to his/her/their internal environment as: *"inverted oceans"*, which is explained as exhibiting: *"Calm currents above, The ability to lead to shore, Despite internal frustration"*. As such, irrespective of internality and its association with leadership, it's shortcoming for self-leadership development is highlighted. With reference to enablers to shift such a control expectancy, Iceberg's self-reflective poem that is aimed at freeing him/her/them from such internality ends with the line: *"Now, back to considering those worries"*. The participants' perspective highlights the shortcoming of cognition[38] to shift control tendencies, and supports the notion of them being embedded as a personality trait according to psychodynamic theory.[39]

On the contrary, when overwhelment is accompanied by excessive control by the caregivers, a belief in a link between one's actions and the outcome is at risk of being sabotaged. Instead, the child may grow to develop a reliance on control by powerful others; the polar opposite of an internal locus of control known as external locus of control. Externality is said to lead to learnt helplessness,[40] and is greatly associated with many psychological problems including proneness to depression, helplessness, and hopelessness. There is a consensus of a lack of leadership qualities associated with externality, with little or no challenge to it in the academic literature. Even when challenged, these studies tend to be highly nuanced and restrictive in scenarios.[41]

One of our research participants, Vanessa Kimoro, in her poem: *"Faith"* (2.2.2), repeats the line: *"Still, I rise"* throughout the poem. Her belief in God, as the powerful controller of her fate and destiny, depicts an external locus of control. She proudly shares how the suspension of self-control and a belief in control by God allows her the courage not to surrender to difficulties encountered in life, and to be immensely resilient. However, in the explanation of the poem, she shares one example of the difficulty she faced when she was inappropriately touched by a taxi driver. She states: *"That was the last day I ever entered a Taxi"*; thus, challenging the extent of her resilience. While the event may not have led to psychological breakdown by assigning control to her powerful God as the protector, her perception of her immense resilience in the example shared is questionable. Nonetheless, she shares how assigning control externally bears the potential to shift responsibility and support resilience.

It is evident from literature, and our research participants, that there are aspects that challenge any notion of an optimal position on the internal-external scale. As such, it leads to the question whether one can juggle the two polar opposites to optimize the benefits from each end of the spectrum of control perspectives. The possibility of doing so is potentially greatest for those who are bi-locals,[42] and exhibit a shared responsibility of internality and externality,[43] or those with a balanced locus of control.[44] While the benefits of such an expectancy[45] are empirically researched, which include optimal subjective well-being,[46] there is a lack of a definitive understanding of how such an expectancy is formed or how it operates.

One of our research participants, Andrew Theunissen, in his poem: *"Leading me"* (2.2.3), presents his perception of control in the line: *"The change inside I can control, the rest not so"* which depicts a balanced locus of control. The benefits of such a personality disposition permits coping with a fast-changing world, and the acknowledgement of control by oneself, yet the influence of (generally, powerful) others. A prime benefit arising from this is that failure is seen as attempting to accomplish leadership goals and reap the benefits singlehandedly. He states in the line: *"Failure is going it alone"* and in the last verse inspiringly expresses the bounty of joy and success, positivity and fulfilment felt when uniting with others.

2.2.1 THE WAVES OF WORRY

Worries
Or are they really worries?
Maybe just false imaginations
Satisfying a yearning for critique and control
Activating a perverse urge to plan for the worst

Like an inverted ocean
Waves hidden beneath
Calm currents above
The ability to lead to shore
Despite internal frustration

Progress has no doubt been made
A relaxed facade being preferable to visible tension
Yet strides must be taken
Leadership comes from within
And changes should come in the form of actions

And so, false imaginations must not be a source of worry
Rather, a little perspective should help
A lack of control is not lack of leadership
But rather too much control may indicate the exact opposite
Now, back to considering those worries

Iceberg

Iceberg's Explanation: I am a constant worrier and this impacts my leadership style quite a bit. Historically, I have been quite dictatorial in my leadership style because I have been so used to worrying. However, in recent years I have become more aware of my personality, and how that impacts various facets of my life, including my leadership style. The reason why I worry is that I get a kick out of preparing for worst-case scenarios. If I do not prepare, I feel incomplete, almost like an addict who is unable to get their drug of choice.

Hence, I've come to the realisation that I must develop a more rational relationship to uncertainty and control, in the sense that worrying too much may actually lead to poor leadership on my part. I must also consider the various types of people that are present in the world, as not all people are like me.

2.2.2 FAITH

High or low,
Up or down,
Still, I rise.

Fall on my knees, surrender and all seems better.
Still, I rise.

Oh, I wonder, without my minder, where I would wander,
Still I rise.

Lost, but found,
Safe and sound,
Still, I rise.

Perfectly imperfect,
Still, I rise.

Vanessa Kimoro

Kimoro's Explanation: This poem reflects the importance of my faith in God to me. There are many times, especially this year, feeling alone in a foreign land. Difficulties that have come with accommodation and settling in made me question my choices for coming here. A Taxi experience, where a man tried to touch me, but luckily did not manage to get any further, I believe that God protected me that day. That was the last day I ever entered a Taxi. I have had some very good moments, and also difficult ones, away from family and friends, and when I feel that there is an ear to listen, I fall on my knees and surrender to God, which somehow lifts a load of uncertainty and sadness. I never used to understand the act of getting still with one's maker, but today, I realize that it is the most powerful tool to date. I can say, in all this, I have remained true to myself, and I know that this part of my story has a purpose in my journey.

2.2.3 LEADING ME

The World is fuelled by change abound;
Change around me, change in me, change;
What goal is mine? What direction calls?
The change inside I can control, the rest not so;

To be a leader seems to have it all figured out;
The work, the people, the relations – to set a common goal;
The more I lead, the more I seem to have to grow;
The ideal self, a canvas yet to be completed;

What holds me back? Why thoughts of failure?
To crumble, to fall, to fail. Or simply failing to try;
Or is it the people, the connection, the stories – the void of want;
Failure is not ego, mistakes or loss. Failure is going it alone;

Excitement, fulfilment and success abounds;
The future bright with all that could;
When I aspire to paint that canvas;
Not I alone, but we.

Andrew Theunissen

Andrew Theunissen's Explanation: This poem is the culmination of the ideas of a rapidly changing world in which we have to figure out how to be relevant, my own leadership journey, and personal growth.

I am intrigued by how quickly the world is changing. Technology is booming and the global population is growing into alarming numbers. Yet, at the same time, our society has taken these changes in its stride. People adapt as part of their nature while it causes them new problems at the same time. However, I struggle to visualise my future role as an engineering professional, given the ambiguity and uncertainty. It is a weakness that I am working on and striving to be more comfortable with the ever-present change.

My own leadership journey relied on most parts of doing what I do and striving for excellence. I have achieved more than the norm and as a result, I was handed leadership responsibilities. However, my personal reflections have highlighted the ability to make meaningful connections with the people around me as a blind spot that needs to be developed. Especially in leadership roles, I tend to be very task-driven at the expense of the team member or subordinate. The last few months have helped me to explore this problem and potential ways to rectify it. The biggest leap was the acknowledgement of this shortcoming in the first place. I will grow further if I can grow my interactions with people.

Lastly, I wanted the poem to end on a positive outlook for the future. This reflects my new-found excitement and motivation to actively mould the "ideal self" that I want to strive to. It brings across the act of having to actively choose to work towards it. It is not a passive process, but rather a continuous journey. This journey will only be achieved through the people around me, my close relationships, my work relationships, and my interaction with people in general.

2.3 THE CONFORMING LEADER

Different from leadership associated with the latter stages of psychological development, the focus of a leader that is fixated in the conforming stage of psychological development is one of fulfilling the organizational needs and intensely controlling aspects of the organization to achieve it. This is dually complementary in the case of family businesses, particularly where

29

joining one's family business is destined for an individual by the parents. An acceptance of the legacy, as our research participant, Nomandlovu Dumse expresses in her poem: "Purposefully" (2.1.1), is well-suited for such a leadership position. A similar person-organization fit[47] can be expected to exist where the business is aimed at satisfying the needs of the family as the proprietors, or in non-family-owned corporates, an example of such leadership is termed: 'transformational leadership', where the focus of the leader is on motivating the employees based on the shareholders' needs.[48] Individuals suited to such leadership, amongst other qualifications, must be comfortable in conforming to the greater needs of the organization or of the higher leadership that operates within the organization. The similarity is drawn from the conforming stage of psychological development, due to the comfort in the harmony of achieving one's own needs while co-operating with the needs of the caregiver and the greater needs of the family at large.

In reference to the stages of self-leadership development to follow, it may be questionable as to whether the attributes of leadership associated with this stage qualify for leadership, or are better acknowledged as followers of leaders that are given leadership positions. One of our research participants, Babar Dharani in his poem: "Soldierly" (2.3.1), recognizes this vital question of agency,[49] emphasizing that the relationship within any corporate between the shareholders and the executives is that they are agents of the principals. He acknowledges the need for qualifications and qualities to acquire such leadership roles, and the influence on others due to having such a position. However, he compares such roles to that of a soldier who follows orders and executes the demands of the proprietors or that of senior executives. To achieve organizational goals, team members must be challenged, engaged, sold the organization's vision, and given interesting, achievable, yet challenging goals to motivate the team and the members. As such, while leadership skills are indeed required, they are needed so for enhancing followership. However, Dharani highlight that other skills are not required for such leaders; arguing that such leadership requires limited individuality and creativity. He challenges the level of happiness of those who are further developed along the self-leadership development stages, particularly when faced with the realization of being *"underutilized"* in respect of the limited skills required as a conforming leader. As such, he presents an argument that while the stages of development of self-leadership align with psychological growth, and the desirability of psychological growth, there are leadership positions and requirements that are potentially better suited to each stage of development.

2.3.1 SOLDIERLY

Armed with esteemed qualifications,
I am told I am skilled and suited to lead,
Only to find myself in leadership positions,
Sealing the fate of so many,
But working similar to a soldier, motivating my team by selling them the greater vision

Of safeguarding commercial interests of the corporates,
While being self-driven by my salary,
And at best, for a 'star' on my C.V.

My actions, directed; my purpose, imposed on me.
My identity stagnating within family constraints,
Converging to transform into one of my narrow-minded colleagues,
Or at best, becoming one of the gourmands I service.
My individuality, diminishing! My creativity, hampered!
My skills, underutilized and homogenized! Becoming increasingly replaceable.
Craving for happiness in a soulless city,
Wishing to tear myself away from the barracks.

But how to do so when my ammunition has led to success and leadership roles,
When I am told I am winning, privileged, and lucky.
Consciously questioning their definitions, and seeking the courage to self-define them,
But the answer lay in prioritizing and safeguarding my sanity,
In the pursuit of happiness, meaning, and purpose,
In a city surrounded by nature, in an institution that shares my values,
With colleagues, whom I look up to, helping to make me increasingly unique.
Content, in living my personally defined success.

Babar Dharani

Dharani's Explanation: The poem is a reflection of my earlier jobs and working in the family business. The privilege of having prestigious qualifications, leadership roles at a young age, and handsome salaries were certainly useful for boosting an amplified self-esteem. However, in the absence of alignment with organizational values, the burden of conforming to the organizational requirements (evaluating others, motivating team members, achieving set goals each quarter, scrupulously controlling the organizational finances) when I was not motivated by a self-defined purpose, placed a heavy burden on my level of happiness and sense of freedom. I felt like a cog in a large machinery, easily replaceable, and increasingly being moulded to become like the people I worked with and worked for – people I did not want to be like. Trapped in the rat race, and succeeding at it, makes escaping the most courageous act. An act I tried to undertake by self-defining my goals and many fundamentals of life rather than conforming to the definition prescribed by society, but could not have undertaken if it weren't for the seismic burden 'conforming' placed on my mental health that left me little choice but to break free.

3 DIFFERENTIATING

The progression of children from being predominantly involved in interactions with people at home, during infancy and early childhood, to commence interacting with community members and society pushes them onto a journey of socialization. The increased variety of the people encountered during socialization allows them to develop variations in their identity compared to that of the caregivers and other family members. As such, the stage is termed 'differentiating', as it involves the development of aspects of oneself that differentiate one from one's family members. While during this stage individuals may largely conform to societal and cultural norms, the knowledge obtained from socialization allows individuals to form collectives with unrelated individuals in the community that is founded on some common grounds like social identity groups, such as race, gender, socio-economic background, et cetera or shared interests.

This stage is said to commence from eight years of age, when the child leaves the home and the protective elements within it and: "… takes responsibility for its self-protection by belonging to a group, community or gang".[50] If the needs associated with this stage, such as a need for acceptance by the group or feeling protected, are not met during childhood and teenage years, they occupy a central and significant position in one's psyche that can trap one in this stage of development. Indicators of people trapped in this stage include either those who are highly competitive and status-seeking or, on the contrary, those filled with self-doubt that results in them continually holding back, procrastinating, or hiding in the shadows. While similar attributes can be observed for personality development imbalances in earlier years of development, the imbalances developed during socialization are considered less foundational than core-personality attributes which are developed during ages two to seven. Nonetheless, their significance is highlighted by many of our research participants in their poetry.

One of our research participants, Elmarie Eises in her poem: "The butterfly" (3.1.1), shares feelings of being rejected by such a group during this stage of psychological development, and the consequences thereof. She attributes these feelings to have arisen from socialization with those outside the family circle in her line: "My heart beats, not for my present parents, or my siblings, much less for uncles and aunts. My heart beats for you, whose ducks are in order, whose chicks can be counted before their arrival"; thus, sharing her need to belong to a group outside her immediate and extended family that is associated with the stage of differentiating. She shares that she felt rejected due to certain attributes of the members of the group that were absent from her life. She explains these experiences as feelings of being: "… rejected by people that I cared about" and goes on to share the consequences of it as: "… so I thought as a defence mechanism I should rather keep people at a distance". She openly shares the consequences of this for her in her adult life in the explanation of the poem, where she states: "It makes me see in me, in-adequacy, in-efficiency, in-ability, in-stability", and being: "sluggish". By doing

33

so, she highlights the significance of social psychology as foundational experiences in these formative years.

Unlike Eises, another of our research participants, Chike M Nzerue in his poem: *"A letter to a dream killer"* (3.1.2), shares another facet encountered during socialization. Children are inclined to make sense of themselves and one another; hence develop self-identity, to satisfy the core motive of establishing relationships and functioning well in groups and prospering. Since identity is largely founded on comparisons to others, its cognition is based on an assessment of oneself with regard to looks, attributes, and characteristics 'seen' in others. This frequently leads to a ranking of self-attributes to others. When a self-assessment leans in one's favour, it permits the development of self-esteem. On the contrary, ranking others above oneself sows the seeds for self-doubt. "… self-doubt is problematic since it is inimical to… [one's] entire social enterprise".[51] He metaphorically depicts self-doubt as his *"dream killer"*; thus, sharing that acceptance into a group to socialize may prevent one from acquiring a fixation at this stage of development. Further elements which are significant for the psyche can develop once one is able to avoid a fixation at this stage.

3.1.1 THE BUTTERFLY

Ask me I know what beauty looks like
I've seen it in the wings of a butterfly, with amazing colours in
patterns of rings
One comes out of the other, the other goes into one, the other
under another and one on top
Please stop! This is dementing, it's taking me on a roller-coaster,
mentally
It makes me see in me, in-adequacy, in-efficiency, in-ability, in-
stability
If only you had the ability to be in me, you would see that too
Don't dare deny that you were the one fast tracking ahead of
sluggish me,
You, to whom thousands flocked. Destitute, you left me
With two or four whose grip I wear like a tight around my
thighs
But I tend to be careful I and loosen the ties, because tights
aren't really my thing
I keep them away at arm's length lest they hear my heart beat
My heart beats, not for my present parents, or my siblings,
much less for uncles and aunts
My heart beats for you, whose ducks are in order, whose chicks
can be counted before their arrival

Ask me, I know what beauty looks like
It's in the sound of sirens, accompanied by the red and blue
flashes
Shining so bright it's piercing through my chest of treasure
Flashes so strong commanding to remove my hands from the
misery
And in a flash, I was cardiac arrested, I was arrested, until I
rested
In peace, I rested. In His Word I rested
Like the caterpillar on a fresh leave kissed by the morning dew
It was then that I remembered that the caterpillar is a future
butterfly

So, in my pursuit for beauty I walked to my mirror
Ah! It is the butterfly with amazing colours in patterns of
rings…

Elmarie Eises

Eises' Explanation: The butterfly poem is a reflection of me in a state where I would always compare myself with others. I was unsatisfied with my own life in terms of the physical things that I have, my relationships, and generally the person that I am. In addition to that, I felt like I always had to fight for what I wanted. No level of success that I have reached so far came easy.

At the beginning of the poem, I see this butterfly that symbolizes beauty and/ or perfection and this butterfly actually resembles me. But, when I look at its physical features, I was confused and I move into a negative mind space where I only see my inadequacies. Even if anyone would tell me otherwise, I would believe them for a moment but revert to the same thinking.

I felt resentment and I was rejected by people that I cared about so I thought as a defence mechanism I should rather keep people at a distance so that if they leave it, I would easily make peace with that and move on.

Nevertheless, I was less bothered by what was going good in my life. I had family and relatives who cared so much about me. I was wondering how I could copy that kind of life I see others have.

Then, came a point in my life when I let go of negative thinking. I wanted to. I think I was terribly conflicted. It was the time that I surrendered my life to Christ, and I can say that I am in a better space. Not that I do not encounter these thoughts but, I encourage myself by saying that the "caterpillar is the future butterfly". The ugly, slow, creepy things in life evolve into beauty in due time. Also, the metamorphosis (such as the butterfly) that I experienced made me see my strengths and traits that make me beautiful. It gave me contentment.

3.1.2 A LETTER TO A DREAM KILLER

For my harness of composure
Through cold mornings dewed
With doubt so I mine the treasure
Of my labour, I thank you.

For forging me into a troubadour
traversing valleys decked with blossoms
of despair, to knock at love's door
I cherish your picaresque company.

For the courage to stare down doom
And merrily dip in and out of its stream,
Though Asclepius be banished from that room
Where scars become stars, I hail you.

I have nothing but a raised glass
To thee that turned a geek
Into a freaky badass-
With a steady diet of disdain.

Chike M Nzerue

Nzerue's Explanation: This poem is a quartern with 16 lines broken up into 4 quatrains. It was penned in response to a class exercise in a strategic leadership course at Saïd Business School when the Professor was teaching about the power of storytelling and myth-making in strategic leadership. The challenge was to write a letter to someone in the past or present who had helped you achieve your dreams or helped destroy your dreams.

- *The quartern with its illusion of control of 4 quatrains tightly packed into a "straight jacket" is an unlikely form to capture the challenge of chaos at every turn that defines a life pursuit of excellence, yet it does. It is alternately rhymed in abab format. Asclepius is a messenger that brings good tidings in Greek mythology.*

- *The villain here is self-doubt, and how it fuels the poet's drive to be that which he doubts he could be in the first place. Self-doubt, to the poet, is a worthy friend lurking unseen, yet omnipresent, asking rhetorical questions when he gets too comfortable. It is a talisman against unbridled hubris, and in the end, its penchant for cynical introspection helps make the poet's dream come through. Thus, the title is an ironic twist.*

3.2 SOCIAL PREDESTINATION

From birth and during infancy, children form the initial foundations of their identity to mimic the image of their primary caregivers. To verify children's self-image based on visual characteristics, the doll experiment[52] tested children of ages three to seven by presenting them with four identical dolls with different shades of skin colours to check the accuracy of their self-identification based on race. It was noted that even at such an early age, children could accurately identify which doll represented them. However, with age, this self-image created by the child is compared, contrasted, and challenged during socialization. Rather than attachment theory,[53] which is fundamental at earlier stages of development for laying the foundations of self-identity, social psychology and sociology theories become more relevant to this stage of psychological development. These prescribe to the fact that identities evolve based on a fundamental psychological process of in-grouping[54] some people that one encounters, and othering[55] some people while socializing. In-grouping develops social identity based on similar attributes and qualities of the people within the group, while 'othering' differentiates one from others.

Social identity is said to develop through taking on this responsibility, which is profound until twenty-four years of age. During this time, the interactional process between the person and the people around the person, as well as the society at large, lays the foundations for one's identity.[56] While it is difficult to draw a comprehensive list of social categories that one assigns oneself to while developing one's identity, as the psyche can in-group some and out-group other people, based on a host of variations between people, race emerged as a dominant factor in our sample of research participants. While race is acknowledged as a major social identity worldwide, its prominence in our sample may be attributable to the fact that many of our participants have either experienced Apartheid first-hand, or have lived in a greatly segregated society based on racial differences.[57]

One of our research participants, with the pseudonym TarliQue in the poem: *"Colour"* (3.2.1), equates his/her/their racial identity of blackness with societal oppression, while acknowledging societal privileges can stem from a host of aspects of one's identity. As such, TarliQue supports the fact that people are said to prescribe to multiple social groups that collectively form their identities. The theory of intersectionality[58] recognizes that one's social and political identities co-exist within one's identity; as such, race is one such identity within a host of identities one prescribes towards. "An intersectional approach is a useful framework for evaluating and assessing how social identities of race, class, gender, sexual orientation and (dis)ability are brought to life through socialization".[59] Their co-existence and contribution to one's identity are complex, as social categories mesh and intersect with each other to form one's identity. However, acknowledging our sampling limitation discussed earlier, our research participants and their expressions regarding being a racially marginalised group makes their race a single prominent factor associated with a loss of privilege. As such, our research participants' expressions are better supported by a comprehensive definition of intersectionality that incorporates the assignment of privileges to identities. "Intersectionality refers to the idea that people have multiple identities and that people experience and perform/ live within multiple, intersecting, and concurrent positions of privileges and oppressions".[60] As such, by validating intersectionality, our research participant acknowledges the possibility to lever other sources of identity to break away from prejudice and marginalization.

However, the social category that presents an individual with the source of oppression emerges as being, single-handedly, the most salient in the poetries of our research participants. Our research participant, Angel Myeza in her poem: *"My encounter with blackness"* (3.2.2), shares her growth to break away from the *"psychological prison"* that society has imposed on black people. However, in doing so, she takes us back to that age when she states that: *"I knew, but I didn't really know"*; thus, expressing that at that age she was aware of her race, but she was unaware of what being black entailed in the minds of others. Thus, she highlights the significance of socialization to the development of racial identity. She refers to that time of not knowing about the perception others have of black people as: *"ignorance was bliss"*. She shares how the eventual awareness of her racial identity triggered questions about the negative connotations in society associated with blackness, such as: *"Has blackness always equated to negative self-perception?"* to better understand and challenge negative connotations associated with blackness.

This corresponds with the findings of the experiment by the Clarks.[61] They asked children, who had identified themselves as represented in the colour of a doll, to choose a doll they would like to play with. They found that the children chose the doll that represented Caucasian skin tones. Similarly, our research participant, Razelle Naidoo in her poem: *"Purpose"* (3.2.3), highlights the challenges of self-acceptance of her physical self in a society that assigns positive attributes to those who look contrary to her. While the message of the poem is to trigger cognitions around racial bias, racial identity, and its repercussions on people-perception and self-image, she acknowledges and highlights that societal prejudices, stereotypes, marginalisation, and oppression can fester in the psyche since the realization of one's racial identity. When one is: "discriminated against because of your gender, sexual preferences, religion, or race; and if you developed fears about not being able to meet your survival, safety, or security needs, you are likely to have difficulties moving through [to] the individuating stage of development".[62] She shares how her belief in God, as the creator of all represented, nourished her belief in racial egalitarianism, and acted as an effective enabler to escape this fixation.

Similarly, another of our research participants, Namuziya Sikatali in her poem: *"Positive lucid dreamer"* (3.2.4), also shares experiences of being regarded as: *"... lazy, stupid and selfish!"* due to her race. She mentions: *"reaching out to like-minded dreamers"* when challenged by others for dreaming. She regards integrating such people as conducive to being a part of a social group while challenging the status-quo by daring to dream of an alternative path to follow for a differentiated future for herself, and thus facilitate a shift, or at the least, lend a hand in changing the stereotype associated with the social category.

Our next research participant presents a useful perspective regarding the tension between belonging needs, restrictions these place on oneself, and the need to out-group others to satisfy one's belonging needs. Jeanne Odendaal in her poem: *"My poem"* (3.2.5) expresses how in-grouping may satisfy one's belonging needs;[63] however, the flip side of the coin entails that social expectations from the group, to which one belongs, weigh heavily on one's shoulders. Additionally, in-grouping necessarily entails out-grouping of others. She expresses these two aspects of belonging in the poem's first line where she states: *"... so many violations of personhood and demonisation of the outsider"*. She presents a solution to survive this double-edged sword, of a need to belong yet avoid the burdens of societal expectations and out grouping of others, by using an extract from Rupi Kaur's poem. He claims an enabler to personal growth to have risen from: *"... when I stopped searching for home within others and lifted the foundations of home within myself"*. In doing so, Odendaal shares another vital balance needed by humans. Social identification theory conceptualizes the need for individuals to belong to a group, and yet be seen as unique. These seemingly contradictory needs exist simultaneously.[64] An optimal balance of the pull factor to a group and the push factors from a group is needed within each individual's psyche, between the degree of in-grouping and individuality, to ensure one's belonging and uniqueness (individuation) simultaneously.

This section ends with our research participant, Khavitha Singh in her poem: *"Go forth young one"* (3.2.6), in which she writes to her younger self, guiding her through the journey to self-leadership. She acknowledges the need for *"boldness and courage in your heart"* not to succumb to the fear felt from the *"judgement of others"* as these place immense pressures on one to fulfil expected behaviours, careers, and other aspects of one's life that can dictate one's destination – hence lead to social predestination. She acknowledges the pressures of predetermined destiny, but informs her younger self that it is still malleable based on her own decision-making. She acknowledges that during her younger days, she was: *"deeply impacted by the opinions of others and the need to 'fit in'"*. She is well aware that this awareness does not allow the need to fit-in to have evolved only later in her adult life; thus, supporting our stance of a staged development of self-leadership.

While academic theories find a fixation at this stage to arise from a rejection by the group one aspires to join, which is supported by our research participant Eises (3.1.1), the challenge is also recognised as joining a group and balancing belonging to the group with differentiating oneself sufficiently from the said group to individuate oneself. It is only through this individuation that one can lead the group one belongs to. However, largely absent from academic literature is the specific reference to the struggle faced when the social group one identifies with is perceived to be 'inferior' in society. Such prejudice and marginalization trigger an enhanced need to differentiate oneself from the group, while simultaneously experiencing the need to belong to the group. Our participants share some enablers through their lived experiences. For example, cognitively questioning prejudice and rejecting being pigeonholed for self-leadership development is shared by Myeza (3.2.2). Intersectionality, which allows various social identity factors to simultaneously be embraced within one's identity (Crenshaw, 1991), is shared by TarliQue (3.2.1), which permits leveraging on alternative aspects of one's identity to differentiate one's-self from one's social group. Such differentiating shifts one onto the individuating stage of psychological development, and allows for leading the group one belongs to. Additionally, forming ties with other like-minded individuals, as suggested by Sikatali (3.2.4), entails joining other individuated people (integrating stage) to collectively serve the cause (serving stage) of egalitarianism.

3.2.1 COLOUR

There is no such thing as colour it's all propaganda
An insidious attempt at stifling creativity so I do not believe in
colour

There is only that which is bright
For He did not say let there be colour He said "let there be…"

Blue, which is how you usually feel though he died for you
You say you do not listen to music that is secular
Well, I do not like to discriminate music by shape but by
number
So that's fifty shades of that colour
Which is a movie that is longer than any round shaped song
But then I could be wrong

There is no such thing as colour "black" we were taught way
back
That in order to see an object light reflected back that colour
into our eyes
But, what if black is just some colour that you do not recognize
That your eyes have no receptors for?
What if darkness is a range of light we cannot comprehend and
so…

There is no such thing as colour
Face your fears, choose problems you enjoy, overcoming them
is what gives you joy
Forgive others, forgive yourself, accept your flaws and work on
your strengths, love yourself more... and by far
You are amazing, just the way you are

Cause trying to be positive all the time is like a light without
darkness
Tap into the wisdom of the great Pompi and learn how to play
the "silence"

I say you are complete, you are worthy, baby, to me you are
more than good enough
With your dark skin, light skin, stretch marks, pimply, long,
wide hips, short, tall, big, fast, slow... by far
Whether Earthling or born on Mars, you are amazing, just the
way you are

There is no such thing as colour, be you to the full
And if your idea of God cannot love you the way you are, then
maybe He does not deserve you

TarliQue

TarliQue's Explanation: This piece is about bringing light to discrimination of all sorts (gender, creed, sexual, etc.). It is about putting off all idolatry and seeing God for who he/she really is. The word 'colour' is used to depict all of our differences. That ultimately, it's all just a construct and colour doesn't really exist... There is no such thing.

3.2.2 MY ENCOUNTER WITH BLACKNESS

I knew, but I didn't *really* know
Ignorance was bliss, or so I thought
I didn't really know, even though I *thought* I knew
Now I know that I didn't know

I didn't know blackness meant being constantly expected to
make yourself small to make room for 'other-ness'
I didn't know it meant being expected to be apologetic for your
mere existence

41

I didn't know blackness meant being expected to be a 'non-everything'
I didn't realize that being black meant being expected to only exist in
relation to 'others'

Has blackness always been synonymous with fear?
In my encounter with blackness, I have seen so much fear in my people
it overwhelms me
I want to reach out and hold the entire black community to my bosom
I want to block out this debilitating fear with so much love, that I
completely obliterate it
I want to hold my people by the hand and tell them to look up instead
of always fearfully casting their eyes down
I want to tell them to look up and know that its ok

Blackness in my people carries so much uncertainty, it breaks my heart

Has blackness always been synonymous with pain?
So much pain! I want to ask Him why? Why this race?
All that is black carries so much baggage, so much hurt!
Why?

Has blackness always been synonymous with trauma?
Blackness seems to carry with it so much emotional and psychological
trauma that we don't yet know its full extent
When did the trauma start and when will it end?
The war that is waged against blackness continues daily in different
forms, in multiple battle fields
Blackness faces a persistent enemy who wages war in every territory
and from all fronts
Blackness faces its enemy in boardrooms when a triple threat – young,
black female – walks in and the enemy says: you are not good enough
The enemy says to the black girl that: she is too feminine, too young,
too educated, too aggressive, not assertive enough, too sensitive, too
outspoken, too big for her boots, not enough experience, dress too
tight, skirt too short, buttocks too big, accent not right, intimidating,
hair too nappy, makes client uncomfortable, qualifications must be
verified, her work must be checked by her 'senior', she is not ready for
that promotion, her 'doek' is not appropriate for the office...the list is
endless!
The enemy is a strategist – he is prepared for war on the streets, in the
media, in the schools

Has blackness always equated to negative self-perception?
Is black incompetent, never ready, a criminal, a failure, an absent
father?
Is blackness all things 'small'?
You are black, so you cannot be ambitious?
You are black; thus, you cannot succeed?
You are black; thus, wealth will elude you?
You are black; therefore, you must settle for 'last-best' and 'never-best'?
You are black therefore poverty and squalor are your 'normal'?
You are black therefore; you shall always have a master?

I am black!
I *am* black, and I reject all these associations with blackness!
I have faced my blackness and I didn't know, but now I know
I know that black *can* be successful, wealthy and ambitious
I know that black *is* best
I have seen my blackness be beautiful, ambitious, excel, dominate!

I have encountered *my* blackness
I have encountered *my* blackness and gained emotional and
psychological liberation
I have encountered *my* blackness and refused to settle for anything less
than best
Black you *are* beautiful
You are resilient
Blackness, you can be proud
I didn't know, but now I know
Blackness, I am glad I met you!!

Angel Myeza

Myeza's Explanation: This poem can be best described as a 'coming of age' story. It's a story about my coming of age in my journey and in my relationship with my blackness. I emphasize on 'my' because it's important for me to point out that this is a personal story and journey and therefore CANNOT be generalized. My encounter is exactly that – mine. It cannot and should not be compared to anyone else's.

My journey (my encounter) evolves and continues to evolve. It starts off with a general awareness of what I believe society paints blackness to be. It's a general awareness about what society expects black people to feel, and how they are expected to behave. They are expected to 'know their place'.

I then move on to talk about how these expectations from society have resulted in imprisoning black people in a psychological prison of fear. I use the word 'debilitating' to describe this fear because it is so all-encompassing that it filters through all spheres of a black person's life rendering them almost incapable of any action that may even attempt to free them. This realization brings out maternal, protective feelings inside me that makes me want to lock my people in a loving embrace in an effort to take this fear and pain away.

I go on to reflect on the fact that black people have experienced constant and ongoing trauma through their life experiences. That the 'other' is a strong enemy that wages a psychologically ravaging war that is subtle in its approach. The war I refer to is how society has made very unacceptable discrimination and treatment of black people somehow normal and hidden it behind words such as 'you don't have enough experience' or 'your dress code is inappropriate' or 'you need coaching' or 'you are too aggressive'. These are subtle ways used to beat black people into submission, make them believe that they are indeed not good enough and that they are the problem. Black people are made to believe they have something 'to fix' before they can be accepted as full members of society – be it their hair, their accent, their skin colour etc.

And the enemy is slowly winning the battle because in paragraph 6 – I note with despair that even our own perception of ourselves has been infected with negative images.

This realization during this journey is what finally gets me to stand up and say: "Wait a minute!! I am black, and I am NOT all of those things that the 'other' would like to have me believe I am".

This is a surreal realization. It makes me want to laugh out loud! It makes me want to scream from the rooftops that I have seen through the 'bullshit'! I have seen through the lie! I know better! I know the TRUTH!

As I come of age and get to these realizations, I am almost at peace with myself and in my skin. I LOVE the skin I am in and I am finally at one with my blackness.

3.2.3 Purpose

My dark skin.
My curly hair.
My long nose.
My curvy figure.

Your fair skin.
Your straight hair.
Your small nose.
Your straight figure.
You are liked.

I like to learn.
I like my morals.
I like my values.
I like my faith.
I like not what they like.

They like to party.
They like boys.
They don't like my morals.
They don't like my values.
They are liked.

God made me beautiful.
God has a purpose for me.
God knows my self-worth.
Jesus loves me.

Razelle Naidoo

Naidoo's Explanation: This poem is about the author's struggle in life to find love based on who she is. Her imperfections have led to her to finding true solace and acceptance but just not where she expected it to come from. She grew up feeling like an ugly duckling amongst the beautiful swans. She desired to be like them for everybody noticed and adored them. However, she was never created to be them for she was special. She struggled for many years, not fully understanding why she had to look the way she did. The author then goes on to describe how her character and love for her relationship with her saviour, Jesus Christ, has made her the odd one out once again. Nobody valued what she did. Nobody understood her values, morals and her pursuit of virtue. She was never liked for these qualities.

The author then sums up the poem by giving us insight into how this feeling of being excluded has impacted her. She never felt beautiful. She didn't think that she had a purpose in life nor did she know her self-worth. The last paragraph reveals how she found what she had been looking for her whole life in God. She was created beautiful by her creator God. She also reveals that she believes that God has created her with a purpose, and that he knows her self-worth. This is how she has come to know her self-worth. It is through knowing the God that she serves, that she is able to see how beautiful, worthy and purposeful she actually is. What she desired from people, was always available in God.

The author then chooses to end her poem in a very powerful statement about how she is loved by Jesus and that is enough for her. This poem is an illustration of how the poet has learnt to use her narrative as her testimony and to show the world how her believed imperfections were the things that made her beautiful on the inside and out.

3.2.4 POSITIVE LUCID DREAMER

I tried a little dreaming
I made friends with tomorrow
I lived in it for a moment
Swinging on its edge today
knowing it is borrowed

Tossed to the zenith of a crazy dream,
It led me to places of new beginnings.
Who says you cannot be you?
Who says you cannot dream a little more?
How did you feel when you experienced tomorrow?

Wake up dreamer!
You are lazy, stupid and selfish!
I am stronger on tomorrow's edge,
When I live my dream, I can be me.
On the other side, tomorrow is fleeting and farfetched,
But what if I catch it,
What if?

It all started with a dream,
I live today knowing it was with me,
In a cycle of mystery.
Yesterday's tomorrow is now my today,
And I had it before it came to me.

Namuziya Sikatali

Sikatali's Explanation: This poem represents my journey through life and all the changes that I have undergone which have been a result of dreaming and reaching out to like-minded dreamers. It all starts with making friends with my future self and people I look up to. I do not see myself for who I am today but rather, who I will be and that is cardinal in the pursuit of what I want. Lucid dreaming is not easy to explain and often is mistaken for weird behaviour and is very addictive. This does not make it different from something that makes us happy and the biggest control is to manage oneself well by creating a balance of how much of it is done. When you have lived in your future, it is difficult for someone to tell you what you cannot be. It is my source of inspiration for the goals that I have set and I live them out before I accomplish them.

The term 'lucid' is defined as something that is clear and well-articulated, but this poem is an oxymoron because there is no clarity in it. There is a mystery that lies in throwing oneself to the zenith of the next day which I relate to a make-believe celestial realm. It is only in the mind that I can be myself and not be questioned by the limitations that come with external opinions of who you should be as an individual. It is when I took the journey to accept my authentic self that I knew I could dream a little bit more today than I did yesterday.

There is a lot of external pressure to succumb to the status quo and just reach for what is available. This is based on what is termed as 'cultural norms', to take what is handed to you and be grateful. There is no right or wrong way to live inside one's head and because life is short, no one remembers what you had, but what you did, and how you make them feel. It is not easy to go through this process because there have been numerous times I have nearly given up. There is also the uncertainty of failure but with that is the "what if?". This is the lingering conversation that can lead to regret because of not knowing what lies ahead and not having experienced it to speak about it.

Lastly, a dream is very mysterious and what I have come to conclude is that everything is repetitive, and patterns are to be followed. When you are living, you are guaranteed a tomorrow and you have it with you. You have had it all your life and this is the mystery because it is known to us. The dream was my starting point and the question I ask myself every day is:

How is the life you are living now going to get you to your dream?

3.2.5 MY POEM

so many violations of personhood and demonisation of the
outsider
fed by fragmented morsels of misinformation
the synecdoche of mirrors

I am you
am I, am you?
is there virtue in hiding in plain sight?
I refuse to follow a path of fear disguised as practicality.
let me use my voice.
to speak. to listen. to move.
henceforth,
I am sending you all my sugar.

Jeanne Odendaal

---

it was when I stopped searching for home within others
and lifted the foundations of home within myself
I found there were no roots more intimate
than those between a mind and a body
that have decided to be whole

Rupi Kaur

Kaur's Explanation: My submission is a combination of ideas: my own, and those of one of my favourite poets, Rupi Kaur. Rupi is a 26-year-old Indian born Canadian poet, writer, illustrator and performer. She writes freely about trauma, feminism and life as an outsider. Sometimes criticised by literary heavyweights for writing too simply, Rupi continues to speak her truth.

My submission starts with my own poem, an 11-lined mirror, reflecting on a season of becoming:

My own and other women's, in especially the 2017/ 18 #MeToo zeitgeist. The first stanza touches on the concept of othering. Female leaders are often confronted with harsh discrimination and regressive mindsets, masked as trivialities. There are generations (of women) force-fed on misguided information; misrepresented by those with monopolist outlooks. 'Personhood violation' is much more than a female issue. It is a human issue.

The second stanza speaks of 'the synecdoche of mirrors'. A synecdoche is a figure of speech in which a part is made to represent the whole, or vice versa. It is when we hold a mirror to ourselves and our preconceptions (the good, the bad and the ugly), that we stand a chance to truly see. If we can commit to seeing, feeling, we can start to acknowledge and embrace the power that lies in our similarities. Vulnerability is the connective tissue between humans. As per researcher and author Brené Brown, vulnerability is directly related to courage. May we have the courage to hold each other in our brokenness, and grow together as a united people.

The third, and final stanza of my poem relates to bravery. It is about tapping into the life vein of being, not becoming. Of embracing the power in oneself, and acknowledging the light within another. As women, as leaders. Without having to tirelessly chase 'perfection,' we can 'send our sugar' and live our truth. Being kind.

My poem flows directly into that of Rupi Kaur's. My interpretation of her words, is that the tireless search for the ideal self is misleading. Surely, there is some virtue in striving to be better and more. But it is when we sit comfortably with the notion that we hold the key to decide and to celebrate who we are, that we are grounded. Wholeness comes in many shapes and forms. And perhaps, through acknowledging that wholeness is not homogenous, we become rooted. Connected.

3.2.6 GO FORTH YOUNG ONE

Go forth young one .... with boldness and courage in your heart
There is no need to embrace the fear of the
unknown nor the judgement of others
These are just a myriad of myths
Born from misinterpretations and insecurities

Your destiny is predetermined
But carefully guided by your decisions
Your defining moments

Life is beautiful
Filled with wonder and amazement
Embrace it
Leave a legacy

With your abundance of love and capability

Khavitha Singh

Singh's Explanation: This is a poem that I have written to my young self. I remember when I was younger, I had deep insecurities born from a series of challenging times. I was not sure of what the future held, deeply impacted by the opinions of others, and the need to "fit in". This poem encourages my young self to banish those burdens and insecurities and instead embrace the wonder that life has to offer. It represents words that I needed at that time of my life reminding me to lead a life that is meaningful, one that my children and I can be proud of. I only realized this much later in my adult life … .

3.3 THE DIFFERENTIATED LEADER

Similar to 'the conforming leader' (2.3) who is foundationally motivated by catering to the needs of the family, a leader who is fixated at the differentiated stage of psychological development is foundationally motivated by a belonging need to the community, or social-group. While such leadership can allow for the greater good of the community, the social limitations of the community are embraced by such leaders rather than challenged. It may even entail the reversal of certain progressions by the leader to revert to cultural norms and restrictions imposed by the group, either based on cultural, social, or religious values that the community prescribes to.

Our research participant, Lauren, in her poem: *"Leadership claustrophobia"* (3.3.1), addresses the mismatch between her aspirations as a leader and the requirements of the leadership positions in commerce. She states in her lines how: *"rules and regulations have never sat well"* with her, and as such an asset she possesses as a leader is to: *"exemplify them for you"*. Founded on the motivation of freedom, authenticity, and differentiation, she confesses in the explanation of her poem that: *"Being a leader in a corporate context"* has not worked well for her, thus, suggesting that those more attuned to following protocols to be better suited for such leadership roles. Similar to Dharani (2.3.1), she emphasizes the significance of agency theory[65] in corporations, that makes leadership positions, such as those of corporate executives, to be agents of the corporate shareholders. This limits the freedom available to such leaders. Restricted by such an environment, she shares that her motivation to adhere to the protocols emanate more so from the consequences she expects for deviating from these for those whom she leads, rather than to be founded on a drive to satisfy her requirements prescribed by those who lead her. She states this as: *"I … experience more pressure to conform due to those I lead, rather than my leaders"*. As such, highlighting the mismatch between her stage of self-leadership development and the one required by the leadership position she holds.

Similar to socialization, that permits the development of self-image and in-grouping of those regarded similar to one, cultural and societal norms also exert pressures of fulfilment of expectations based on image. For example, our research participant Regis Mukumbuzi in his poem: *"You are human"* (3.3.2), reflects on the societal image of a leader. The poem starts with expressions of pureness during childhood, that is eventually corrupted by self-image and its associated roles. For example, Mukumbuzi reflects that his: *"leader ideology was centred on the perfect being – with no emotion"*. The non-emotional man as deemed perfect for a leadership role, pigeonholes one into roles, such as those based on gender identities that lead to gender-role associations,[66] and sows the seeds for aspirations to be someone other than oneself to be a leader.[67] This he regards as being a *"slave to self-doubt"*.

3.3.1 LEADER CLAUSTROPHOBIA

Rules and regulations have never sat well,
And needing to exemplify them for you, can be my personal hell.
Protecting your freedom at the expense of my own,
Allowing you to live authentically, yet I've become a clone.

Messages from above softened, before being spread below.
Personalisation of the impersonal as I kneed the words like dough.
A tactful hint added to your singing,
To make sure management agrees their song is winning.

The expectations close in worse than solid walls
Until I'm stuck by more than just protocols.
But who built these walls of expectations?
Are they mine or yours?

Lauren

Lauren's Explanation: This poem is a response to the first half of the Advanced leadership course, which included the concept of leadership freedom. It is written as if the reader is a member of the author's team. Being a leader in a corporate context is not an experience I personally experience as freedom. I have linked this to claustrophobia as I experience feeling stuck and not having an escape, despite being fully aware this is irrational, as the only real thing preventing me from leaving is myself.

As an individual, I have the option of not doing as management asks when I believe this is counterproductive, because the only one who will be negatively impacted is me. When I am representing others this becomes more difficult, as I know my actions and choices can impact others. I also know it's in their best interest to act as management wants and therefore, I need to emulate this behaviour to encourage them to do so. Therefore, I can experience more pressure to conform due to those I lead, rather than my leaders.

3.3.2 YOU ARE HUMAN

You are missed.
Your playfulness,
Your spirit ever radiant and contagious.
Such energy, such untamed drive.
Alive, much like a raging African veld fire,
Yet subtly, inside you're pure.
Pure as snow,
Serene as the Northern lights.
Your sturdiness runs deep from within.
Who would not be charmed,
By the gaze of your eyes or
At the crack of your smile?
A personality that lifted people,
That lifted the world,
So, we thought
So, we thought you had it together.

But the world caught up with you.
Corrupted you,
Ensnared you into the shadows.
Darkness grew in your once captivating persona
The smile, those calling eyes all washed away
Melted away like man, to time
All the flattered hearts sobered up with great pain
Pain such as of a bride left at the alter
Doubt settled in and made itself at home
It spoke softly yet firm
You are not good enough
You are not worthy
You are a shame

Yet the same world that takes also brings hope and promise
The hope and promise of the caterpillar to the butterfly
The hope and promise of the phoenix as it rises from the ashes
Help others, help yourself
How else will you appreciate the mystery of life
If you are not vulnerable
The beauty comes in rising from a fall
In accepting your flaws
In accepting you're human

Regis Mukumbuzi

Mukumbuzi's Explanation: The motivation for this piece comes from being increasingly exposed and being made aware of the idea that leadership business is messy and it goes beyond the perfect being. Growing up through my childhood the heroes had always been the cool children, those that seemed to be flawless. However, no one has created a very reasonable explanation. Therefore, my ideal leader ideology was centred on the perfect being – with no emotion, knows exactly what to say and when and to whom, could get everyone on their side and loud enough to draw the required attention.

I wrestled through time with wanting to understand myself and fit into this leader ideology. The younger me would have wanted to experience every adventure including failures. I lived up to the adventure lifestyle, I thoroughly enjoyed my childhood, even more so being a toddler. Some of the memories, I obviously don't remember in detail but my parents captured these pictures for me. I felt I could conquer anything. I want to remember that and honour that time and perhaps keep that child-like yearning close especially for my own little daughter. I want to let go of any fears and if I ever do, choose to draw lessons from life's hard cards and grow instead of hiding away and being ashamed.

Life as a child is very beautiful, you have very few cares, someone is watching over you and your every move. When you are awake you are spirited, free to do whatever you want, you are limited only by your imagination. I would like to believe I see the world from many vantage points and that picture or rather those vantage points are far from being exhausted. I also see how the world has created these silos where we have put ourselves in and lost that "childhood" energy, adventure, spirit and almost carefree attitude. I simply want to remind myself that when you fall hard, don't close yourself in or not accept any help, choose to find the silver lining and grow through learning from it. I am also not saying we should be childish. I am rather saying we should keep the curiosity of a child as we develop into mature beings.

The world will always test you, it seeks to break your guard walls. It feeds on your negativity. However, as we grow, we always resort to making a plan, building these walls around us so we don't expose our true weaknesses. Think about how to best avoid a crisis – on a daily basis – this is the plight of the average person. We lose the curiosity to self-doubt and a whole host of negative emotions. This is not the end though. Grow knowing that we possess the power to be better beings by being ourselves, by not being afraid of failure, not being a slave to self-doubt. These things, among others, make us unique, beautiful and worth the effort to be more as ourselves.

4 INDIVIDUATING

Individuating, as a stage of psychological development, is associated with a desire for self-exploration. In doing so, freeing oneself from parental programming as well as challenging societal norms form the key attributes of this stage of escaping social predestination. An unindividuated individual is regarded as: "… a mere fraction of our intrinsic complexity, treated as interchangeable with other members of that cluster".[68] Thus, while differentiating makes us belong to a group, gang, or cluster of people, individuating makes us unique within that group.

As such, norms associated with social categories are cognitively acknowledged during individuation, and challenged where necessary. For example, gender as a social category is described as a socio-cultural product rather than a fixed individual attribute, like sex. It is said to be: "determined through social norms but ultimately internalised by individuals".[69] Gender presents a crucial social identity for most people. However, gender conformity accompanies gender identity. It entails social expectations of attributes, behaviours, and role associations with the gender. For example, masculinity may be associated with expectations of being physically strong (attribute), inclined to lead (behaviour), being a provider (role), et cetera.

These social expectations vary based on cultures. Certain social groups exhibit greater uniformity in these social expectations, while others allow for more variation. More restrictive definitions are more likely to be challenged, and by doing so, one can lend a hand to widen societal definitions of the said social category. The trigger that allows one to deviate from the norms are the negative emotions felt when adhering to the norms. Cultural norms, such as patriarchy (the father or eldest male as head of the family) and patrilineality (descent reckoned through the male line), extend beyond the family into society. They act as fundamentals that assign political, economic, and social power and leadership in favour of men. These benefits for men have been normalised to such an extent that they have been overlooked for generations – but this is changing. Demands for voice, gender equity and eradication of gender-based violence are evident in the immense support for social media movements such as #MeToo, Time Up's and #MenAreTrash worldwide. While feminist movements, victim support, improving existing legislation, and bridging gaps between law and reinforcement have all contributed positively to the cause, the role of individuating in achieving this transformation is also significant.

Our research participant, Shivani Ghai in her poem *"Be!"* (4.1.1), challenges not just gender-role association,[70] but also gender-behavioural expectations of women in her community. She describes them as: *"stifling"* and as: *"shackles"*. Evident from the intensity of these words in the poem, the emotional triggers for rebellion, and a need to break free from these emerge. Her poem starts with an expression of a variety of her behaviours, and the community's perception of these to be misaligned with the cultural and social expectations from women. As such, they work as effective enablers for individuating. Similarly, our research participant, Mandy Ritchie in her poem: *"Microagressions"* (4.1.2), shares facing: *"double standards"* between her siblings, stating: *"... younger brother, who was awarded different freedoms"*. In reference to gender stereotypes, Ritchie states in her poem: *"I can be a girl AND not want pink everything, I can be a boy AND not want blue everything"*. Ritchie encourages turning up the volume when judged in terms of stereotypes to challenge over-generalization.[71] As she encourages this, she also voices a challenge to the perceived dichotomized notion of blackness and greatness.

Similar to the social category of gender, a number of our research participants share that they are facing expectations from historic oppression of their social groups that demand subservience, or a settlement for unequal and unfair treatment based on race. Stereotyping, pigeonholing, and prejudice encountered by our research participants emerge as major triggers for them to challenge social expectations from society and self-individuate. Just as Ritchie levers on intersectionality, a framework that acknowledges individual identify to be founded on belonging to multiple social groups,[72] she adds her racial identity in addition to her gender in discussing these triggers. Another research participant, Jacobs Sihela, in his poem: *"Lamentations of a Disinherited Self-Seeker"* (4.1.3) mourns the lost knowledge of his ancestral historic contributions to society imposed by *"... living in an anti-black world"*, which allows dominant cultures to dictate his perception, knowledge and his own perspectives of his identity. In his poem, he tries to: *"... remember my Ancestors who built pre-colonial African civilizations and empires"* in seeking pride in his existence, without which, he is predestined to stereotypes of his 'blackness' from society. Thus, he shares historic and ancestral knowledge, achievements, and positive attributes of the culture to enable self-pride which can allow individuating by learning not to conform to the current societal expectations.

A significant aspect of individuation that is shared by our research participants who shared their belonging to social groups that have been marginalized, based on race or ethnicity, is a striving for a return to the cultural fundamentals that were overpowered by alternative social groups and their norms. This perspective is contrary to prominent theories around individuation, as it is derived from the voices of those oppressed and marginalized in recent history, who continue to feel aspects of the subjugation currently. The difficulty that arises in categorizing such initiatives, of a return to ancestral perspectives, values, and beliefs as 'individuating', is due to the definition of individuation. The process of individuating is regarded in academic literature as: *"... dis-embedding yourself from your parental and cultural background and beginning to align the motivations of your ego with the motivations of your soul"*;[73] thus it suggests a journey to individuation is one of: "becoming more fully yourself by finding and expressing your own values and beliefs".[74] As such, these perspectives deviate from the definition, and are more attuned with the differentiating or conforming stages of psychological growth.

However, the perspective of our research participants presents a nuance to the academic literature. This is because parental perceptions, values, and beliefs have been altered as a result of the domination by other groups. As such, a return to one's ancestral perspectives bears the typical 'individuation' emotions felt from unburdening one from societal expectations. Additionally, in recognition of a loss of knowledge and way of ancestral life, attributes selected to and incorporated into one's identity are investigated, researched, picked, and chosen amongst a host of elements from one's ancestral history. It is debatable whether this selection process depicts 'individuation', as some known ancestral beliefs may be foregone.

4.1.1 BE!

You're too loud, they said, don't be!
You're too proud, they said, don't be!
You're too wild, they said, don't be!
Manners should be mild, they said;
Mine won't be!

You're too bossy, my team said, don't be!
You're too bitchy, my team said, don't be!
We prefer it when you're bubbly, my team said;
Clients like 'em ditsy, my team said;
I won't be!

You're too emotional, my boss said, don't be!
Is it hormonal? My boss said, don't be!
You look hysterical, my boss said, don't be!
You should try to be more rational;
I won't be!

You're so feisty, he said, don't be!
You can be so pushy, he said, don't be!
Feminists are frumpy, he said, don't be!
You'll make a great mom, he said;
I won't be!

Abrasive, don't be!
Aggressive, don't be!
Ambitious, don't be!
Frigid, don't be!
Irritable, don't be!
Vulnerable, don't be!

Oh, won't we be?

Shivani Ghai

Ghai's Explanation: An embodiment of the author's struggle to be authentic as a woman in social and cultural contexts where authenticity has double standards.

The poem begins with the author's exploration of her childhood growing up in India, and in an Indian home internationally. The author recalls the stifling of her childhood wildness by frequent reminders to be mild-mannered and other aspects of how girls should behave while growing up next to a younger brother, who was awarded different freedoms.

It continues to her college and professional experiences in team settings, where she was constantly told that she looks pretty when she smiles, and her ambition and pursuit for excellence were perceived as dominating. In the same world, she saw male counterparts commended for their assertiveness while she was chided for her assertiveness.

In a male-dominated industry, her menstrual cycle was a constant topic of discussion as she tried to passionately make a point. Her vulnerability and compassion were seen as weaknesses by the same people who told her she was too harsh. Her words seek to define the tightrope all women seem to have to walk in the professional contexts.

The poet then treads into the realm of her personal life where partner after partner misunderstood her, stifled her, tried to contain and tame her. The poet acknowledges that traditional gender roles will not shackle her, perhaps at the cost of a family.

The poet concludes with a war cry for all women to stop being bound by social, cultural and gender norms and just 'Be!'.

4.1.2 MICROAGGRESSIONS

Snide remarks, everyday exchanges, commentary of denigration,
Disparaging, belittling, undermining, prejudiced, derogatory,
Sometimes humorous to the maker, always offensive to the subject,
Intended or unintended – who are you to judge me?
Speak up, speak out, shut those people down.

Those little "jokes" you think are funny, made at others' expense,
Racist, sexist, homophobic, ageist, genderist,
Don't assume because I look like you, that I feel the same way as
you do,
Don't assume I see the world through your eyes and myopic bias,
Speak up, speak out, shut those people down.

I can be a lesbian AND be pretty,
I can be black AND achieve greatness,
I can be black AND get a job based on my own merit,
I can be a woman AND not know how to cook, sew or iron,
Speak up, speak out, shut those people down.

I can be a girl AND not want pink everything,
I can be a boy AND not want blue everything,
I can be C.E.O. AND be a mother, wife, sister and best friend,
I can be any race other than yours AND speak English better than
you can,
Speak up, speak out, shut those people down.

Who are you to criticise me? What gives you the right to speak to
me this way?
What makes you better than me? Where does your superiority
come from?
Is that your white privilege speaking? Is that your arrogance
speaking?
Are you just ignorant? Scared? Afraid of the unknown others?
Speak up, speak out, shut those people down.

I am learning to speak up and voice my disagreement,
I am learning to out your bias, your racism, your narrow-minded
prejudice,
I am learning to call you on your bigotry,
I am learning to open my eyes and ears and speak out.
Speak up, speak out, shut those people down.

Mandy Ritchie

4.1.3 LAMENTATIONS OF A DISINHERITED SELF-SEEKER

I am searching for myself in a hurricane
I have set myself on fire as an attempt to light my own path
My soul has been shackled by ignorance of my true self
The ignorance that was enforced on me after I was erased from my
royal bloodline

I have now been re-created into a non-being whose only goal is to
seek to be seen
My entire existence has been re-designed to depend on my visibility

As I stand right now
I am like an invisible mannequin screaming out to the world to be
noticed
But yet, I remain invisible

To alleviate my oppression
I try to remember my Ancestors who built pre-colonial African
civilizations and empires
I remember Mapungumbwe, Songai, Mossi, Mutapa and Asante
empires
I remember the first physician 'Imhotep' who gave the world
knowledge of medicine
I remember the mathematicians in *Kemet* who taught Pythagoras the
"Pythagoras theorem"
But before I could remember all my stolen and hidden legacies
I am stopped in the middle of my *remembering*

I am told to forget those who came before me
I am told to forget the past and to only look to the future
The wisdom keepers in my village once told me:
The past, present and future are all one
The future is the past that is happening right now

I try to tell them that but they wouldn't listen
My ontology is censured
Coerced to censor my own voice
I am only permitted to speak with a palatable rented tongue

Nonetheless
I continue searching for my true self with silence
I continue searching for my true self in secrecy

Jacobs Sihela

Sihela's Explanation: This poem reflects the personal existential suffering that I am experiencing living in an anti-black world that constantly makes me feel invisible and not-belonging. It's a lamentation of my journey in searching for my true self when the world denies me access to the true knowledge of myself and my ancestry. I have been on a journey of almost 16 years seeking the true history of Africa and its people, I have come across a huge volume of literature on pre-colonial Africa and I believe that literature is intentionally kept away from our formal schooling system.

This poem seeks to invoke the reader to search beyond what they are taught in schools and academic institutions. The words I have used in this poem all came to me intuitively and I have no concrete explanation of why I used those words. I will allow the reader to form their own interpretation and do their own searching.

4.2 GUILT VS. FEAR

In addition to pressures to adhere to social norms that may rub one against one's grain, a stumbling block to individuation are the emotions associated with deviating from parental and societal norms that are experienced as fear. These fears can emanate from questions regarding one's survival, and belonging needs, since, until the stage of individuation, the individual has depended on the primary caregivers, family, and society to fulfil these needs. Any attempts to change this tried and tested provision of the needs are deeply feared. This represents a double-edged sword, comprising of the need to belong yet differentiate oneself from the group. These two correspond with emotions of: "… ontological anxiety and ontological guilt. The former refers to choosing the future in spite of the fear of the unknown and difficulties ahead. The latter refers to choosing the status quo and familiar past practices; it will bring ontological guilt because of a felt sense of missed opportunity".[75] The missed opportunity, or an unlived life, bears the potential to haunt the individual. This is experienced as guilt of not having been brave enough to face one's fears associated with being unique, different from one's family and from one's social group, and/or following a novel path to the norms dictated by them.

Our research participant, Afzal Dalwai in his poem: *"I stood in the wrong spotlight"* (4.2.1), shares that he was accepted by the group he felt belonging towards. He shares his journey of differentiation in the line: *"I embarked on a journey to seek a different connection"*. The link with childhood when a child leaves home to socializing with others their own age, to engage in shared activities that interest them are sketched in the lines: *"… to be more of who I am, A place where I can share my playfulness"*. The development of social identity during this period is expressed in the line: *"I spent time getting to know who I am … connecting with others"*, and: *"it is what makes me, me"*. In the explanation of his poem, he confesses to his risk-averseness arising from this stage. In explaining 'risk-averseness', he clarifies that it entails not merely avoiding risks that may expose him to potential failure, but also his fears regarding potential success. As such, his explanation of being 'risk-averse' is more aligned with a fear of non-conforming to the benchmark of success associated with the social group where his sense of belonging lies. Upon identifying this 'restriction' that the social group has placed upon him, he expresses that he feels that he has not found the 'right' group, or 'gang'. As such, Dalwai calls attention to the fact that, despite his perception of 'success' in socialization, upon achieving the success comes the next stage of individuating from the group. As such, he highlights the stumbling block that societal impositions, for conforming that are internalized during the differentiating stage, can restrict or halt one from individuating.

Similar to Dalwai, one of our research participants, Maijang Mpherwane in his poem: *"Longing to belong"* (4.2.2), expresses the implied necessity to adhere to the limitations imposed by the social group one belongs to. He shares several self-assessments of himself that arise from a fear to deviate from the prescribed norms, including: *"no confidence in self"*, *"unsure of my strengths"*, being *"detrimentally humble"*, and *"… people-pleasing, Conflict avoiding, Pain fearing, Joy foreboding, Fulfilment seeking"*. Despite these attributes that have evolved from a lack of belonging to a group in the title of the poetry, the source of these attributes is assigned to belonging to a community that is associated with a lack of privileges. He expresses this lack of privilege in the lines: *"The politics of poverty still prevail. The cycle too vicious and engraved to exit"*. He expresses how being underprivileged forms his identity, that is generated by comparisons, which leads to a sense of belonging to a group that is oppressed. His belonging to the group is evident, but this belonging entails forgoing privileges associated with being a part of the social group. Hence, he corroborates that there is a challenge to balance the need to belong yet differentiate oneself; however, Mpherwane introduces a nuanced perspective of privileges associated with the group one belongs to, and the battle to belong yet break free from the lack of privilege associated with that group that is introduced earlier in the chapter.

Our research participant, Lauren Williams, in her poem: *"My dear friend"* (4.2.3), sarcastically refers to fear as her dear friend that has been her constant companion. She questions: *"Where did you come from? How did we meet?"* She gives an example of an incident, similar to many throughout her life, where she did not apply for the promotion out of a fear of being unsuccessful. While her poem and explanation do not uncover the root cause of the fear, she explains the reason to be: *"… because I was afraid that I would … be judged"*. Fear, as an emotion in the context of self-identity, is frequently mentioned to arise from a change of one's perception in the eyes of others. The fear arises from a perceived change in one's status or rank[76] in comparison to others. She regards it as a major stumbling block, and her approach to managing fear is one of the cognitive thought processes so as not to allow it to be debilitating in her everyday life.

In conclusion, while our research participants in the stage of differentiation presented examples of rejection from a social group that they felt they belonged to, which indicated fixation to that stage, our research participants in this section present the difficulties faced even when one is accepted in the social group; however, with psychological growth, the group is seen to place restrictions that emanate from adhering to the characteristics associated with the group. This presents a push away from the group, while the satisfaction of belonging needs provided by the group pulls one towards conforming to the norms of the group. The resulting fear of deviating, or the guilt for conforming and giving up a novel adventure, are the corresponding emotions felt from this push and pull respectively. The need to elevate oneself beyond the stage of differentiation requires a degree of deviation from the norms; thus, an art of balancing belonging yet individuation is attempted in the individuation stage of psychological development. Thus, an individuated individual is defined as becoming conscious about the aspects that make him/her/them a unique human being and, at the same time, no more than a common person.

4.2.1 I STOOD IN THE WRONG SPOTLIGHT

I stood in the shadows of others' successes
I did not believe that the spotlight was where I wanted to be
But it was merely the wrong spotlight being shone

I embarked on a journey to seek a different connection
One that allows me to be more of who I am,
A place where I can share my playfulness
Where I can be emotional when we are not being great

I spent time getting to know who I am
Learning that I cannot scale the highest
peaks on the back of my ego
Connecting with others allows for a better ascent
At times it's me being a part of their journey
Building trust that our reason for starting
the journey will get us there

I remain on the journey to rediscover my values
To ensure that it represents who I am,
what I believe, and how I act
Never does a moment pass where my values are unknown,
But never do I believe that my values are complete,
The sensation of discovery burns bright,
It is what makes me, me

Afzal Dalwai

Dalwai's Explanation: I was never one to take risks as I was always ashamed of the failure or the success thereof. I kept on believing my stories about not being good enough or that recognition is not what I want and that instead others deserve it more than me. Thus, I always operated in the shadows. I did what needed to be done to achieve our objectives, but I would never be the one in the limelight. I was not comfortable being the focus of attention, but I would support others in their efforts to be successful. I did not know the reasons for my behaviour, so I decided to undertake an MBA. Mainly to gain confidence in my abilities, to formalise my experience, and to network with like-minded individuals. Over the last 24 months, I learnt that it was not my lack of desire or an inability to lead but merely that the environment wherein I operate is not conducive to my style. It does not foster experimentation, collaboration, and mistakes. Without this, I am unable to be vulnerable at work and embark on projects or initiatives that are uncertain or ambiguous. Therefore, it's not that I don't want to lead but merely that I don't want to lead in my current environment.

My MBA journey was filled with highs and lows, from the first group assignment where we were finding ourselves as a syndicate group, or our individual leadership assignment and to our first fall-out as a group. Through these events, I kept on questioning my behaviour and actions so that I could gain a deeper and better understanding of why I act the way I do. It started with the analysis of my mental models, to my discovery that I struggle with compassion, and finally, to the realisation that I become static when dealing with uncertainty and ambiguity. In this process, I learnt more about who I am and started to become comfortable with the person in the mirror. I realised that I need not lose the best of me, my playfulness in order to become the leader that everyone wants me to be. Instead, I need to use this to bring joy and to better connect with others. Thereby remaining authentic and true to myself. Also, I should not bottle up my emotional outbursts but instead use the passion to motivate others so they can achieve greatness. In this process, I realised that my fear of rejection also played a role in my reluctance to lead, it was mainly my concern that others would not follow me.

Through communicating my vision and building meaningful relationships, I was able to cajole my followers and soon realised that my/our success is built through this trust. While we stumbled and tripped along the way, we were in it together. The moments when things were dark was when I played the role of mentor to shine the light on our achievement and to assist in identifying where we went wrong. It was me being a part of their journey.

Today, I believe that I have an understanding of my values. I know who I am. I am becoming comfortable with who I see in the mirror. I am accepting of the person that smiles back at me. My actions are based on these values and this sense of contentment. Never does a moment pass me by where I believe that I am done exploring. There is so much more to learn and to discover about myself.

4.2.2 LONGING TO BELONG

Unknowingly am but still aspire to be
Unsure of my strength so clear to all
Imagine what could be if I believed in self
Comparisons would be limited to self
The other would appreciate more of self

Every day I would celebrate self
Self-indulge and inhale contentment of self

Sunny days been around
Yet motion of no confidence in self
The politics of poverty still prevail
The cycle too vicious and engraved to exit
A heart so detrimentally humble to self
Neglecting self, over-extending self

I am but a people-pleasing,
Conflict avoiding
Pain fearing
Joy foreboding
Fulfilment seeking
Son of man
Endowed with abundant vitality
Ready to live one day at a time
Driven by the pure pleasure of existence

Maijang Mpherwane

Mpherwane's Explanation: One of the greatest obstacles that hinder my ability to fulfil my dreams and achieve great things is self-doubt. There is a persistent voice telling me how things could go wrong (how unworthy I am of an MBA, how off-track my parenting skills are, how I will struggle to make an impact in my new job), and how I may not have it worked out right (how off point my spirituality is compared to others. Over time it has had an impact on my productivity, and to some extent my emotional and spiritual wellness.

I am constantly in a long cycle of procrastination that impacts my ability to get things done on time. It is only when I get them done ultimately that I amaze myself as to what I am capable of doing while at the same time, decrying the excellence I could have produced if I gave myself sufficient time to get the work done. The doubt I constantly place on my ability to achieve my dreams and fulfil my desires has prevented me from experiencing my full potential. This is despite the fact that those around me see and openly recognize my potential.

Like an enneagram 7 kind that misapplies their talents, I overextend myself in many fronts, resulting in me often appearing scattered and undisciplined. I do this to avoid missing out on the worthwhile experience and to keep myself away from avoiding or discharging pain.

65

I wrote this pain as a way to come to terms with the aspect of my personality that I would like to change. I long to focus only on things that will result in my personal growth.

4.2.3 MY DEAR FRIEND

Wrapped in your cocoon
I feel safe and secure
You have been my constant companion
for as long as I can remember
Where did you come from?
How did we meet?

How is it that during our relationship there
were times that you held all the power
And I felt so small and insignificant
Never feeling good enough

Most times never having the courage to show
up because I gave you the power
But now my dear friend fear, it's time to part ways
I have used you as a crutch for far too long

Release me, so that I can be free
Free from fear of judgement, free from fear of failure, free
from fear of failure to succeed, fear of not being perfect.

I have given you this power for way to
long. I am taking back my power
Now my dear friend, it's time for me to
be free to be imperfectly perfect.

Lauren Williams

Williams' Explanation: The poem is about my relationship with fear. I often feel that in the past I have used this as a crutch so many times. There were promotions or jobs I didn't apply for, opportunities I let slip through my fingers because I was afraid that I wouldn't get them and be judged as not being good enough. Or on the other spectrum, I was afraid that I would get the opportunity but that I wouldn't succeed at it.

This has been a continuous theme in my life, not only in a work context but outside as well. I would never try new sports or activities because I was fearful that I wouldn't be good at it.

I have tried in the last two years to delve deeper into this to really unpack where this stems from. Was it my upbringing?

The most important growth that has occurred personally is being aware that fear is my constant companion but not giving it all the power. Rather use this awareness to drive me to do better.

4.3 JOURNEY TO INDIVIDUATION

Several factors play a role to facilitate the individuating process, that ranges from aspects which are internally founded within individuals to environmental influences. For example, the degree of difficulty experienced in extracting oneself from the influence of their parents is higher for those with controlling parents who were harsh in their punishments. Similarly, those living in authoritarian or repressive regimes are more afraid to socially detach from the norms and express aspects of themselves that either deviate from the norms or challenge them because they are conscious of the repercussions of doing so, such as punishments by the state or the courts, as well as fears of social rejection and alienation rather than acceptance of unique perspectives, behaviours, or attributes.[77] Internally, some people believe that they have a dominant role as drivers of their futures and others may regard powerful others, fate, or luck to dictate how their lives unfold. As such, one's locus of control, self-efficacy, and other personality attributes can facilitate or hinder individuation.

Irrespective of external or internal factors that may play a vital role in individuation, people seldom consciously segregate which of their life choices are founded on personality and societal factors, and which aspects are consciously driven through cognitive decision-making — a conscious evaluation and assessment of our values.[78] A lack of such questioning is highlighted by our research participant, Amanda April in her poem: *"Questionable truths"* (2.1.4), where she encourages the reader to develop a questioning mindset. She terms it as breaking away from: *"... slavery of the mind and heart"*.

A vital question arises as to what triggers one's cognitive mind to acknowledge social predestination,[79] while other aspects forming one's identity are followed with ease and remain unquestioned. In respect of the society as a whole, research has noted that: "[a] belief in predestination is more effective when heterogeneity of beliefs is high, when the desire for homogeneity is high, or when accurate signals about ethics are important".[80] The societal rigidity of moral classifications of good and bad promises that followership of the 'good path' shall be awarded happiness within ourselves and others who also play a decisive role.[81] Many scholars have argued morality to be a psychological means for encouraging followership and maintaining the status quo at the expense of one's authenticity.[82] However, in respect of individuals, our research participants share triggers that allow individuals to challenge the status quo and exhibit bravery to refuse predestination, instead seeking an alternative dream.

Our research participant, Audrey Loiselet in her poem: *"Prisoner of routine"* (4.3.1), highlights a major stumbling block to escaping predestination which she metaphorically expresses as *"the city"*, and explains to be: *"... the little world you tend to become a prisoner of"*. She advises in her line: *"If your life is all mapped out, deviate"*. While acknowledging the immense courage needed to do so, she presents a host of enablers, such as: *"... free your mind, experiencing new things, going out of your comfort zone"*, as well as accepting one's strengths as well as the weaknesses. She concludes with her belief that individuating is a recipe for one's happiness.

The goals of individuation in academic literature are said to be: "(a) know yourself, identify your most important values and the behaviours that align with those values, (b) become responsible and accountable for every aspect of your life, and (c) learn to manage your fears and develop your emotional intelligence skills".[83] One of our research participants, Joe Hooper in his poem: *"In knowing thyself"* (4.3.2), addresses the first goal in the above quotation of knowing oneself. He effectively illustrates the emotional turmoil of getting to truly know oneself by expressing the positive in the line: *"After-rain smell"*, and the negative as burnt bridges. In the explanation, he expresses how knowing oneself is akin to a phoenix rising – a mythical bird that is born again rising from the ashes – thus, acknowledging the pain as well as the glory associated with the journey of individuation.

Hooper explains this journey of self-knowing to have: *"... slowly surfaced, in moments of stillness.... And it came not without costs"*. As such, following suit the next poetries, Kurt April in his poem: *"Silence"* (4.3.3) and Camaren Peter in his poem: *"Yet what was there to be learnt ..."* (4.3.6), elaborate on such moments of stillness that enable individuation, and sacrifices that are a vital part of the journey. April in the line: *"During silence, I seek to choose"* links times of silence with decision-making, when silence facilitates cognition. Additionally, it is said that: "The conditions that moderate the impact of these skills are also examined along with the ways in which cognitive capacities shape subsequent leader behaviour".[84] As such, silence that is illustrated as an: *"... art of intentional contemplation"* emerges as a condition that is vital for cognition. Since cognition and cognitive skills are strongly linked to leadership emergence, as well as effective leadership performance, it links individuation with leadership.

Similar to Loiselet, April regards constant busy-ness a stumbling block to individuation. However, April acknowledges the challenges associated with silence that most people can relate to. As such, meditation, mindfulness, spirituality, and as one of our research participants, Robert Sutton, in his poem: *"Mammon"* (4.3.4) highlights, the proximity to nature and the avenues it can provide which facilitate achieving silent moments. Pets, plants, bonsais, gardening, or other means of appreciating nature in clinical application is referred to as 'eco-psychology' -- proven to heal the mind through enabling an escape from the mismatch of the mind to the human-made built environment.[85]

April expresses moments of silence during the journey of individuation as an: *"... inwardly felt-journey, mostly travelled alone and not with others, a returning, that leads to full presence, raised conscious awareness and a form of human healing*". While travelling alone, the possibility to facilitate such a journey is shared by one of our research participants, Johan Carlson, in his poem: "*What happened?*" (4.3.5). He explains how this confusion, arising from getting to know himself, was facilitated[86] by a leadership course. He confesses it to have led to remarkable changes in him, which he presents in a humorous fashion that makes the reader laugh. He shares how individuation brought the awareness of a lack of need for glamorous material things, such as a black Jaguar (F-Type), caviar, champagne, fancy suits, and golf, which Jung[87] referred to as having 'too narrow a spiritual horizon'; instead, aiming to "*settle for less*". He acknowledges being 'a mess' thanks to this journey of individuation, but similar to Loiselet, he recognises that he is happier due to it. Jung[88] links a narrow spiritual horizon with unhappiness and its expansion as a recipe to escape neuroticism.

The journey to individuation emerges as turbulent, and the reward a growth in respect of self-leadership development accompanied with happiness. As with each stage, due to the seismic change during the journey, it is expected that there are likely to be sacrifices made along the journey. Our research participant, Camaren Peter in his poem: "*Yet what was there to be learnt …*" (4.3.6), talks about sacrifice in the context of the struggles to end Apartheid. He explicitly describes the pain of sacrifice, equating it to an open wound that will not heal. However, he acknowledges that: "*… sacrifice is not brokenness … For sacrifice is not a dearth of spirit, But a commitment to it*". He elucidates sacrifices to be immensely painful, but they are evidences of courage, an act of freedom, and of enduring power.

The journey to individuation can be regarded as an end to 'playing the game' and 'covering' that our environment expects one to abide by. As such, it marks an end to 'illusion'[89] that prescribes the way one has to be in the environment, making one a product of the environment rather than of one's authentic self. Individuation marks the end to being taken up by the game that the environment introduces us to play and instead maturing to rise above the game, and begin to increasingly define the rules for life by oneself.

4.3.1 PRISONER OF ROUTINE

Vers de nouveaux soleils

Escape from the rumours of the cities,
If your life is all mapped out, deviate.
A page is still blank to host your heresies
Choose uncertain roads, dare to defy fate.

Lace your wind shoes and become a thief of fire
Move mountains with your dainty arms
Cross countries, campaigns, idyllic farms
Flee from this district and now respire

Tweak strengths and weaknesses, make your life a poem
Read between the lives and write life between the lines
Ignore the slanders and sing your own anthem
Hands free, head up, look up: the sun shines

In the early morning hours, anything is feasible
Start all over again, reset the cycle
Revive the flame and start over the fight
Sharpen your blade and stab your fright

Break the chains and escape the jail
Redraw the moon so it will light your quest
Become the wind in the night and push the sail
And flee to the dreams that tear your chest

Audrey Loiselet

Loiselet's Explanation: The reason why I wrote this poem is that one can easily become stuck in one's own daily routine and forget about what one's dreams are. But you must never forget that with faith and courage, you can live your dreams.

The "city", in this poem, represents this routine, this little world you tend to become "prisoner of". However, this "city" is a place one can escape from, with courage. Leaving this place is a way to free your mind and leave your dreams.

There is always a way to deviate from the path that you think is set for you. There is always a new story to write if you dare to leave your routine. As the image of the white paper shows, it is never too late for a new start.

The metaphor of the wind shoes is for becoming an empty vase again, free from prejudices and with your mind so light that you can run from opinions to opinions. One of the thieves of fire is to have the ability to take energy and power from all the new feelings, thoughts, and places you discover. The image of the mountains stands for not listening to the people who have told you that you were too weak to make big things and live your dreams. You are able to achieve huge goals. But first, you have to free your mind, experiencing new things, going out of your comfort zone but finding also a new breath.

Knowing and embracing your strengths and flaws will allow you to be the best version of yourself and give you solid foundations for you to build your life (the poem) again. You can even rewrite your story based on what you have lived when you write between the lines/lives. The part on the slanders/anthem is all about forgetting what people think about what you are doing but do what you want to do and be proud of it. It will bring you happiness.

You just have to wake up a morning and escape from the constraints you've been giving to yourself. You just have to sharpen your assets and grab your courage to face the fears that inhibit you from living your dreams.

The metaphor of drawing the moon is for, in the darkness of the unknown, setting the frame that will allow you to meet your goal. The image of the wind that pushes the sail is for you being 'you first' cheerleaders, your will is your first motor.

4.3.2 IN KNOWING THYSELF

After-rain smell
And gold flecked sunrise
Still in our morning armistice
Last night we fought fire with fire
And burned our bridges so well
Our familiar refrain
Of repeated pyrrhic victories
Our life's leftover shards and ashes
Pedestalled for appreciation
And in that morning quiet
As we pick up our pieces
We know that in falling apart
We learn to carry each other
Anew

Joe Hooper

Hooper's Explanation: This poem is a synthesis of regrets, realizations, and growth that occurred during my time in the EMBA programme. Perhaps it can best be phrased as a melancholy mash-up with some phoenix-like attributes that were gleaned over the many modules and since I completed the studies. Over the course of the programme I tried to balance work (which included moving to three countries over 21 months), the demands of an academically demanding programme, and sharing this mad journey of life with my wife and family. I also turned 40, which meant nothing and yet still meant something oddly enough.

Along the way, I drifted loose of my anchors. Which is ironic, as the EMBA programme focuses so much on self-awareness and understanding how your actions can affect those around you; it's so easy to know this, and so hard to

71

understand. Perhaps that is the summary of my Oxford experience. So as the demands grew on all sides, my perspective just seemed to vanish. It was a little like getting lost in music for hours and hours, only to snap out of it to realize you do not actually like the tune that is playing. I was not an especially pleasant person at times. And that hurt those around me. Often, I think.

My inner circle is comprised of such special and simply amazing people. In this time, I felt they tolerated the worst of me too frequently. The process of breaking and rebuilding and breaking and rebuilding happened too often in such different ways. The energy and effort required increased in magnitude and shook me to the very core. It built a resilience of a sort as well, with transgressions laughed-off over a bottle and papered over by other wonderful moments. Relationships not necessarily as strong in the same way, but strong in the way they are different.

And somewhere along the way, I understood what this Oxford journey was about: knowing thyself. Such knowing took longer than I thought, and it didn't come about the way I thought it would. It slowly surfaced, in moments of stillness after some of those difficult times. It came with perspective. And it came not without costs. Knowing thyself – for me – is about appreciating both the cause and effect, and my role in it.

4.3.3 SILENCE (I)

Silence
Long my enemy
Demands my attention

Silence
Is a form of fluidity
Not an enduring stillness … never stationary
Often welcomed
Sometimes rejected

In silence
My stories come
Incomplete
With present anxiety
Fast, uncontrolled

During silence
I seek to choose
Symmetry … control of my stories

Inspiring vistas, grounding spaces
I feel embraced
Vulnerable
Yet powerful

Silence births vivid emergence
Rendering an irrelevance of the present
Sometimes deepening my presence
Always inward
Yet, pushes me to move outward

Kurt April

April's Explanation: Silence is often associated with the negative actions of communication and implies concealment, sometimes indicating hostility or disagreement, or the skilled interview/conversational technique to induce unease in the other person in the communication. However, the silence being written about here is about the more disciplined art of intentional contemplation. In deliberate silence, there is nothing to be known – what must, emerges from the holding space as full-body realisation(s). We can't force it. In fact, we have to do the opposite. Let go, surrender, and be open to accepting the direct experiential knowledge and wisdom that emerges from the practice of balanced self-perception. It is an inwardly-felt journey, mostly travelled alone and not with others, a returning, that leads to full presence, raised conscious awareness, and a form of human healing – so directly opposed to the busy-ness and information push of modern lifestyles. As a result, one literally has to separate oneself from the resonance of modernity, and hone in on a simpler thread. Change happens deeper than at a systemic level.

4.3.4 MAMMON

There's a dragon in these rocks, watching out,
Over the bay I sit sheltered,
Under the serpent's neck, protected
from relentless social blustering.

White surf bites that monster island,
Set apart from the Mother City,
Disturbing the sun's warmth,
with the overshadowing cloud of temptation.

Resting watchful while stilettoes clack,
On dirty streets, noisy and moving,

I hear a thundering voice breathe,
Calling for those lost on the mainland.

Robert Sutton

Sutton's Explanation: There was so much to take in all at once upon arrival in Cape Town. The beauty of the place, the ruggedness of informal settlements contrasted with the opulence of Camp's Bay and the V&A Waterfront, the homeless sitting uncomfortably adjacent to luxurious restaurants and hotels, never letting people forget that all is not well. A city built for the future but spiritually and emotionally shackled by its past, not yet flying free.

As these initial impressions began to settle, we continued our learning in class and on field trips giving us a broader and deeper understanding of the history which has led to the current social, economic and political situation. What struck me the most was a brief but incisive description of how Apartheid began: Out of a brutal conflict between the British and the Dutch, the mutual desire to protect wealth, dominance and prosperity rose to the fore, and agreements were made regarding the division of the spoils to the cruel, deliberate and planned exclusion of indigenous and/or coloured communities.

Sitting atop Table Mountain, under a formation that actually looked to me like a dragon's head pushing forth from the rocks it dawned on me that people struggle with the same temptation and lure of wealth today as much as they ever have, and the fear of hardship, the fear of discomfort, the fear of financial and material insecurity still drives people to directly or indirectly cause harm to their brothers and sisters on earth.

In consideration of this, I reasoned, it becomes ever more important to take time out, escaping the so- called 'rat-race' to find some solace; time to think and reflect on meaning and purpose, to confront the temptation to strive forward for success and riches without due consideration of deeper consequences both to self and other. People often seem to find security beneath their endeavours, being 'under the serpent's neck, protected', affirmed by their carefully chosen wider social circles which are likely to be caught in similar temptations to get ahead despite the costs.

I saw Robben Island and was struck how, in this beautiful city reaching for a better future, there is the constant reminder of the 'monster island' where people were imprisoned and abused; a physical memory of what the temptations to dominate, protect wealth and get rich can drive people to do. The warmth of the sun which shines on the city perhaps cooled by those memories. And yet, the problem persists.

While some people go about their lives in luxury, striving for the next distraction of social entertainment, the 'dirty streets' harbour malcontent, disparity, and poverty. But it must be said, those affected are not innocent of the same desires for wealth and prosperity which leads some to crime, others to drugs, alcoholism, and street life. The expectation of a new world order post-1994 has, in reality, left many people behind and promoted disillusionment.

The dragon of temptation does not spare the rich or the poor and calls out over the Mother City seeking those lost in the struggle. Using individual and collective desperation and confusion as an entry point, the serpent sends out its low 'thundering voice' luring people further into anger and resentment. My poem's title 'Mammon' is a deliberate reference to the Biblical lesson that you 'cannot serve both God and money' (Mammon being the god of wealth and riches). In other words, it is very difficult to do that which is right if your primary focus is only wealth without due consideration for the world and humanity. But as I gazed out over Cape Town from my sheltered vantage point, I saw in the Mother City a real living hope which has birthed growing movements of people who, together, seek to ignore the dragon's call and build a resilient, inclusive future.

4.3.5 WHAT HAPPENED?

Dear Kurt, I now just don't know what to do.
Sell my possessions and move to Karoo?

Started the program, thinking I would go far.
I saw all the glamour and a black Jaguar (F-type).

But I find my music, well mostly by chance.
Which is quite funny as I clearly can't dance?

Thought I liked all the caviar and champagne in my life
Now I skip all that nonsense to spend time with my wife

And instead of golf now I'd rather play soccer
The suit has been changed and I dress like a rocker

But not that I'm leaving GSB as a mess
I know myself better and will "settle for less"

My life has changed in more than one way
I'm much happier now what more can I say

Johan Karlsson

*Karlsson's Explanation: The intention of this poem was to, in a light-hearted mood, describe the impact this elective has had in my life. It has truly been a life-changing experience where the focus has shifted from using the MBA as a platform for career growth to a more internal and private focus. The questions are now rather what I can do for myself and people around me to increase the amount of happiness in **our** daily lives.*

The first verse indicates that I am still struggling with finding my purpose but at least now realise that something must change in order to find happiness.

The second verse describes my expectations of what this program could result in... and my favourite car is a Jaguar.

The third verse is how I find the direction to happiness, but also that I really like my job and my colleagues and that the missing pieces required to find my happiness probably can be found in my private life by loosening up and allowing myself to 'dance' more ... this as my inability to let go was evident during the dance session.

The fourth verse describes the realisation that the important things are closer to home than keeping up appearances, and to aim for the expected signs of success.

The fifth verse ties into the previous, as my passion is soccer and that I really don't like playing golf but that it is expected of a modern businessman/woman to play ... but I am now fine with doing what I want.

The sixth verse describes the overwhelming feeling of changed direction in life and the uncertainty ahead, but that I am fine regardless of the outcome even if it is "less" in purely monetary terms.

The seventh verse tries to close the loop tying into the initial statement in not knowing exactly what to do but also describes the overall liberating and positive emotions of finally realising the need for change, but also that I am currently in a happy place already.

4.3.6 YET WHAT WAS THERE TO BE LEARNT...

Yet what was there to be learnt when the troubles had duly
passed,
But that struggle meant sacrifice and that sacrifice was
unending.
That what was lost could never be reclaimed,
That there was no salvaging of it.

And so it is,
That there are many tales of glory,
But few of sacrifice,
In the myths and fables,
Of struggle and revolution.

For struggle is not momentary,
It is ever-ongoing,
And what is endured is a thing of sacrifice,
A thing that time cannot repair.
A thing of endurance,
And not of interruption.

A rupture in time that can never be sealed,
Like the scarred flesh of a wound,
A rupture in time that can never be sown back,
That can never be remade whole.
A mark never born alone,
That's what sacrifice is.

There are tales of struggle that soar very high,
But they can never convey with the fullness of truth,
What sacrifice wreaks in the circles and cycles of life.

And it does not do it once,
And it does not do it twice,
But it does it still.

It spreads outwards into the lives of others,
And they are bound to it as were you.
It is an unending trauma that sacrifice inflicts,
An open wound that will not heal.

Between pain and loss, it moves,
Yet sacrifice is not brokenness,
And about this I must be clear,
For sacrifice is not a dearth of spirit,
But a commitment to it.

For brokenness reigns when you are unable to struggle.
Brokenness is not struggle.
Yet painful it is,
It is not struggle.

Yet lasting it is,
It is not struggle.
It does not sacrifice,
It hasn't the choice,
But to endure its plight.
Brokenness does not know,
And it does not venture to seek out choice.

Yet that is not the whole of it,
For there are those that know not either,
Neither sacrifice nor brokenness have they endured.
And yet their notions duly fool them,
That struggle is their pledge.

For that struggle that they pledge,
Knows nothing of the edge,
Of revolution.
That severs as it turns,
And turns for evermore.
The spirit is its engine,
And struggle is its chore.

Space may bend,
And time may follow,
And matter may call them both,
But of struggle it is certain,
It knows no safely guarded berth.

Camaron Peter

Peter's Explanation: This piece reflects on the permanence of sacrifice, that which is lost in the devotion to struggle cannot be reclaimed, and that the suffering that it brings affects more than the sufferer alone. Families, friends, and children in the greater network are affected. Some of that suffering persists over generations, long after the original sacrifice has been made. Yet, although that sacrifice is painful, it is still an act of courage, or an act of freedom amidst the denial of it. That is its enduring power; that it is so embodies in the human spirit that the quest for freedom will never end. It will persist through time and space, for as long as humanity exists.

4.4 CONQUERING COMPLEXES

Since the concept of individuation is a Jungian idea, it demands a psychological investigation. From such a lens, knowing oneself entails becoming self-aware of one's inner world. In other words, it requires introspection into parts of one's psyche that are outside the conscious mind — the personal unconscious, collective unconscious, and the shadow.[90] Investigating the unconscious requires introspection into one's archetypal self and one's complexes.[91] Additionally, individuation is regarded as: "the shift of psychic balance from the area of consciousness with the ego as its centre, to the totality of the conscious and unconscious psyche. This 'totality' has its own centre, which Jung has called the 'self', in contradistinction to the 'ego'".[92]

In the absence of one getting to grips with the unconscious parts of one's psyche, aspects held within it have the capacity to control and dictate one's behaviour as instinctive reactional behaviour in response to the environment that may trigger them. Drawing the analogy from physical reflexes, these behavioural reactions are regarded as 'psychological reflexes' since they are out of the control of one's conscious mind. Stimuli that trigger such responses are popularly known as 'pressing of one's buttons'.

Complexes are essentially childhood experiences that have exceptional imprinting on the individual's psyche. The memories of those events are responsible for complexes which are stored by our psyche in 'full-colour high-definition'. Not merely from a visual perspective, but the vivacity of the experience may exist in respect of any of the senses. When encountering a similar sensory stimulus, these complexes take one back to the moment in childhood. The nostalgia is so profound that it dominates one's response to the situation.

Complexes are more easily understood with examples within one's own psyche or examples of such complexes shared by others. Our research participant, Jordan April, in his poem: "The waiting room" (4.4.1), artistically sketches an image of a childhood experience in the waiting room of a dentist's practice. The recollection is vivid, precise, clear, and shared with all sensory recollections and emotions experienced. When such stimuli are experienced later in life, they 'press one's buttons', and psychologically place one in the mindset that was experienced during the time of the initial experience. There are physical signs associated with triggering of one's complexes that lead to physiological changes, such as the stomach-churning, quickening of the heartbeat, or one's palms becoming sweaty. Additionally, the behavioural response to the stimuli is always disproportionate to the situation at hand.[93] Many of the memories that lead to complexes within the psyche, from a cognitive assessment as an adult based on realism, may not qualify as out of the ordinary, unique, or even significant. Nonetheless, the psychological experience and imprinting on the psyche is prominent, which is the reason for such experiences to be recalled so vividly. Also, while April's recollection is one of the fears of visiting the dentist, complexes need not always be negative memories. Certain positive memories, and even dreams, may be recalled or dreamt in colour.

In psychology, "'Hotspots refer to memories of detailed moments of peak emotional distress during a traumatic event".[94] Frequently associated with post-traumatic stress disorder (PTSD) and the field of trauma counselling, hot spots are defined as: "… specific parts of the trauma memory that cause highest levels of emotional distress, and that are associated with intense re-experiencing of aspects of the trauma".[95] However, we have chosen to use the term 'hot spots' to describe specific aspects of the encounter or experience that bear the potential to trigger the complexes that may not necessarily justify a classification of a trauma experience. This is because complexes can be argued to be psychological traumas, though a physical traumatic element does not necessarily accompany them, and thus differentiates them from traumas. Additionally, the existence of 'hot spots' is similar to that in the research of PTSD. For example, in the case of Jordan April, it may be any of the variety of sensory details described in the poem that is potentially a 'hot spot'. Unlike traumas, 'hot-spots' of complexes may not always represent such extreme scenarios that require the attention of clinical psychiatrists. However, they play a foundational role for individuation as: "… the complex … is never exhausted as a rich source of reflection and learning".[96] As such, the first step to conquering complexes is the identification of 'hot-spots', through recognition of physiological effects described earlier, or a disproportional response by one to the stimuli. An awareness of one's complexes can allow for a degree of cognitive control over their tendency to draw one back to the childhood memory to help to control a response that is incoherent to the event.

Our research participant, Saa-ima Natha in her poem: *"Blemishes"* (4.4.2), uses the metaphor of drilled holes in the wall to create an image of the psyche punched with holes due to such complexes and 'hot spots'. She describes 'hot spots' to be: "Holes in the wall, though very small, Collectively, leaving a wall diminished"; thus, highlighting their psychological significance. She expresses how complexes are drilled into the cement without consent, that leave scars that never disappear. However, she does not challenge the ability to heal one's complexes. She states in her line: *"Nothing is a permanent fixture. But a mark proves something existed"*. Thus, conquering complexes requires bringing them to the conscious part of the psyche, i.e., becoming aware of them, and acknowledging their prominence. Such acknowledgement and identification of complexes do not render: "… one fully conscious of such psychic reflexes, but rather that it better enables one to recognize their presence when they do emerge" (Hollis, 1998, p. 46). As such, they stop being "blind spots"[97] that trigger psychological reflexes.

Identifying 'hot-spots' and complexes associated with them, we need to allow them to move to the conscious mind, which eventually permits the memories to fade over time, thus deflating the emotional pressures bound within the memory from releasing unexpectedly. Our research participant, AJ Nel in his poem: *"My journey, as a poem"* (4.4.3), vividly describes wounding in life's journey. The wounding, as well as its healing, are expressed as a continuous process, as *"pursuit for a better you"*. Thus, Nel highlights the numerous complexes within one's psyche, and the constant need for their identification, and their mastery, by decreasing their prominence to one's behavioural response, as a vital aspect for individuation.

However, in addition to the academic literature that largely regards time as a healer for complexes to fade, Kurt April in his poem: *"Owning forgiveness"* (4.4.4), expresses forgiveness as an enabler to overcome complexes. While the identification of complexes, and linking them to childhood memories may still be precursors for this enabler, and additionally the relevance of time as a healer is unchallenged, forgiveness presents a potential catalyst to facilitate and speed-up conquering of one's complexes. He defines forgiveness as: *"... an act of no longer feeling resentful or angry towards oneself and others for some real or perceived flaw, error or mistake"*. April continues to provide a host of measures to assist in the difficult process of forgiving oneself and others, which include: unlearning habits, acknowledging the compromised truthfulness of the past, learning from God's forgiveness, facing truths about others, cultivating new passions, transforming relationships, and pursuing disciplined living. April regards the pursuit of forgiveness of others and ourselves, but also seeking forgiveness from others in pursuit of peace.

An unwounded psyche is an impossibility. Our research participant, Lynne Molloy in her poem: *"Perfection"* (4.4.5), in recognition of the fact that everyone of us has experienced wounding, urges the reader not to pursue the image of an unwounded perfect self. She regards perfection to be an elusive place, and its pursuit redundant. She explains that the striving to be perfect is to embark on: *"... a journey of avoidance and self-deception; about evading and pushing down all of one's troubles and flaws"*. Since wounding is inevitable, and experienced by all, seeking perfection and denying the opportunities of growth that conquering complexes can unravel is to deny the cloud its silver lining. As such, instead of concealing complexes by aiming at perfection, conquering them by identifying hotspots, making acquaintance with one's complexes to become conscious of them, and either allowing them to fade due to cognition or actively embarking on the challenging process to forgive those that were the sources for the complexes can allow for healing and peace.

4.4.1 THE WAITING ROOM

It was still and quiet
Except, the ever-present tick of the old plastic clock hanging on
the wall
A smell
Images provoked
Of rubber gloves and mouthwash hung in the air
Behind the bolted door, the dentist worked.

Across the room
The little boy fidgeted
Uncontrollably
His brown hair stuck out in all directions.
His coat was old, his tracksuit bottoms were tight around his ankles

His black shoes hung off his feet with the laces draping
downwards

His mother incessantly ignored
The boy's fidgeting
The dentist sounds
In baggy red patterned trousers, a multi-coloured striped dress
Faded red bandana on her head
Tightly sealed
Over a mass of scruffy brown curls
Her face, pale
Her hand, on top of her lap.

The waiting room's white walls
Not a spot of dirt
Red seats covered in plastic material
A woven navy carpet

Eyes panned across to the large wooden door as the silver
handle turned
The door creaked
Open
The dental nurse appeared
She was young
And tall.
Her ponytail hung over one shoulder
Her cheeks were blushed red
Mascara made her eyelashes look like spiders' legs
Pink lips.
She looked down to her notepad
Called: "Miss Mines, if you'd like to come through, the dentist
is ready."
The mother with the odd attire stood up
So too her little boy
She took a deep breath
Walked slowly towards the door.

The boy, beads of sweat furrowed his brow
The nails at the end of his fingers dug into his palm
Leaving its presence behind
His pupils dilated as they took each pulse-raising step

The mother sustained a painfully slow pace as to avoid what lies
ahead
Side by side with her boy as if they were rounding the corner to
the principal's office
She whispered to herself
As if she was praying for it to end, swiftly
As the steps which remained lessened
It was time
The pearlescent silver handle of the great door turned, to reveal.

Jordan April

April's Explanation: When we are scared and when we are fearful, everything around us becomes vivid in detail. Our senses are heightened and our body has physiological reactions, particularly when we remember previous trauma about the same or similar experiences, or when we anticipate perceived trauma. We notice like we never noticed before during our normal day-to-day activities (colours, details, smells, words, anxiousness, and thoughts running amok under the grip of strong emotion). The boy, in the poem, uses a grounding technique (digging his nails into his palm) as a distraction. Typically, older or more experienced loved ones or people who care may step in, to support, to comfort with words and action, or to provide distraction, as is the case of the little boy's mother in the poem. Isolation and loneliness are not ideal in times of stress and trauma – we all need support, we all need to belong, we all need to know that someone cares. We need someone to help us know that everything is going to be okay.

4.4.2 BLEMISHES

Blemishes on the cement
Drilled without consent
Trying to patch it up,
but the marks are clear
like a wound again sheared
leaving scars that never disappear

The nail was hit on the head
The frame seemingly perfect
Until the picture depicted
something that no longer existed

Even time changed with time
the clock hands worn and misaligned

The clock hung had to be taken down
to keep up with the era now
It was the final nail in the coffin
Realisation didn't need a boffin
to see that change happens so often

Nothing is a permanent fixture
But a mark proves something existed
Though bright pictures may be a stark contrast
To the grim blemishes that forever last

Holes in the wall
though very small
Collectively leaving a wall diminished
the impression of a canvas unfinished
Yet the masterpiece piece of life flourishes
for driving nails in its walls takes courage

Saa-ima Natha

Natha's Explanation: We often confuse the idea of perfection with being perfect. Imperfection is often highly valued just like our favourite worn-out couch that is far more comfortable than the new one. This poem was a reflection on the Wabi-sabi philosophy by comparing it to the way houses become a home. I was staying at my parents' house in my childhood room for a while and saw a strip of purple paint sticking out from behind the dresser. My shelf had been removed after my old room was repainted leaving a blemish on the wall. I stood up to move the dresser as it was distracting to see this strip of bright purple against the rest of the now cream coloured walls. Instead of touching the dresser, I ended up touching the purple strip. I remembered the books that the shelf carried and the trinkets it carried that I got as presents from my school friends. I loved that purple colour so much back then and made my room up in purple. I studied within those purple walls and cried. I painted and wrote short stories. What was a mere blemish now held many memories and it now was no longer just a mere blemish? It was a strip of character. It's what made this room once mine. It reminded me that we're constantly shifting furniture and painting walls to try and change ourselves. Sometimes it does not work out and sometimes it works out perfectly but we wouldn't know unless we tried. Our houses become homes only after many years of traffic and damage and shifting things about. In the same way, we realise our authentic selves, and being left with some blemishes on the way can only be proof that we were willing to try and doesn't have to be a reminder of where we failed.

4.4.3 MY JOURNEY, AS A POEM

Blades taken to calloused hands
Quick slice, blood flows
Momentary pain

Fresh new skin
Soft, supple, sensitive

Temporary

AJ Nel

Nel's Explanation: Our MBA leadership journey has, to me, not been linear at all, but rather iterative – a continuous cycle of learning, identifying weaknesses, developing strengths to combat or improve on those weaknesses, executing on your learnings, and then reassessing for weaknesses again. My poem aims to capture this cycle metaphorically, by comparing our learning process to the removal of callouses from your hands. Initially, our leadership journey forces us to look inward, recognizing our bad habits, stumbling blocks and so-called weaknesses – the callouses formed from hard work over the last few years that lead us to this point, the start of an MBA and ultimately (hopefully) a significant change event in your life and career.

We are given the tools to make sense of these callouses, and are invigorated by the courses and our peers, again seen metaphorically as the removal of these callouses, replaced with fresh learnings, perspectives, and skills. However, we often slip back into the same habits, and even our new habits and learnings become routine and therefore callouses form again. The fresh skin is temporary, you must work hard, and then start over – reflect on where you are, cut what doesn't work, keep what works, and continually "refresh" your hands in the pursuit of a better you.

4.4.4 OWNING FORGIVENESS

Forgiving … it demands from me
Accountability
Justice
I am committed to its importance

It is difficult to break the cycles of orthodoxy
Enmeshed in patterns of negativity and destructiveness
It is difficult to unlearn habits

85

Difficult to remember the past truthfully
Difficult to embody

God's forgiveness is the only true lesson
To help me narrate the truth about my life, my darkness
Dying a death to my old self, my old
selfishness, my old self-concern

A true reconciliation through costly forgiveness
Facing the truth about others
Reconciliation of brokenness
Restoration of communion
Living anew

Cultivating appropriate sorts of passions
In transformative relationships

I am called to disciplined living
Through inhabiting exemplar spaces
By exhibiting good character
In favour of establishing a committed community of forgiveness

Kurt April

April's Explanation: Forgiveness, never a weakness, is a form of compassionate strength towards others and ourselves, the knowledge of which is often lost or forgotten when it comes to forgiving ourselves. It is an act of no longer feeling resentful or angry towards oneself and others for some real or perceived flaw, error, or mistake. It does not, however, mean forgetting – on the contrary, it encourages us to act in wisdom to protect ourselves from the future, further harm, but not to let the pain or disconnection affect us any longer. The orientation and action required are of reaching out to re-establish connection and humanity, which ultimately alleviates suffering in the world. It re-establishes the possibility for healthy future communion with others and the world. Peace emerges when we choose to stop contending with others and ourselves, just as we would have liked for ourselves if we transgressed someone or something and require forgiveness from others. Forgiveness and the act of forgiving grow easier with use, unlike physical courage which depletes with usage.

4.4.5 PERFECTION

The home my heart has longed for
The apex of love long out of reach
Of meaning made plain
Of safety

Of acceptance
Travelling a road paved with pain, cast as resilience
With fragility, concealed as pride
With guilt, veiled by innocence
With shame
With disgust
A lifelong journey
A pursuit demanding life
On a road unending
Until finally
Oh, relief.

Lynne Molloy

Molloy's Explanation: My poem is about avoiding one's shadow and seeking perfection as a means to fill all the holes and hurts in one's life. The hope is that by reaching this elusive place of perfection, everything will be alright. All problems will be solved, all hurts will be healed, and all needs will be fulfilled.

But really, this is a journey of avoidance and self-deception; about evading and pushing down all of one's troubles and flaws, driven by a desperate and misguided hope that by achieving perfection, these will all fall away.

It is a journey that will take one's whole life – will demand one's whole life – if you're willing to give it.

But perfection can never be reached, and this effort at life will really be a sham. By following this path to perfection, the only hope for relief will be achieved when the path finally ends:

And looking back, is a life like this not pointless? Although suppressed, the pain, fragility, guilt, and shame have been harboured and carried throughout the journey, under the illusion that attaining the impossible will make them disappear. Is this not really a weak attempt to justify avoidance as a noble cause? Is attempting to suppress the shame not really the route of a coward? Nothing can make these shadow elements disappear, not even perfection. The point of life is not to aspire towards perfection. Perfection is the one true enemy of authenticity. True meaning, love, safety, and acceptance can be achieved through knowing oneself honestly and facing up to one's shadow. This way, life can be lived, rather than feigned and tolerated until it is finally over.

4.5 WABI-SABI

If the journey of individuation is one during which one becomes aware of the extent to which one is directed by one's ego, then an exploration of parts of the unconscious psyche provides a valuable perspective on the ego. By unravelling one's complexes and exploring the shadow psyche, an acknowledgement and understanding of shameful experiences allow one to view oneself as being imperfect; thus, helping to deflate the prominence of the ego in one's daily life. The role of the ego as a stumbling block in acceptance of self-imperfections is clear in psychology.[98]

A necessary facet of individuation is being comfortable with imperfection.[99] Our research participant, Deneshan Govender in his poem: *"Imperfection"* (4.5.1), effectively presents acronyms for the ideological notion of perfection. In doing so, he challenges perfection in its definition, as being a *"subjective"* notion, that varies based on *"context"*, which requires a benchmark for comparison, and is therefore, *"relative"*. This fundamentally places the notion of perfection in the earlier stages of psychological development where comparatives with family members or people in and around one's society during the conforming and differentiating stages of self-leadership development dictate the existence of the notion of 'perfection'. As such, during the individuation stage, one escapes these comparatives and externally influenced expectations of 'being', instead choosing to be who one truly is, and living one's true life. The principles of the Japanese philosophy of Wabi-sabi encourages one to embrace one's shortfalls, celebrate the way things are, and make the most out of life rather than how one is conditioned to think that they should be. Embracing of this philosophy is a pivotal tool for individuation that casts doubt on the concept that emerges in earlier stages of development of perfection, and begins to develop a novel perspective that what in earlier stages would be regarded as 'imperfection', at the stage of individuation is viewed as 'authentic'. He concludes with his regard of imperfection as synonymous with *"living"*, highlighting the need for its acceptance. He ends the poem by equating imperfection with uniqueness, by claiming it be: *"far from the usual"*, and laying the foundation for its potential for uniqueness and for utilization of one's imperfections as assets, rather than regarding them as liabilities.

Our research participant, Gerald Chimenya in his poem: *"Why worry?"* (4.5.2), shares how the pressures of attaining perfection can lead to the negative affect of constantly worrying, undermining oneself, and comparing oneself with others. Despite cognitive knowledge about the impossibility of its attainment, as well as questions regarding its existence, he highlights 'self-vanity' as a stumbling block to authenticity that results in one continually pursuing perfection in vain. Wabi-sabi philosophically views as 'dishonest', the embellished compliance to uniformity that often characterises aesthetic perfection and instead encourages the individuality of personal narratives. He extends the pressures of an expectation of perfection on one in society to that experienced by our leaders. This instils fears in the leaders that any signs of imperfection would be demotivating for the followers, and a source for disrespecting the leader.

Another research participant, Seshen Moodley in her poem: *"Dear perfect self"* (4.5.3), talks about how the illusion of perfection has fully controlled her life. She expresses how sometimes her ideal image of perfection appears so close and attainable that it appears: *"... as close as a whisper"*, and at other times the attainment of perfection is felt like a: *"... teasing laughter from a distance"*. Thus, her poem addresses perfection as being similar to a mirage. She identifies an enabler that assists in diminishing the aspiration to be perfect – exhaustion. The recognition that the perfect-self is a mirage, hence an illusion, with time and development of cognitive understanding leads one to acknowledge the immense energy consumed in its redundant pursuit. She ends the poem with the beautiful line: *"... someday, Perfect you will realize that imperfect me was worthy of being chased too"*; thus, awaiting a beginning to start an appreciation of self-imperfection.

Our last research participant in this section, Kurt April in his poem: *"Beauty in imperfection"* (4.5.4) furthers debunks the perception of perfection by supporting beauty in one's imperfections. He lists some hardships people experience such as grief, loss, traumas, and loneliness that can leave people feeling imperfect, flawed, and broken. His expressions are well-aligned to existential humanism[100] that focuses on the "positive existential givens" of hardships.[101] The healing process, enabled by *"... small memories, [and] shadowed delights"*, brings repair, facilitates character-building, and transformation. He ends with the line that one's imperfections are: *"Our gifts, Embedded in our imperfection"*. Wabi-sabi propels one in the acceptance of things in their current form or state, and finding beauty therein, in common irregularity, facilitating authenticity, truthfulness, and weakening the power of the ego.

4.5.1 IMPERFECTION

Subjective

Contextual

Relative

Living

And sometimes far from the usual code, much like this ode.

Deneshan Govender

Govender's Explanation: This poem is meant to reflect what the writer feels about imperfection in his life. The succinct nature of the poem is intended to point out that the writer does not consider the concept of perfection as important. Additionally, the unusual structure of this poem is meant to highlight that imperfection can be seen as abnormal.

Intended meaning of adjectives/lines used:

Subjective: perfection is a matter of opinion and left up to interpretation.

Contextual: often the circumstance or situation calls for a particular action so imperfection can be defined by the circumstance or situation.

Relative: something or someone can be imperfect when compared to a particular benchmark or someone else respectively. For example, a memorandum to a scientific test versus an examinees answer.

Living: it is impossible to live a perfect life because living involves making mistakes and learning or not learning from these mistakes. There is no memorandum to living and we are all different and complex. Being imperfect is part of living.

Far from the usual: Imperfection can be interpreted as far from normal and this line is used to highlight that the writer recognises that this poem is far from a usual poem. Moreover, the line is used to point out the writer's comfort and acceptance of being imperfect.

4.5.2 WHY WORRY?

Is this poem going to be meaningful?
Is it going to sound good?
Is it going to be well-received?
I worry.
Will the sun rise today?
Will the moon and stars shine tonight?
Will the fish swim in the ocean?
I worry.
I sit quietly, watching the beautiful blue skies
As the sun shines
And the birds fly over singing sweet melodies
It is indeed a beautiful day,
Still, I worry?
As I look up while reading this poem
I realize I am surrounded by wonderful people

People so beautiful that one wouldn't want to change anything
about them
Still, I worry!
Vanity, this is vanity of vanities
As a wise man once said
"if you cannot change it then, why worry?
If you can change it then, why worry."
Vanity of all vanities I say.
Am I perfect, I ask
Am I perfect, I worry
In the end and with comforting words I conclude,
I know I am perfect in my imperfection!
So, why worry?

Gerald Chimenya

Chimenya's Explanation: The title of my poem is "Why worry". The struggle that I have faced in my life is that of portraying myself as perfect, the struggle of portraying an image that I am perfect and that's what the world should see about me.

As a result, I have been struggling to find my proper and real image. I have this week started to ask myself, how much vulnerable should I be? What is it that I have been hiding and struggling with? Whenever I make a mistake, I beat myself up, I accuse myself and I engage in much self-talk that sometimes ends up being toxic to the extent of feeling sick. I sometimes have countless sleepless nights and I worry a lot about what is going to happen.

As I worry, I always want to make sure that I have made the best decisions. This has caused me difficulties in engaging with and embracing uncertainty and ambiguity because I am afraid of making mistakes. I have always believed that as a leader I should be perfect because if my imperfection is seen by those around me, they will be demotivated, and they will not respect me. Even when I preach, I always worry about whether the message I preached was good enough or not.

I have come to realize that it is because of my struggle with 'perfection' that I tend to worry. I have come to realize and learn that I should be comfortable and that I should not hide my imperfections. This will enable me to develop courage and grow and not set high standards for myself which I may not be able to attain. I should rather look at my ideal self, that even with those imperfections I am able to serve the purpose that I should serve.

In my poem, I use the sun and the moon as examples. It is not up to me whether the sun will rise or not. I cannot do anything about it. So why worry over things I cannot change?

In the end, my lesson is that I am perfect in my imperfections.

4.5.3 DEAR PERFECT SELF

Dear perfect self

You have eluded me for far too long
At times you'd be as close as a whisper
And at another, I'd hear the echo of your
teasing laughter from a distance.

You played this game in full control
Completely invested in finding you, I did not notice that I'd lost
my way
With each waking day, there I would try, to become clever and
smart
Little did I know, that you've mastered this game of elusive art.

Now so deluded and so exhausted after playing
Remind me, why was it important to find you again?

Do forgive me as I won't play anymore
You are not at fault, of that I'm sure
To play this game alone, now you must endure

So, in the end as I walk away, my hope for you, dear perfect self,
Is that someday, Perfect, you will realize that
imperfect me was worthy of being chased too!

Seshen Moodley

Moodley's Explanation: This poem speaks to the ever-lingering internal voice in my mind, that voice that since time innumerable, which has always been critical of my imperfect self. This voice was also the motivation behind doing the MBA, which constantly said to me: "You will only be good enough once you have done your MBA".

My Leadership journey taught me that the perfect self always eludes you with its moving line, each time I'd think I was close to attaining my perfect self, the line would just shift outwards, again and again, becoming a vicious circle of chasing the elusive perfect self.

Furthermore, my journey has been liberating in the realization that actually this imperfect self that I am is in fact good enough. Accepting and surrendering to this realization has been a large part of my journey and I have used my poem from the point of imperfect me, as an avenue to express some of my feelings to my perfect self. At this stage, I wanted to make peace with being my imperfect self and find closure in what has been a relentless pursuit of my perfect self.

4.5.4 BEAUTY IN IMPERFECTION

Grief
Can be silent, unseen
Felt loss, hardship, trauma
Loneliness
Learning imperfection

Left flawed
Broken
The heart's usual whispers overtaken

And invites us to be who we really can be
Anew

Our heart is called upon to break
But
Small memories, shadowed delights
Brings repair
Richness, imperfection
Colour to one's soul
Not fixed ... vessel transformed
A new way of knowing
A new being

Our brokenness
Our gift
Embedded in our imperfection

Kurt April

4.6 AUTHENTICITY

Numerous definitions of authenticity emerge from the literature. They include thoroughly abstract descriptions, such as being one's true self, to further dissecting the concept, such as splitting it into three dimensions of: self-awareness (the subjective experience of being in touch with oneself, i.e., knowing who one is, for example, one's strengths or weaknesses), authentic living (the degree to which individuals live in accordance with their own values and beliefs), and external influence (the extent to which an individual accepts the influence of others).[102]

A useful, yet concise definition of authenticity for the context of stage development theory that prescribes to stages that require conforming, either with family or societal perspectives, defines authenticity as: "... seeing through your own eyes, instead of through the eyes of others";[103] thus, establishing authenticity as growth beyond the surviving, conforming, and differentiating stages of psychological development. With reference to Jung's concept of individuation, the definition embodies a move from the 'persona' to the 'Self', or from the 'false self' or 'partial self', to the 'true self' or the holistic Self (written with capital S).[104] Authenticity is the attempt to live one's life according to the needs of one's inner being, rather than the demands of society or one's early conditioning, which places it in the individuating stage of development.[105]

One of our research participants who decided to stay anonymous, in the poem: "*Many??? – Am I good enough?*" (4.6.1), shares a question that has haunted the participant in everyday work and social life: "*Am I doing it the correct way?*". The participant highlights the 'façade' that was created and which him requires constant maintenance. In the explanation of the poem, the participant shares what he/she/they believes was the seeding of this aspiration of being perfect. Anonymous claims it to have developed from early childhood learning that taught her/him/them: "*... to be successful in order to receive recognition*" from primary caregivers. As such, the participant shares conditional love as an enabler for ego significance in the latter stages of development, that works as a stumbling block for being authentic. The participant also highlights the significance of control over life and one's surroundings as attributes of perfection that are learnt. Anonymous goes on to share an enabler for authenticity in the statement: "*I allow only a few people to enter my personal sphere in which I expose my vulnerability*"; thus, linking authenticity with vulnerability.

Being one's 'true self' entails knowing oneself thoroughly, which includes bringing elements from the unconscious mind to the conscious mind. In addition to complexes (4.4) discussed earlier, the shadow is a part of the unconscious psyche. 'Shadow work' refers to introspective psychological self-reflection that can lead to greater authenticity, creativity, and emotional freedom. One of our research participants, Kerry Littlewood, in her poem: "*The shadow*" (4.6.2), talks about the challenges of exploring the shadow psyche to gain consciousness about it, in order to fully reveal oneself. "The shadow is an element of the unconscious representing all things opposite of the ego, which are typically those impulses, wishes, fears, and desires that people feel are the most disturbing, frightful, and shameful".[106] She regards such introspective work as fundamental to enable authentic living. Unlike complexes that bear the potential for reverting one back to one's earlier stages of development as soon as they are triggered, the shadow is said to lurk, sit and wait, always judging one to have a profound influence on one's fate. Not only is it deeply distressing to address the fears and secrets that the psyche keeps locked-up in the shadow, but the fear extends to a hesitation towards transformation, and fears of one's transformed self that unlocking the shadow would reveal. She shares this fear in the line: *"What if I do not like, This true-self deep inside"*. However, she believes that should one find the courage to address the shadow, it can lead to inner-peace and reveal one's purpose.

Theoretically, "Individuation is a complicated process of intrapsychic differentiation and transformation that occurs throughout the second half of life.[107] It involves confronting both the shadow and anima complexes".[108] While our research participants have shared their experiences with complexes and less so with the shadow psyche, the anima (an element of the unconscious representing the feminine side of men) and the animus (which exists for women, representing their masculine side) were absent in our sample. The shadow and anima are said to: "… join and are confronted by the ego through what Jung termed the transcendent function, a process of integrating conscious and unconscious contents through the free exchange of libido (psychic energy) across the boundary of consciousness".[109] As such, it may well be that the anima and animus are not distinguished from the shadow psyche by our research participants, and thus not addressed in the data. Alternatively, it may be less profound for it not to have been mentioned by any of our research participants.

From a staged development point of view, several definitions of authenticity place it within different stages of development ranging from individuation to beyond. Nonetheless, there is largely a consensus for it to belong to the individuation stage. For example, a simple definition of authenticity is for one to recognize oneself for who one really is, and self-acceptance of that discovery;[110] thus, placing it in the individuating stage. Some scholars explicitly state: "The task at the individuating stage of development is to find your authentic self".[111] Also evident in the quote: "… Authenticity does not automatically mean self-actualization because the project of becoming fully human is fraught with difficulty",[112] is that authenticity precedes self-actualization. "The result of successful individuation is a more balanced and integrated personality".[113]

4.6.1 Many??? – Am I good enough?

In everything I do
In my private and professional live
Among my friends and family
Among colleagues, supervisors and in University

I ask myself the questions
Am I doing it the correct way?
What can I do differently to become better?
What does it take to be better than others?
I do everything to be perceived as successful
Is that really what I want?
Am I putting up a façade around me?
When can I show the world my real ME?

Anonymous

Anonymous' Explanation: I believe this poem touches all of the three areas – imperfection, purpose, and authenticity. All my life, I have been taught to be successful in order to receive recognition. Be it in school as in achieving good grades or sports as in being ahead of others. Therefore, I developed success in the eyes of others as a main driver and motor in my life. I constantly find myself in competition mode and comparing myself to the people around me. This raises the question of whether I am good enough or what I can do to create a better version of myself. In this context, I try to avoid showing weakness by all means. I want people to see me as the version of myself that I am in control of and that I show the world. I want them to see me as smart and successful. I am creating a façade around my true me. I allow only a few people to enter my personal sphere in which I expose my vulnerability.

4.6.2 The shadow

Quietly watching, intent to observe
The shadow sits and waits
Judging with hypocrisy
As it contemplates my fate

Thoughts consume the silence
As the shadow dares confess
My deepest fears and secrets
Trapped feelings I suppress

What if I do not like
This true-self deep inside
What if I cannot change
These confessions I confide

Quiet reflection, calm the storm
These thoughts, they are not real
Embrace what you are afraid of

And allow yourself to feel

Unmask the authentic self within
And true peace will unveil
Know the shadow from the self
For your true purpose to prevail

Kerry Littlewood

Littlewood's Explanation: For the past two years, I have been exploring the shadow and its effect on our conscious sense of self. How we have become so adept at hiding our true authentic selves that we begin to represent the masks we wear. This poem explores the fear of discovering who we really are.

By acknowledging the shadow and embracing what we tend to be most afraid of, we begin to create awareness. It is this awareness that begins the process of feedback and acceptance. Reflection provides us with the ability to unmask our true authentic selves: the good and the bad and the opportunity to turn this feedback into action.

It is the acceptance of this shadow that will give us the freedom to live a life full of purpose, a life worth living.

4.7 THE INDIVIDUATED LEADER

From an individuation point of view, the emphasis on future leadership development is clearly on self-knowledge and self-understanding. These personal attributes are argued to form the basis of mature leadership. On the contrary, an immature leader is unlikely to have the ability to handle ambiguousness, complexity, and ethical dilemmas faced in leadership roles.[114] As such, individuating firstly underscores the importance of being honest and truthful to oneself and others, which entails avoiding the unfulfilling nature of merely saying what one thinks others want to hear, and thereby becoming entangled in political webs and loss of values.[115]

Our research participant, Tintswalo Baloyi in her poem: *"Leading through imperfection"* (4.7.1), challenges the perception of a hero in society. She questions why an alternative to the projected image of a leader is offensive to people. Baloyi sees it as a challenge by those conforming to those who are living with authenticity. She concludes by challenging people putting on personas, and encourages the reader to be authentic. In the explanation of the poem, she shares her leadership style. Baloyi states: *"Vulnerability and being personable ... as a leader, gets so much more from your employees as they know and understand the sincerity and purity of your connection"*, thus, highlighting the use of 'weaknesses' as assets for authentic leadership.

Gandhi stated that leader imperfections are vital assets that enable them to embark on a journey with their followers.

"My imperfections and failures are as much a blessing from God as my successes and my talents, and I lay them both at His feet. Why should He have chosen me, an imperfect instrument, for such a mighty experiment? I think He deliberately did so. He had to serve the poor dumb [mute] ignorant millions. A perfect man might have been their despair. When they found that one with their failings was marching on towards ahimsa, they too had confidence in their own capacity. We should not have recognized a perfect man if he had come as our leader, and we might have driven him to a cave. Maybe he who follows me will be more perfect and you will be able to receive his message".[116]

Additionally, individuation not only helps a leader to tolerate his/her/their own imperfections, but also to become accepting of the imperfections in others. Insight into their own strengths as well as their weaknesses permits such leaders to similarly see those of others. As such, by becoming accepting of others' weaknesses and strengths, they can better manage a team to leverage the strengths of individual team members, as well as lend a helping hand to improve weaknesses of individual team members, making them growth-oriented.[117]

Authentic leadership forms a part of this stage of the psychological development of a leader. It is regarded as "behaviour that draws upon and promotes both positive psychological capacities and a positive ethical climate, to foster greater self-awareness, an internalized moral perspective, balanced processing of information, and relational transparency on the part of leaders working with followers, fostering positive self-development".[118] It includes listening ardently, telling the followers the hard truths while being compassionate, but fundamentally making decisions based on that which is aligned to one's authentic self.

4.7.1 Leading through imperfection

What is this look, walk and manner that one should embody as a leader?
Why does the fact that one walks, talks and dresses a certain way, insult you so?
Why does one's ability to lead authentically make you despise one so?

What is the infliction you suffer from laughter in the workplace?
Why does candour amongst colleagues repulse you so?
Why do long faces and long hours equate to hard work?

Here is a question for you?
Why do you look, walk and act like you do?
Why can't you be you?

Tintswalo Baloyi

Baloyi's Explanation: I am a SX4 which means that I am feeling my feelings all of the time and, most importantly, I am always looking to show up as my authentic self. This said, I have found that my manner of 'being' seems unacceptable to many. I use the word 'seems' as there is an element of it just being my perception and not the reality. But with that said, my peers act, dress, speak in a certain manner and even reserve their presence to "the few".

I have never seen myself as being superior in any shape or form, and struggle with segregating myself from my team and others purely based on level of seniority. I socialise with people with whom I have a connection, and that isn't based on hierarchy but rather on the sincerity of the interaction. I really wonder why as individuals we have let ourselves have our manner of 'being' dictated to by a culture that is toxic to those around us. I don't lead with fear. I don't expect my team to stop telling jokes and relating with each other, purely because I am around and they need to do busy work and look serious.

I think that if, as individuals, we stopped wearing marks and having work personas, there would be less burn-out and depression in the workplace. Vulnerability and being personable, as an individual and especially as a leader, get so much more from your employees as they know and understand the sincerity and purity of your connection.

Authenticity and vulnerability-based trust are paramount in this age of leadership.

Lessons from this poem:

Be who you are.

Lead through authenticity.

Vulnerability-based trust gets more out of the team than fear.

5 SELF-ACTUALIZING

One of the earliest, and arguably the most popular, perspectives of the self-actualization stage of psychological development is Maslow's[119] placement of 'self-actualizing' at the top of the pyramid of human motivation. With the four lower tiers regarded as deficiency needs, and self-actualization needs deemed as "being needs" or "growth needs",[120] it is associated with a healthy, balanced, and integrated personality, that radiates love, utilizes creativity, and ensures an ethical and compassionate attitude towards others.[121] Consequently, self-actualized individuals are said to reap the benefits as higher life satisfaction,[122] stable contentment,[123] and happiness at a eudaimonic level.[124] The profoundness of the association of self-actualization with many of these attributes and rewards is clear since these, by definition, embody the concept of self-actualization. For example, eudaimonia is defined as: "... actualization of our human potential, focusing on optimal functioning, personal growth, and the presence of a strong purpose in our life project".[125]

Its placement at the top of the pyramid,[126] and its association with a host of positive attributes make its attainment enticing and tempting. However, to attempt to achieve self-actualization, one must first understand what self-actualization means. A 15-item self-assessment of self-actualization[127] has been validated to discriminate between groups of people nominated as self-actualizing and as non-self-actualizing. The below three items from the inventory estimate the same,[128] the last two of which are in reverse scale (R):

- I can express my feelings even when they may result in undesirable consequences.

- I don't accept my own weaknesses. (R)

- I have no mission in life to which I feel especially dedicated. (R)

The first amongst the questions emerges as a test of one's ability to rise above conforming and differentiating stages of psychological development, whereby adherence to family and societal expectations are no longer sought, despite potential "undesirable consequences" of not doing so. It can be argued that this establishes one to have progressed into the individuation stage of psychological development, that permits authenticity (4.6) in the expression of one's feelings and behaviours. As such, the fundamentals of self-actualization are said to be embedded in authenticity.

The second question that queries an acceptance of one's weaknesses aligns well with an acceptance of one's imperfections, as discussed in the chapter section 'Wabi-sabi' (4.5). However, self-actualization requires more than mere acceptance of one's imperfections. By developing a greater knowledge about oneself through an exploration of the unconscious psyche to reveal the 'Self', knowing one's complexes and having delved into one's shadow psyche help one to better understand the foundations of one's emotions, one's behaviour, and one's motivations for the behaviour.

Lastly, finding one's mission or purpose is sought and understood at the self-actualization stage. However, incorporating one's purpose into one's everyday activity requires integrating with people who share the same values and purpose in life, or whose purpose and values align or complement each other. This is stated as: "you will be looking for a vocation or calling that allows you to fully express your authentic self",[129] which is discussed in the next stage of development of 'integrating'.

Based on self-actualization's definition of achieving one's full potential and becoming fully human, or more comprehensively stated as: "... becoming more fully yourself by finding and expressing your gifts and talents",[130] self-actualization is a stage of deeper authenticity that is uncovered through not only knowing oneself and accepting one's weaknesses, flaws, and imperfections, but furthermore, instead of hiding or covering up these imperfections, growing to accept them, thus accepting one's vulnerabilities. Since hiding one's imperfections is energy-consuming, by embracing them one can free oneself from the tenacious grip these can have on one, freeing one and the energy trapped in keeping up the persona of perfection.

5.1 KINTSUGI

Wabi-sabi recognizes and appreciates that ageing, scarring, and traumas do not lead to a loss of beauty. On the contrary, it philosophically regards perfection as 'insincerity', the sterile and unnatural uniformity that promotes a monotonous and inauthentic vision of aesthetics. Founded on the fundamentals of Wabi-sabi, kintsugi is the Japanese art of pottery repair. Its intense attention to detail emerges from the fact that in addition to the use of urushi, a plant-based adhesive lacquer resin to glue the fragments of the pot together, it is followed by a dusting of gold or silver along the cracks as well as for replacement of the pieces lost or deemed unsalvageable. Not only does it present a radically different care of possessions than the West, it also represents a deviation from traditional Eastern beliefs that traditionally regard broken objects to be inauspicious. For example, breaking of glass in an accident is seen as symbolic of a good omen in Hinduism; however, retaining it in the house is seen to be the contrary. As such, the incorporation of kintsugi in the traditions of Japan represented a deviation from traditional approaches towards the value of things that are broken, as their repair is not considered an act of frugality but of craft that make the pottery more valuable than unbroken pottery. Kintsugi's appreciation is such that pots may be intentionally broken to allow for such creativity and craftsmanship to be applied to them as a means of beautification and value addition.

While the practice originated along with the traditions of the tea ceremony developed between 1573 and 1615, its origins are expected to be influenced by the Japanese geo-ecology. The frequent experience of earthquakes on the islands encouraged the adoption of a philosophy to repair and re-use and beautify broken objects; thus, appreciating their history and the event that caused them to break. Additionally, several aspects of Japanese cultural perspectives support the philosophy, such as regret experienced from waste, the melancholic expression of life's impermanence, and family bonds in regard to inheritance and succession. However, its rise to become akin to being elite commenced with Sen no Rikyū, a historical figure with the most profound influence on the Japanese tea ceremony. Rikyū is said to have ignored a significant tea jar during a tea ceremony, withholding praise for it for the time until it was broken and repaired. There are also tales of his intentional damage to the handle of a flower vase to allow an opportunity for kintsugi craftmanship. Since then, kintsugi products are highly esteemed and used in culturally significant practices such as the tea ceremony.

"Instead of covering up or disguising this nature, kintsugi highlights and enhances it to celebrate the beauty in what is broken and strengthened anew".[131] As a craft, it is a means for repair and beautification. It facilitates the long life of objects in an otherwise increasingly disposable society, and it shows deliberate and conspicuous care for any object. Gold or silver that traces the lines of the cracks or infill voids are regarded as beautification of it — beautification that is coaxed out of brokenness. Additionally, kintsugi allows for an appreciation for the afterlife of the object. Also, over its use over time, it became a means for testing the authenticity of ceramics, as the distinctive features of kintsugi became identifiers of age, history, as well as representative of its origins (foreign-made or local ceramics).

Kintsugi's went beyond ceramics to found fundamentals of philosophy. This has allowed for its extrapolation to various experiences of life into the broader field of transformative repair. From a personal growth perspective, just as: "Kintsugi is shown to demonstrate the propensity of repaired objects to embody dual perceptions of catastrophe and amelioration",[132] its philosophy represents hope in times of despair. It promises a life of quality after the hardship experienced, as the repaired pot does not only revert back to its original use and value, but evolves into something stronger, more beautiful, more valued, and hence more appreciated by having been broken and visibly mended. "Kintsugi repair of a broken pot can be understood as a visual metaphor for how virtues … can be like "veins of gold" that positively reframe physical and mental scars".[133] The broken pot expresses the trauma experienced by people during their lives, and not merely the recovery from such negative experiences, but the personal growth that emerge from it.

However, the first step to self-healing is similar to the use of urushi as the glue to put the pot back together again. Thereafter the gold can be used to enhance it. Applying the metaphor to personal traumas, our research participant, Kathy Harvey in her poem: "Future and past" (5.1.1), presents the struggle to equate hardships with anything positive during the experience. In the explanation of the poem, she states: "*I couldn't imagine something positive emerging as a result*". Instead, she highlights what is needed during the difficult experience is self-care, self-compassion, self-empathy, positive self-talk, and visualizations of life after recovery from the trauma. These support hopefulness and provide strength to oneself at the time when scars are inflicted or during the time when the scars are still sore and not fully healed. Only upon healing, and recovering from the soreness of the traumas that were inflicted on them, can the scars be decorated as personal assets.

Our research participant, LNT in the title of his/her/their poem: *"Who am I but a broken vase?"* (5.1.2), depicts ego-depletion by applying the philosophical concept of Wabi-sabi and imperfection to herself. Additionally, in her poem she talks about how people desperately try not to let others see their imperfections. However, if the scars are representative of the pieces of evidence of one's life's journey, attempting to hide them is to: *"... plunge [them] into darkness"*; thus, portraying that hiding such valuable learning experiences as a waste. Only through embracing of one's vulnerabilities can the light be shone on individuals, entailing that acceptance of one's imperfections allows one to be acknowledged and recognized as a potential leader. Not merely for achieving leadership aspirations, she emphasises recognition and appreciation of moments that have shattered us, similar to a broken vase, that can allow for inner peace to thrive.

Another research participant, Euston Witbooi in his poem: *"One word at a time"* (5.1.3), takes us on a journey through his childhood in which he recaps former stages of self-leadership development. However, his journey does not end at self-acceptance of the imperfection. "Wabi-sabi acclaims beauty in common irregularity, while kintsugi celebrates beauty in visible signs of repair, like scars".[134] Witbooi shares how the scarring that his stutter has inflicted on his personality, in the true spirit of kintsugi, has given him an opportunity to heal the scars with gold. He states: *"I see the good in what my stutter has given me and the value it has added to my character"*. He attributes his focused listening skills and writing skills as a direct consequence of healing from the scarring that his stutter inflicted upon him. These heightened skills are the 'golds and silvers' that he has healed his scars with, which have permitted him to view the scars as his assets, rather than his shortcomings. While his personal reward from kintsugi is unashamedness of his imperfection, the reward to others of having healed his scars is that he is: *"... empathetic, encouraging, and endearing"*.

Similarly, our research participant who decided to stay anonymous, in the poem: "The veil of my own making" (5.1.4), gives the reference of a tree in the wind-swept area of Cape Town (Sea Point). Despite being: "Whisked, tossed and toiled, In the winds of life", Anonymous invites others to: "Come, sit in my shade". A key development upon acceptance of one's imperfections, weaknesses, and traumas experienced is their potential as a unique 'selling proposition' that differentiates one from others. Thus, beyond acceptance and healing, it is the gold and the gift to others that are representative of kintsugi philosophy. Anonymous shares that the courage to weather life's hardships and offer the learnings from it to others is enabled by spirituality.

The primary leadership development goals at the self-actualizing stage of psychological development are said to be: "(a) release any fears you may have about fully expressing who you really are; (b) find your purpose in life, the work that you love to do; and (c) express your creativity".[135] Our section of Kintsugi ends with our research participant, Kurt April in his poem: *"Necessary imperfection to enact change"* (5.1.5), in which he acknowledges the role of suffering that triggers a desire for change. He challenges the notion of the necessity of a sense of belonging, and replaces it with the necessity for imperfection. By doing so, he suggests psychological growth from the conforming and differentiating stages of psychological development to individuation and self-actualization. While he recognises the need for 'a vision' to embark on such a journey of change, he regards it necessary for a leader to have the capacity to go 'against the follow' in the pursuit of such a vision; thus, challenging the notion of change-leadership at earlier stages of psychological development. In the explanation, he emphasises the concepts of Wabi-sabi and kintsugi as enabling self-actualization that he regards as fundamental for effective leaders.

5.1.1 FUTURE AND PAST

To care, to touch
To have, to hold
A pivotal moment to decide

For the bravery of it?
Or for the fear?

Don't be afraid to hope
To be deliberate about the future
To be happy and hopeful at the end
Not just at the start

Kathy Harvey

Harvey's Explanation: This poem was written at a time of great personal crisis, which coincided with great opportunity in my professional life. The hopes and fears I felt about this opportunity became entangled with the negative emotions and beliefs caused by this threat to my personal well-being. Suddenly, I could imagine my world collapsing, but unlike the Japanese vase which becomes more beautiful when it is mended, I couldn't imagine something positive emerging as a result. In the poem, I am imagining wrapping my arms around myself, reminding myself of my strength of spirit, and visualizing a better future. Re-reading the verse, I see it as a message for all of us to be compassionate about ourselves and others, and to harness compassion and empathy to realize our potential and the potential of our families, friends and colleagues.

5.1.2 WHO AM I BUT A BROKEN VASE?

Who am I but a broken vase?
Trying desperately to not let you see,
The broken sides of me.
I turn those sides
Away from the light,
In fear that you
Will discover who I am.
But who am I but a broken vase?
Carrying the scars
of life's journey.
If I continue to plunge into darkness my imperfections,
soon there will be no light to illuminate my richness.
Vulnerability – turn on the light,
and show all that I am about,
the load will be shed,
and with all its pain,
the light will shine in,
with all its peace,
Who am I but a broken vase?
with nothing to hide
for all to see

LNT

LNT's Explanation: Following on from the initial Leadership course, I have been inspired by people being able to share their stories both positive and negative. I was intrigued by the absolute empowerment that sharing one's story brings about. I was still uncomfortable about showing my imperfections though. I was comfortable sharing stories that were about me, but not about my failures and flaws.

During the Advanced Leadership course, I was confronted with being an Enneagram 3 and, for the first time, I owned both the positive and negative descriptors of an assessment. I understood my deep-rooted fear of failure. For the first time I engaged with my beliefs and behaviours, in an attempt to understand whether they were being fed by fear or by love. It was an emotional journey passing through denial, blaming my parents for how they raised me, to overcompensating for the failures by taking on even more successful feats, and culminating in acceptance.

I have always strived to be perfect, to be an achiever, to be attractive and to be liked. So much so that it meant that I would hide certain aspects of myself in the fear that those aspects do not describe who I have created as a perfect self. I would intentionally seek out people and things that would make me look and appear successful. I realised the more I did this the more withdrawn I got, the more successful I got the more I had to hide.

This poem is a reflective piece to give myself permission to be flawed and show off my flaws. It is a transformative piece linking how the reveal of my flaws will be necessitated by choosing to be vulnerable and allowing myself to be okay with the change people will see. It reveals the state of relief and peace that will come with the illumination of the broken parts of me.

My intention with the poem is to empower others, who are on the same journey of hiding imperfections, to illuminate their imperfections. Key takeaways should be that it is okay to be vulnerable.

5.1.3 ONE WORD AT A TIME

One word at a time, I navigate an oral minefield.
With my heart in my mouth, I stumble over barricades of speech.
It has been this way ever since I can remember, January to December.
What is wrong with me? A perennial question with meandering answers.
A truer definition of loneliness you'll never find.
How can certain sounds and words be so unkind?

One word at a time, I fight against my past to create my future.
A battle may be lost but the war is alive and well.
Some days I am so eloquent you would never tell.
Will I learn to control or better yet overcome? Or is my destiny to return to the oral slums?
The answers to these questions are mine to determine.
Assertive self-acceptance is the route I have chosen.

One word at a time, I express my essence unashamedly.
With my heart on my sleeve, I am the general of my speech.
My greatest weakness has given birth to my greatest strengths – I am empathetic, encouraging and endearing.
There is nothing wrong with me!
A truer definition of aloneness you'll never find.
The universe, in its entirety, is so very kind.

Euston Witbooi

Witbooi's Explanation: 'One word at a time' is a poem documenting my journey thus far living with a lifelong stuttering problem. My stutter, upon reflection, is a defining character trait and has invariably impacted the individual I am today. It has made me an avid, focused listener and forced me to become a decent writer. When I was 12 years old and in grade 8 (high school), I knew that I had to do well in the creative essay assessments (for English and Afrikaans) to compensate for my limited oral ability at the time. I forced myself to read one book every weekend to develop my writing and spelling skills. This is an example of a positive influence my stutter has had on me amongst the many often overbearing negatives.

The poem is divided into three distinct stanzas representative of my feelings towards my stutter in the past, the present and the future. The first stanza depicts my feelings and my reality a mere three years ago. Before I decided to proactively do whatever was necessary to overcome my stuttering, I was a solitary, self-pitying individual who had no understanding of my speech impediment. I felt like an outcast and believed that I was the only person on Earth going through this never-ending ordeal.

The second stanza is representative of a very definitive period in my life. Over the last three years I have learnt to understand the physical and psychological aspects of my stutter, which has been instrumental in changing my view on my potential to overcome it. The speech programme I am currently attending has taught me that assertive self-acceptance is paramount to my journey of overcoming. I have learnt that if I am courageous enough, continually expand my comfort zones, and never avoid public speaking situations, then I will progress on my journey.

The third stanza expresses my outlook going forward. I am genuinely optimistic and extremely motivated to continue progressing towards overcoming. I have made peace with who I am and what my mission is. I see the good in what my stutter has given me and the value it as added to my character. I would not change anything about me, and I am proud of who I am. Aloneness in this context is defined as simply the joy of 'being' or fullness, where nothing or nobody else is needed to feel complete.

5.1.4 THE VEIL OF MY OWN MAKING

Like a Sea Point shrub
I have been whisked
Tossed and toiled
In the winds of life

A sight of awkwardness
Bent and gnarled
In defiance of the mental constructs
Onto which I cling

I must stand alone
I must conserve what I can
And yet, my purpose is collective
Come, sit in my shade

The fault lines
between purpose and reality
Separated by meanings
The veil of my own making

But my Father is the gardener
With each storm
Cutting and pruning
Oh, the beauty of the weathered and aged!

Like a Sea Point shrub
Exactly the kind of 'tree'
It needs to be
Come, sit in my shade

Anonymous

Anonymous' Explanation: In my walks along Sea Point promenade, there is one particular tree that always catches my attention. It grows sideways from the daily wind and the storms it faces. I see this tree as a perfect metaphor for my own journey.

Like this Sea Point shrub, I have faced hardships; 'tossed and toiled in the winds of life'. I have struggled not only with outward appearances that I have not liked, but also been confronted by my own prominent weaknesses, especially when it comes to relationships with others. Rather than standing tall and full of lush leaves, I often see myself as 'a sight of awkwardness – bent and gnarled'. These feel like imperfections, deviations from the mental constructs I have for what I 'should' be – the gap between my real self and my ideal self that mirrors the difference between my mental construct of a tree, and the Sea Point shrub in mind.

Some of the things I tell myself are that I must be completely independent – 'I must stand alone'. And yet I feel like my purpose is often at odds with my patterns of withdrawal. This I consider to be a fault line in myself – a paradox and an imperfection. While I know that meaningful connections with others is part of my life's purpose, the meanings of the world I formed in early childhood often get in the way of that. This I call 'the veil of my own making' because it is a way that I create space between my purpose and my current reality, almost self-sabotaging because of the hardships I have faced and my beliefs about myself.

Then, a turning point. Quoting from John 15:1, I turn the attention to God as the gardener. Jesus says, "I am the true vine, and my Father is the gardener. He cuts off every branch in me that bears no fruit, while every branch that does bear fruit he prunes so that it will be even more fruitful". Hence, with each storm I face, I hope to see a bigger purpose. Sometimes we need to be broken down. It is in times of suffering that there is sometimes the most room to grow. As a result of my own challenges, I feel I have emerged more beautiful for my wear and tear. There is something to be treasured in people and things that are damaged and scarred, vulnerable, and imperfect. The things we have experienced make us beautiful.

The last paragraph ends with me contemplating that I am exactly where I need to be right now. That even writing this poem feels like an important part of my journey. I end on the note, "come, sit in my shade" because it is an instance of me living my life less according to habit and fear, and more according to my purpose, as a result of acknowledging the things I have been through and the meanings I have formed.

5.1.5 NECESSARY IMPERFECTION TO ENACT CHANGE

You are the change
Being of service
To the world
Others

Requires not a sense of belonging

Requisite imperfection, vitality required
Energy from the world's dark abyss
Borne out of necessary suffering
Out of disconnection, across boundaries
With vision – granted

While being in the world
Seeing the lack of flow
Not fully aligned with the world
You – flutter

Vision enacted
Broken it may be
Wounded you remain
But stepping forward
The sun will shine
For others
For your own soul

No substitute for the imperfect you.

Kurt April

April's Explanation: Perfectionism speaks to a mindset of constant moving, of never arriving, unyielding, and if one ever achieves it, an ultimate prize of a finished state without any flaws or errors. It encourages a disdain for imperfection in ourselves and others. We get angry with ourselves and others for not meeting the supposed standard. It emanates from a place of: (1) judgement ("As I am now, is not good enough"), and (2) comparison ("There is always something, or someone, better or worse than me"). Leadership literature is filled with development techniques to help individuals on a pathway to perfection – to fix this, to change that, to cut out those – engendering a life of perpetual unease with ourselves – and to gloss over or even hide those things/experiences that may cause us to appear flawed, imperfect or broken to others. The Japanese concept of Wabi-sabi, embedded in Zen Buddhism philosophy, conveys a complex set of meanings which can best be summarised as an appreciation of the impermanence, asymmetry and small details in life and everything that surrounds us. Wabi-sabi gives us a more constructive lens for thinking about leadership, and the acceptance of transience and imperfection – a liberation from the caves of opinion and comparison. Wabi-sabi philosophy is also beautifully expressed in a practice of fixing broken pottery with gold, called kintsugi. Here, a broken object is carefully mended back together and the cracks are not just repaired with glue, but further enhanced and decorated with gold or silver. Rather than lamenting over a precious object being broken, the object is not only repaired but made more beautiful in the process. The so-called imperfection actually enriches the original object, and appears even more beautiful. Kintsugi is a powerful metaphor for overcoming hardship, trauma, loss and approaching our own perceived imperfections, weaknesses and traits which we may see as undesirable. Things, and people, are often much stronger and more unique when emerging, or bouncing back, from struggle, suffering or brokenness. In kintsugi, breakage is an essential part of our true history, and not something to disguise. We all bear scars from adverse conditions in our lives and our relationships – and this could be our very gifts to the world later on in life,

e.g., having overcome social injustice, one might spend part of one's life fighting for
social justice, for looking out for the most vulnerable or marginalized in society, or
having come from poverty one may find the connection and strength to help those
currently in poverty or out of work – our so-called scars or imperfections in our
history/lives, can become our actual gifts to the world.

5.2 TRAUMAS

A major aspect of self-actualization is a recollection, reflection, and cognition of the traumas experienced in one's life, and utilising them as experiences of unmatched learning to heighten one's emotional maturity, as well as connectivity with others and compassion towards others. Using the metaphor of Kintsugi, the trauma represents the shattering of the pottery, only upon which it can be mended to be unique, stronger, valuable, and more beautiful than before.

Traumas are defined as the psychological response to usually a single, deeply distressing incident that overwhelms the psyche.[136] While such incidences can occur at any point in one's life, they therefore can occur at different stages of psychological development, the maturity hence psychological processing of the traumas are different at different stages. For example, during infancy and early childhood, traumas are not recollected by the conscious psyche, and are therefore scars that permeate into the unconscious mind that can exert seismic forces on the psyche that shift the normal course of personality development. As such, they can: "... significantly shape personality development and influence adult behaviour".[137]

The heightened significance of traumas during the early stage of psychological development is due to the fact that early stages represent times of lower emotional maturity. As such, the intensity felt, and its corresponding psychological impact is profound. Unlike during childhood, during adulthood, the extreme stress faced during a traumatic event challenges one's coping mechanisms[138] rather than shifting the trajectory of personality development. How a person responds to trauma is subject to significant variations based on details of the event itself, personality trait variations, coping mechanism adopted, as well as societal perceptions and social support available.[139] Psychological responses to traumas range from assimilation (a distortion of the experience as a coping mechanism, such as denial), to deflection of personality development through accommodation (an alternation of self-belief), and over-accommodation (extreme distortions of beliefs about the self and the world).[140]

Most commonly reported incidences of trauma include physical assault, road traffic and other accidents, witnessing death, armed robbery, sexual assault, and medical traumas. One of our research participants, Beneta Bale in her poem: *"In my silence"* (5.2.1), shares two traumas in her untold story that she shares for the first time. Firstly, she shares the ordeal of a physical assault which led to the murder of her ex-partner. Secondly, she shares her medical trauma in contracting the human immunodeficiency virus (HIV) from him. Due to the stigma surrounding HIV, she confirms it to be: *"... hidden deep within. Hidden very carefully and deeply ... It is a part that stays in silence Within me"*. Thus, she expresses how the social stigma regarding HIV presented her with a binary choice to either suffer in silence, or to voice her trauma and face exclusion and marginalization. She shares how such suffering in silence exacerbates the pain associated with the trauma and acts as a stumbling block to healing; hence, hindering deeper authenticity and self-actualization.

Interestingly, our same research participant, Beneta Bale, shared another trauma in her second poem: *"Soil – not of home"* (5.2.2), when her friend passed away. Unlike her previous poem which led to her silence, the trauma addressed in this poem triggered: *"... a creative frenzy and started writing pieces and mapping chapters for my novel"*. She explains that her friend who had passed away was a well-known artist, and the trauma triggered a striving in her to live by the legacy of her friend. Thus, in conforming and following the legacy of her friend lay a recipe for her healing from the traumas shared in both her poems. As such, Bale presents two opposite responses to traumas that can either fixate one to a stage of psychological development, or trigger personal growth emerging from the traumatic experience. Comparing her response to traumas in the two poems, one where she is silenced and the other which triggered the sharing of her story, she shares the significance of trauma responses for one's growth. On one hand, the result of having experienced trauma was learnt helplessness, which bears the risk of growing into heightened fear and anxiety to a deep depression and can also result in death. However, if the emotional pain induced by the trauma has its roots in learning, the cure or healing for the trauma can lie in storytelling about the traumatic experience.[141]

A trauma response that embraces vulnerabilities, associated with the trauma experience, is shared by another of our research participants, with the pseudonym Toti in her poem: *"Iron girl"* (5.2.3). The double entendre title of her poem represents the strengthening that emerged from living in a metal shack (hence iron girl) during her childhood, that enabled her to represent herself as a superhero figure – 'Iron girl'. She expresses the feeling of being *"robbed"* of housing, and clearly draws a link between this trauma and her self-esteem. Despite this experience's financial, psychological, and emotionally negative impact on her as a child, she shares how she leveraged this negative experience to enhance her appreciation and acknowledgement of the importance of a house to a family, and for the children in particular. She goes on to share how she used this learning to develop a passion to acquire, build, and furnish beautiful homes as a career; thus, drawing a purpose and financial success out of the ordeal.

Traumas have the potential to trigger people to challenge conformity, or direct one towards it as a response. As such, not only do they bear potential for valuable experiential learning, but they also represent an enabler for progression along the stage development theory of self-leadership. For example, where conformity jeopardizes personal survival or entails significant personal harm, there are limited options but to reject conforming to the status quo. Edy Kaufman[142] shares an example: "I think for the Jews, after the trauma of the Holocaust ... the idea that you don't fight back is not a proper idea". Unfortunately, the world presents many such examples of atrocities inflicted on entire communities that traumatized certain social groups. Our research participant, Camaren Peter in his poem: *"Cardboard City (1993)"* (5.2.4), expresses the Apartheid era to be one during which: *"... it was the colour of our skins that had rendered us incomplete citizens"*. And despite the end of Apartheid, the line in the poem referring to the era as when: *"Humanity failed itself, as it would do so over and over again"* conveys continued conformity to the fundamentals of inequality and a lack of compassion and empathy, like an impulse or an automatic reaction. In doing so, Peter highlights the need to fundamentally deflect from conforming to the norms. In the case of Apartheid, it means not merely to halt segregation and privilege based on race, but to fundamentally embrace egalitarianism.

A life without traumas and psychological wounding is an impossibility. This section ends with a research participant, Chike Nzerue's poem: *"Pandemic Blues"* (5.2.5), that reminds us of how our society, and each one of us has experienced the trauma of the Coronavirus – the COVID-19 pandemic. A response to traumas may be founded on any founding psychological theories such as self-preservation from an evolutionary psychology perspective, behaviourism, or cognition. Assimilation or lower defence mechanisms of coping,[143] such as denial, deprive one of the opportunity hidden within the trauma to leverage and use it for self-leadership development. While denial may be necessary to protect the psyche and survive the traumatic experience,[144] cognition that utilizes our thinking processes can assist to derive personal growth benefits from it.[145] Acquiring knowledge through perceptions regarding the trauma, reflecting upon and assessing the incident, imagining alternatives, remembering and grieving to evolve into problem-solving encountered due to the trauma, et cetera, may be the secret to unlock a trauma's optimal advantage for emotional maturity and self-leadership development.

5.2.1 IN MY SILENCE

There is a burial spot hidden deep within
Hidden very carefully and deeply
No one can find this spot within
Unless they care to search deeply

The part of the pain I was left holding
When the casket was lowered
And the rain married my tears
As the earth opened and swallowed my fears.

The part of my being that nobody sees
Was left to live within me
Even when the other being ceased.

It is the part that was shared at some

Intimate moment in the past,
It is the past that ignites painful
And bitter memories in my parts.

It is the part that I will live with
Until I depart.
It is the past that has chosen to
Live beyond the grave.
It is the part that stays buried
Deep within me, for I am brave.

It is the past that has chosen to
Have a presence,
Beyond the beautiful summer nights of passion
Beyond the drizzly autumn morning
By the graveside.

It is the part that stays in silence
Within me.
It is the part that I will be brave
And carry with me to the grave!

Benita Bale

Bale's Explanation: The piece above was written after an ex-partner was murdered in Cape Town. The poem arose out of the emotions that I experienced at his funeral. Although we were no longer a couple, we were still close. Part of our bond was due to the HIV that he had infected me with. We bonded in our search for treatment at a time when none was available in South Africa. He struggled on this journey and instead of succumbing to the dreaded AIDS, he lost his life to a low-life that stabbed him to rob him of a R100 (Rands) note. I felt betrayed by his choice of death. Although I understood that his journey to healing was hard, at the time I felt as if he had bailed out on me, leaving me to face the consequences of a stigmatised disease.

This poem is an extract from a larger body of work, a novel that I am working on: "…. I watched teary-eyed as part of me surrendered to the earth. I was torn between the cool shivery reality of the wet morning and the promising comfort of the earth. My tears spilled over as my heart shattered and bled as the coffin continued on its journey deeper into the bowels of the earth. I felt both betrayed and freed. My comrade in arms was gone."

I am a fun-loving woman and mother to two sons who adore me. I find beauty in life's little moments. I thrive on good books, movies, and taking beautiful seaside walks.

5.2.2 SOIL – NOT OF HOME

Don't bury me in lands that have no red stony earth.
Don't bury me in lands where no peach trees grow wildly
untended.
Don't bury me in foreign lands that don't
have the scent of my umbilical cord.

Burn me on a pier and watch my smoke greet the heavens.
Gather my ashes and scatter them in all the lands that I have
walked.
Scatter them in the sands that I have caressed.
Scatter them in the Oceans that have
warmed my body....... BUT

Don't bury me in lands that don't understand my yearning for
the taste of red soil.
Don't bury me in any one place that can
never have a claim on me.

Scatter my ashes and share them with all the places that I have
beautified.
Scatter my ashes and share them with all
the places that have beautified me.

Celebrate my life with this dance of the ashes
because my song is written and sung.

Dance to it – ALWAYS.
Dance to it with LOVE.
Dance to it with LONGING.
Dance to it with DESIRE.

Whatever you do dance to my song
ALWAYS!!!

Benita Bale

Bale's Explanation: This piece was written on the day after receiving a call from my mum telling me that my best friend was no longer with us on the physical plane. The call came at around 21h30 on the 8th of April after her passing had been announced on the local TV news. She had died in a foreign country, far from home. We both cried on the phone, which is something that we had never done before. The only time that I have cried over the phone talking to her was when I called her to tell her that my marriage had ended and she just listened to my tears quietly yet encouragingly. I can only ever recall seeing my mother cry in front of me at the height of the Rhodesian war when my father was in jail and I was an uncooperative teenager. It hurt and ached down the line between Pietermaritzburg (South Africa) and Bulawayo (Zimbabwe, formerly Rhodesia) as we both wept; her for a daughter so humble and had no qualms about visiting her in her tiny 3-roomed house in a dusty township, and me for a friend who had been a sister, guide and confidante for over 20 years.

My friend was a world-renowned artist. On the day of her passing, before I got the news, I went into a creative frenzy and started writing pieces and mapping chapters for my novel. When I got home, I took down all her artworks and cuddled them and lay on my day bed and longed deeply for her. She had not responded to my email messages for about two weeks. I felt lost. Then I was woken by my mother's call, bearing the most dreaded news.

The following day I wrote the piece above. I felt her talking to me through my fingers and my pen. I later found out that she had wanted to be cremated and her ashes to be scattered back home, at one of her favourite places.

I am a writer of prose, currently working on my debut novel and a collection of short stories. In times of grief, I turn to poetry.

5.2.3 IRON GIRL

Do not see my
warm smile and be
deceived by it
Down below is
my iron mask that
is petrified of just
being me, scared of
being all that I was
created to be

Does is it shock you
that I shop on Fifth
Avenue and yet I
grew up in an iron shack?
From being chauffeured in
a dark blue Volvo to
an iron shack
The pitter putter of rain
on my iron shack always
lulled me to sleep
You are enough girl in
the iron shack

Does it scare you to be
alone? My iron heart,
are you open to receive
and give love? Yes, he hurt
you and abandoned you.
Is there a strong man
out there for me that I
can rely on?
Be still my iron heart
Be steel my iron heart

My iron mask
My iron shack
My iron heart
My iron life
His banner over you is love
Be still
Be steel

Toti

Toti's Explanation: Iron ore is brittle, but when you infuse it with carbon, it becomes steel and something strong yet very malleable and can have multiple uses. 'Be steel' means be malleable, not easily broken like iron.

My iron mask is the warm smile I wear to hide the hurt and the feelings of inadequacy.

My iron shack represents the time when my family and I went through a tough time, and my mum moved us into a shack. It affected my esteem for a while. Lack of a proper house to call home robs you of something. However, I use this to fuel my passion to acquire and build, furnish beautiful homes.

My iron heart represents past hurts of abandonment by my absentee dad, and all the boys who broke my heart. God's banner over me is Love, which comes from the Songs of Solomon 2:4 that says: God, my heavenly father, loves me, his love fills the holes of abandonment and rejection. Though my earthly father abandoned me, my heavenly father always has my back.

5.2.4 CARDBOARD CITY (1993)

The land grew thirsty on the eve of liberation. That experiment – the ruralisation of African people – was failing. The land refused to bear them any longer. What the Apartheid project inherited from colonialism and had formalised, was giving way to the forces of 20th Century society. The "quiet encroachment of the ordinary", as it is now termed, had begun its work of undoing a reality that had established and maintained itself for decades in the post-war South African Apartheid-era world. The city had become a site of struggle once again, and those who had been removed from sight for over 40 years began to creep back into it.

Yet it still wasn't a daytime struggle. It was hidden in the darkness of night, shrouded by long grass in the open fields of traffic islands, and the recesses afforded by shop doorways and alleys across the city. It was a "quiet encroachment" indeed, but there was nothing 'ordinary' about it. It was a shadow that fell upon the city, a shadow hidden in the moonlight of the night. It cast a new face upon the city, and even though it would be gone in the morning, each night it appeared as though some errant artist had sketched over the previously overlooked parts of the city that hosted the unrecognised potential for settlement – albeit temporary – that had now become exploited to its hilt. These sketches had popped up into three dimensions, and their outlines were that of jagged cardboard edges; the bricks and mortar of this makeshift city.

I witnessed it first-hand.

Each Friday and Saturday night I worked a shift at *Fun Land*. Each night I got on the microphone,

"Everybody's a winner at the Camel Derby!"

119

Ten per cent of the takings is what it took for me to give myself to such dubious employment. "The city where the *fun* never sets" blared the advertisements as I enticed minors into the transient excitement of consumption, one that was disguised as play by the blinking lights and honking hooters of the Camel Derby.

The walk home was a long midnight one, from Point road to Overport, one that took me through the full swathe of the city proper. I saw many huddled-up bodies, eyes closed, yet foreheads crinkling as if to ward off the dull glow of the sodium lights that lined the streets. A cardboard box the only shelter from the night air, thick and humid, rendering this shelter unnecessary, except as a demarcation of territory, however transient, however small. A reminder that each claims a space in the world, and must defend it, whether actively or passively, to remain in it.

I claimed my pay each night and walked home through the shapeshifting city intent to defend it come what may. Yet I never encountered any harm. I never encountered anything to fear. I encountered nothing more than the stillness of night, and I feared the walk through the white neighbourhoods far more than I feared the cardboard city.

The city's established residents began to arm themselves more than they had before. The fear of crime and violence merged with the fear of the shadow that the informal, shifting and discontinuous refugee camp – one that had seeded and cultivated rapidly within the city – had cast upon their everyday expectations; of maintaining an abnormal arrangement undisturbed. And refugees they were, from centuries of ignominy, deception and greed. People who had lost everything; whose new beginnings had been skewed to meet the ends of their oppressors. Yet they were met with suspicion, beatings and bullets, as was historical tradition.

Humanity failed itself, as it would do so over and over again in the city of my birth, and elsewhere. That impulse, that automatic reaction; too often rising up before compassion, before empathy, before insight. That notion of possession would negate society's evolution, its potential to go beyond the normal scuppered by the average of us. And so, the average of us is what we reaped in the transition of the city.

Camaren Peter

Peter's Explanation: This piece accounts for the changes that unfolded in the City of Durban during the transition to democracy. Ravaged by drought and political violence in KwaZulu-Natal, many fled their rural villages and towns to find sanctuary and employment in the city. They slept in cardboard boxes, fitting themselves into wherever they could find an unused space, and woke early to avoid persecution by the authorities. At the time I was in my first year of university; I took a weekend job at a games arcade at the beachfront shopping mall called "The Wheel", and would have to walk home through the city at night in order to get home. So, I became a first-hand observer of this human crisis, and felt very much a part of it myself. I had been out on the city streets at night since the age of 13, and was no stranger to it. Yet I was a denizen of the city as much as they were, and I recognised their transient belonging as mine too; after all, it was the colour of our skins that had rendered us incomplete citizens of the Apartheid city. Yet there was nothing to be afraid of, except the paranoia and neurosis of a white-dominated city that felt itself under siege, and this made the city far more dangerous than its new refugees did.

5.2.5 PANDEMIC BLUES

The malice of a virus
And the wreck of its storm
Wreathes us in a dark cloud:
Pandemic blues, earthy-
Not flat or round
But Copernican- you have
To feel it to fathom its wound,
Its phantom limb fervour,
Weaving a dark chill in our souls.
It has growth rings like trees
But ages poorly in its bowers
Shrinking in time-
Slow hours petal its flowers.
Enigmatic, heavy as lead
None can yet measure
Its work; hoist its burdens
Or be left in tatters
The muted silence of bees
Flutters hearts in frightful solitude-
Eyes bleary with sears of virtual tears
From last moments shared
Behind glass doors

Knead our bread of sorrow:
We must thread the needle of hope
Until we slay this Lernaean hydra.

Chike Nzerue

5.3 MAGICAL OTHER

Similar to the intensity of traumas during the earlier stages, the intensity of love relations during the early stages of psychological development is also heightened. Falling in love, at a young age, is a highly intense experience. It leads to physical experiences, such as the racing of the heart, to emotions flowing freely from the unprecedented expectations from a relatively unknown person, to building large castles in the sky of 'the perfect life' together. Our research participant, Maluba Wani, in his poem: *"The way I want you"* (5.3.1), through the use of hyperbolas, takes the reader back to the sentiments most have felt during the differentiating stage of one's life. Due to the intense experiences of young love, and its subsequent development and maturation, it has the potential to be a magical journey. The journey starts with a stranger who is seen as the 'Magical Other'.[146] He/She/They is depicted by the psyche as someone with the potential to save one, accompany one, and yield unprecedented happiness throughout life. However, upon maturation, one learns that one can only be made whole and rescued from hardships by oneself, and the realisation that such expectations from a Magical Other are unfairly exaggerated. Not to undermine the support, love, and want of someone special in life to share the journey with, but the projections of perfection onto others get increasingly subdued with experiences of love and psychological growth.

A trauma shared by many of our research participants involved failing by 'the Other' in love relationships. Our research participant, Lele Mehlomakulu in her poem: *"The day the music died"* (5.3.2), shares such a story. She elucidates the journey from her romantic dance with her partner, to dancing for both of them, the subsequent awakening when projections fail and reality emerges, which she metaphorically expounds upon in her lines: *"I remember the day the music died. Not because you stopped playing it. But because I stopped hearing it"*, and lastly to dance her own dance to her own tune, symbolic of individuation. Similarly, TarliQue in his poem: *"Accolades"* (5.3.3), challenges the notion of love in its infatuation state of development, and questions what allows a relationship to thrive. He states: *"Love is neither good nor bad ... Love can be either good or bad ... So, what then sustains us? Respect ... A deep mutual respect is what it takes"*. Thus, he shares a vital element of the journey of growing love between people as a move from infatuation to the development of mutual respect for one another.

Our last research participant in this section, Oelzah Puckree in her poem: *"Rise of the Phoenix"* (5.3.4), writes as a form of emotional expression. Puckree is inspired by storytelling and taps into her own, and the life experiences of others to write truths that enlighten, connect as well as highlight the human potential for change. She expresses how she has been conforming to the gender roles associated with being a woman, by being a loving wife and a devoted mother, which she regarded as being: *"Stuck in this house, trying to get out"*. Despite the efforts exerted towards sustaining a self-debilitating relationship, its end and the trauma associated with it is compared to a Phoenix rising – a mythical bird that is born again rising from the ashes. Thus, she acknowledges the potential for traumas associated with a failing of reliance on the Magical Other to complete oneself can lead to re-birth. This re-birth is compared by Puckree to rocks that the harshness of a raging river can turn into the smoothest of pebbles. The stage of self-actualization is typically associated with the ages of 40 to 49. While all traumas have the capacity to trigger growth, with the average age of divorce being 41 for women and 45 for men in South Africa, the traumas associated with love relationships are probabilistically significant to the self-actualization stage.

5.3.1 THE WAY I WANT YOU

I want you in ways that make the word desire an understatement of
sorts, a misrepresentation of fact, a force to be reckoned with

Like your smile, your kiss, your touch are not just memories but
things in themselves that they linger like toffee or peanut butter that's
stuck in between your teeth

Ooh, the way I want you I could try to describe, but my vocabulary
isn't versed enough so as to do your bare countenance justice and not
kill your vibe even in part as to its celestial construction

Voluptuous, vivacious vixen that you are, the way I want you...
Verdict: cataclysmic... could be cosmic like the death of a star-struck
sun, definition: fatal fusion

Endogenously intertwining, swirling like the clouds on nebula, being
sucked into your neutron star gravity, taking me through the Milky
Way, fingers locked in each groove like a mortise and Tenon

You are not wanted... The way I want you, is base need, it transcends
the elements, it's as if desire was feeding on desire itself, much like the
very fabric of existence needs its building blocks like matter or DNA:
I need you like blood needs iron
Open mouthed, open minded you meet my every stroke... The way
I want you is as a disease with no cure, there's no hope... It's not
alluring, it IS allure...and...

Ultimately, wanting you makes no excuses for your push with every pull, it's forceful in its moments such that the pivot is lost to bliss… Is lost to bliss… of that I'm sure

Wanting you, meeting you, blow for blow, breaking you, burning you, just so I could rebuild your walls with my tongue, refusing to have the poor ventilation in this jail cell be the only thing that makes us sweat

Am not ever letting go, pulling me in like dessert perfume, you are the one I burn for, defiant, I won't let the walls of the Kariba be the only place that's (wet)

Not unlike the way the desert needs the sun, the way I want you is more than just how sugar needs to be sweet, its very essence, the basis of which lays art to its definition, I am drawn to you like magnets, till our poles collide

Jiving and gyrating, adding me to you in sensual summation, subtracting articles of dress appreciating our difference, multiplying all principle and inhibition by any product of zero, rushing to the quotient of how your long legs divide

Intimately into you, so thick, so tight… the things we do should be illegal in a few states… you deserve a ticket on that dash for how your form so fine

… The way I want you, couldn't express it all, so I left the clues by the side about how you make me feel, and how I pray I am forever yours and you are forever mine

Maluba Wanji

Wanji's Explanation: This piece is about falling in love so deeply. The imagery phases from discipline to discipline, art to science, subject to subject. It has chemistry, biology, physics, cosmology, mathematics, etc … the most fascinating part I guess would be that the first letters of every stanza spell out a hidden message for the intended audience.

5.3.2 THE DAY THE MUSIC DIED

All our life, we danced
You played the music and I danced
The music carried on, and I continued to dance
To keep you pacified and happy
To make you love and affirm me
I played small, so you could feel big and strong
I hid my magic, so yours would shine
Because you were my love, my friend, my job, my relative, my
community

I woke up to the music everyday
I danced in tune, even when I did not understand the rhythm
Every day I was reminded
That if I danced out of tune, then I was not good enough
The dance became my oxygen, my shield from shame
It became my protector when I felt vulnerable around you
Because when I danced, you told me I was worthy
Because you were my love, my friend, my job, my relative, my
community

I was worthy for a moment, a good girl for a while
But the dance was never good enough
The music was random
And however magnificently I danced
In your eyes, I could never keep up
I was never worthy,
Never good enough, and never made you feel how you wanted me to
make you feel
Because you were my love, my friend, my job, my relative, my
community

I thought that if I could dance for both of us
I would be worthy, deserving of your love
You rewarded my attempts, and criticised and shamed me for my
failures
But you see... it's a dance
It takes two to tango
How could I get that so wrong?
But I only wanted to feel worthy

Worthy enough to deserve you, my love, my friend, my job, my
relative, my community

You see, together we found a rhythm
Your rhythm
It was good when it lasted
It was not good because I was always last
I let your music define when and how I would dance
When I wanted to tango, you played the salsa
I settled and compromised my own music
Because you were my love, my friend, my job, my relative, my
community

I remember the day the music died
Not because you stopped playing it
But because I stopped hearing it
The dancer in me, struggled to dance without the music
We both were confused
When I stopped dancing to your tune
For a while, I did not know how to continue to dance without your
music
Because you were my love, my friend, my job, my relative, my
community

Then I started hearing a different kind of music
Music which resonated with my own dance
Music so peaceful, so kind, so familiar
Music that only demanded of me to be and do my best
Music which supported me as much when I fell as it did when I was
in rhythm
Music which reminded me, of me
Yet you continued playing your music, demanding of me to dance
Because you were my love, my friend, my job, my relative, my
community

I continue to dance
But this time I play my own music
And sometimes there is no music
And sometimes the music is not as good as your music
But it does not matter because I am a dancer and I dance to the music
in my ear

126

Music that was composed when I was born
And this way I am my best; and you deserve to see that
Because you were my love, my friend, my job, my relative, my
community

Today I have learnt that there are many sounds of music
Each good enough, each deserving
We both do the dance now
Both on our own equal terms
We sometimes complement each other
But I no longer must dance to every beat
I do not have to dance when I do not feel like it
Even though you are my love, my friend, my job, my relative, my
community

Lele Mehlomakulu

5.3.3 ACCOLADES

My queen, you are beautiful, no doubt, as if doubt too broke to pay
attention was asking after your purse
With hair worn down and dishevelled, you are pretty yes... a
pretty hot mess

You are attractive inside out, with your silly mind games, traps,
tricks and conspicuous tests
Rollercoaster riding me, pulling me in, screaming and driving me
out with sticks and stones like you would pests

I know he affects you in ways you cannot even begin to imagine
that when you sit and fantasize, you realize... saving yourself
entails a mental patricide
You are identical to him in every way, you say... well, the elephant
in the room has begun to grow in magnitude and size... to
materialize that which is inside... that which you cannot hide

I know you know I know you know I am not effectively got
together, sane or glamorous either
But then you attack me from within, so sudden, so still,
inconspicuous, you hit me like a fever... and without
anaesthesia...

127

… You dig deep into my chest cavity… with dull knives you cut at,
and harvest my heart with cheap surgery
Thus, you have me infected with the self-same careless gestures
you inherited from him as you leave me in my infirm array… in
my infirmary

Always letting your mind have its way with you… impregnating
your thoughts with twisted sentiments and crazy ideas of me with
God knows whom
When all I want is nothing more than to cherish you and do what's
right by you… what's right by 'our' the fruit of your womb

But there you go again, blowing things out of proportion, perhaps
the only quality you have kept with you from our past lives and
worlds
The reason why we keep coming back to this wretched place life
after life without knowing what fulfilment and real peace heralds

But I thank you for always being the girl of my dreams, night after
night, day after day, every time, complete with the heart-piercing
knives
I am starting to think, maybe not dreams but memories of, or
revenants of, some of our 'not so distant' but past lives

But we have survived… now I see that… from all your tests, trials,
booby traps and tribulations
And from our many deaths I have gained clarity, insight, patience,
pain and mostly lacerations

I have marks on my body that permeate my mind to prove I
passed the path you led by knives and blades
I wear these scars proudly… because you got me… I know what
these are… accolades

TarliQue

TarliQue's Explanation: A tribute to the brutal marks left on the skin (and soul) from… nails marks and mind games form rifts as fight between insecurity and daddy issues causes turmoil while love lives on… and speaking of love, love is not enough to sustain about anything… Love is neither good nor bad… Love can be either good or bad… So, what then sustains us? Respect… A deep mutual respect is what it takes… Am sorry I lost some…

5.3.4 RISE OF THE PHOENIX

In my chest a fire is burning
In the pit of my stomach the flames are churning
You left and then you were returning

Stuck in this house, trying to get out
Release me from your grip I tried to shout
Why did you suppress me? What was that all about?

You tried to smother me with your smoke
Your hands around my throat
You tried, but I never broke

Engulfed in your furnace of self-hate
I decided my own fate
You said you would change, but I fear it's too late

You have torched me with your eyes
And suffocated me with your lies
When I left, did it come as a surprise?

On a pyre of hurt, I set myself alight
Reborn, with no need to fight
You wanted to ground me but instead I took flight

All that is left are embers of the inferno that ravished me for so long
Emerged from the ashes, renewed and strong
Purging myself from your scorching love
My wings spread open, soaring and dreaming of...

Oelzah Puckree

Puckree's Explanation: I wrote this piece as I reflected on the hurt and pain experienced by myself and the women in my life. I was inspired by how we have transcended these experiences and have risen to personal greatness with a peace that comes with a raging river constantly flowing over a bruised rock, turning it into the smoothest pebble. I want to note that the hurt described was not only inflicted by hateful men, but also from women who were meant to be role models and grown children who have forgotten that their mothers brought them into this world.

5.4 THE SELF-ACTUALIZED LEADER

From an interactional perspective, Kintsugi is not only symbolic of self-care, but also of care-giving and care-receiving.[147] Kintsugi can metaphorically represent team or community bonding despite personal or social differences. Similar to the cracks in the pottery which are acknowledged, appreciated, and celebrated, the sensitivities between people and communities require bonds that are strong enough to ensure that these cracks do not lead to weaknesses, but present an opportunity for the beautification of the team in its differences, or society in its diversity. From a leadership point of view, a Kintsugi master can join broken edges within a person or communities, and fill crevices and holes in a way that they are not denied to exist, but rather appreciated for the history and interpersonal and inter-communal differences that form a team or a society. The leadership's role is to reconstruct the missing pieces, ensure a solid foundation for it to stand on, and allow the team or society to work cohesively despite the existence of fractions.

Individuated people have the unique ability not to deindividuate people,[148] i.e., not to view others as clusters and pigeonhole them, but to see them as individuals. This individuated perspective of others gives them the capacity to lend a helping hand to unindividuated people by taking them through the journey of individuation. Our last research participant in this section, Christina Swart-Opperman in her poem: *"Or so they say"* (5.4.1), humorously questions the reader in her line: *"… are you Humpty Dumpty on the wall, pre-programmed to fall?"* There is an expectation of deindividuation from such leaders which must be shared; additionally, not only is individuation an attribute for awakened leadership,[149] but the facilitation of others' individuation is a fundamental role of individuated leaders. In addition to self-individuation, assisting others with such an awakening requires an understanding that people have varied experiences in their infancy, childhood, as well as experiences during adulthood that scar people in unique ways. In acknowledgement of this, they bear a host of varied scars that they need to become consciously aware of for their healing and progression to greater psychological growth and self-leadership development.

5.4.1 OR SO THEY SAY

Once upon a time a story started
not in a faraway land
without brand or band.
or so they say
Do not be concerned yet
I can bet
that you do not know yet
That you can drive a timeline
as
splendiferous, glorious, eventuous, gorgeous

or
are you Humpty Dumpty on the wall
pre-programmed for a fall?
So, choose your timeline as forever
and never say never
the soul is forever
the physical never
Transcend into boundless space
Trimmed with beautiful lace
As death
has not breath
or so they say

Christina Swart-Opperman

Swart-Opperman's Explanation: Leaders are challenged at an interpersonal level by people who are scarred by their pasts. However, leaders are in the privileged position to play a role in facilitating growth, especially when presenting hope for the future (for organizations and thus the individual).

In this poem, the intention is to reflect on personal timelines, as life stories start somewhere. People start off differently in life, with unfolding life stories often heavily influenced by circumstances. As imprints are left on our souls, growth and beauty are often stinted. Stereotyping of us as individuals, groups, and communities is internalised and reinforced by external sources making it difficult to break free from the past.

The message of hope is undeniable: we are not destined to be bound by circumstances or events. Although difficult, transformation can be beautiful and special. The reader is urged to claim happiness and make sensible choices as time is finite. Leaders have a major role to play in this regard.

6 INTEGRATING

While several theorists, such as Maslow,[150] regarded self-actualization as the highest level of motivation, even Maslow, later in his life, acknowledged that aspirations of personal growth and accomplishments can embody selfishness. Thus, the danger of seeking self-actualization without moral considerations is viewed as a threat associated with self-actualization which can make people not merely selfish, but "evil".[151] As such, further segregation of the self-actualization stage led to 'the integrated stage' and the 'serving stage', suggesting these to be higher levels of ego development by evolving above the drives of the ego.

In addition to non-conforming (2), addressing one's personality imbalances (2.2), thoroughly knowing oneself (4.3.2), conquering complexes (4.4), unpacking the shadow psyche (4.6.2), acknowledging one's weaknesses and embracing them (4.5) so as to leverage on these to translate them into one's 'gifts' (5.1), a prime desire that emerges at the self-actualization stage is for a vocation or a job that not only permits one the freedom to fully express themselves (4.6), but to apply it in the context of work. Self-actualizing, by not merely accepting one's weaknesses but also leveraging them for self-development, leads one to a build-up of a desire for opportunities that align one's work with one's true, authentic self. In the absence of being able to do so, it can lead to one becoming increasingly disengaged at work.[152] However, its alignment with one's day-to-day life gives meaning to one's life and a purpose to which one can dedicate their skills, resources, and energy. While developing a mission in life is theoretically argued as a part of the self-actualizing process,[153] an expression of one's true self is deemed the next step of self-leadership development of integrating the purpose into one's daily life, as well as integrating with others whose values and purpose resonate with one's own to collectively work towards a shared purpose.[154]

6.1 VALUES

Values are defined as: "basic convictions of what is and is not of importance in life".[155] Spranger[156] founded fundamentals of individual values using a conceptual model that accounted for six major values which are present in all individuals in varying levels of importance. It is suggested that people construct the unity of their lives around these six values, that were regarded by Spranger[157] as 'deep-value traits'. These include (1) theoretical value (a quest for truth and valuing of truthfulness that facilitates a cognitive attitude of observing and reasoning), (2) the economic value (an emphasis on the importance of what is 'useful' and what is not, that translates into a high level of practicality), (3) the aesthetic value (with a deep interest in form and harmony, leading to an emphasis on grace, symmetry, and fitness), (4) the social value (an inherent love of people leading to altruism and philanthropic actions), (5) the political value (a regard for power as being most important, leading to a power-grabbing and controlling demeanour), and (6) the religious value (seeking higher meaning than everyday life exhibited as spirituality). The theory does not present a comprehensive list of values, but proposes the six as the deep-value traits. In doing so, the theory is challenged for noting certain values, such as the hedonistic, expedient, and sensuous values of some individuals, as core values.

Spranger[158] believed that one's true values are revealed in interests and intentions rather than in concrete achievements and successes. This is partially attributed to the fact that during the earlier stages of self-leadership development, goals and corresponding achievements are effectively 'hijacked' by the drive to conform to family values, or to differentiate from family to abide by social values. Therefore, any fixation or entrapment in the earlier stages of self-leadership development misaligns one's values from one's accomplishments. Our research participant, Afzal Dalwai in his poem: *"Purposefully"* (2.1.1), emphasizes the centrality of values to one's life. This supports Spranger's[159] theory that did not allow for a distinct or complete lack of values.[160]

> "I remain on the journey to rediscover my values
> To ensure that it represents who I am, what I believe, and how I act
> Never does a moment pass where my values are unknown,
> But never do I believe that my values are complete,
> The sensation of discovery burns bright,
> It is what makes me, me."

Also, our research participant suggests that values need to be 'rediscovered' which supports Spranger's[161] perspective of values being more evident in interests rather than in accomplishments. One's values are clearer during authentic childhood years, but are subsequently 'hidden' due to pressures and expectations experienced during the conforming and differentiating stages of psychological development.

In addition to stumbling blocks along the self-leadership development stages, the need to evaluate and incorporate one's values presents several challenges.

- Firstly, being in touch with one's values and beliefs is foundational for the prospect of living by one's values. This struggle of getting to know one's values is addressed by our research participant, Alun Josias in his poem: *"Ode to be free"* (2.1.3), in which he shares an enabler for getting acquainted with one's own values in the lines: *"Purpose, courage, self-love, values … Stop, be still, and breathe"*; thus, aligning purpose (6.3) and values to share similar enablers for uncovering them, such through meditation, mindfulness, or other contemplative tools that facilitate a state of stillness and being present in the moment.

- Secondly, the exploration of these major six deep-value traits can lead to an understanding of the concept of the 'value challenge', which is regarded as the art of balancing the different values to allow for maximum sense-making of the individual's life. Our research participants did not exhibit struggles with the balancing of deep-value traits, but more so with other challenges of identifying one's values as well as the difficulties faced in incorporating them in their daily lives.

- Thirdly, it is a challenge to ensure that the values, which one regards as uniquely founded on one's self-exploration, are not merely adopted due to socialization. Knowing whether one's values are an authentic representation of one's 'real beliefs' is expressed by our research participant, Nidheesh Sharma, in his poem: *"From dented cages to inspiring leaders"* (1.2.2). He states in the explanation of his poem: *"... it is easy to follow the crowd and perhaps make wrong decisions that are against your values"*, highlighting the relative ease of followership compared to self-leadership development in respect of values. However, as shared by Alan Florence in his poem: *"Scarcity mindset"* (6.1.1), it takes courage to foundationally challenge one's socialization, as done so in the line: *"The culture is not serving the purpose of the time"*. Thus, authenticity can unveil one's true values, and testing one's values against societal values can help one to evaluate their degree of gaminess, in contrast with the degree of adoption of family or societal values.

- Fourthly, the differences between one's authentic values and the culture one belongs to can present one with an existential threat. As such, it needs to be addressed by a degree of harmonization with the culture or society one has a sense of belonging to. Our research participant, Razelle Naidoo in her poem: *"Purposefully"* (2.1.1), states: *"I like my values. I like my faith. I like not what they like ... They don't like my morals. They don't like my values. They are liked"*; thus, sharing this challenge faced when attempting to incorporate one's values in one's life while living within societal norms and cultural values that the society prescribes to. The challenge is heightened where the two clash, and demand compromise of either belonging to the society or to one's own values.

- Lastly, after values are known, balanced within the six core-value systems, ensured for having developed personally and not derived from external forces, yet harmonized to fit the society need to be practised, one must incorporate one's values into how one lives one's life (values actioning). Our research participant, Kira Koopman in her poem: *"On finding purpose"* (6.3.3), expresses the challenge of being happy at work in the explanation of her poem: *"... working in a job that is unfulfilling for people whose values are misaligned to your own"*. Thus, she emphasizes the need for value alignment with one's work-life for fulfilment and happiness at work. Theoretically, it is deemed fundamental for work dedication[162] that operates within the larger construct of work engagement.[163]

Our research participant, Alan Florence, in his poem: *"Scarcity mindset"* (6.1.1), gives an example of the above challenges experienced at work while integrating two departments. In respect of discovering one's values, he suggests asking: *"... if I had a blank slate how could I do this differently?"* to help to avoid the traps set by status-quos. The challenge of deviating from the crowd, yet the dependence on the team members is shared in the lines: *"If I am not going to be bold and honest about conversations and values, I cannot be scared of losing membership of the group due to disagreement and resistance to change"*, highlighting the need for courage to live one's values despite threats of facing exclusion. However, the need for compromise entails being flexible and thoughtful of the values of others while living by one's own values. This is expressed in the lines: *"I want to be me and allow the space for you to be you, so that we can meet somewhere in the middle"*.

6.1.1 SCARCITY MINDSET

Scarcity mindset – what is my part?
As I see I could be part of the problem I can get power back.
Not thinking correctly, I could be also intrenching this pattern. I am enough!

How can I fix relationships and be part of the solution?
I want to make it better or leave and open opportunity for someone else to meet me half=way.
What is the reality of what I need to change?
I need to stop being soft about change management.
Say it as it is – let's not mollycoddle and carry on playing the game.

Requisite applicability. Let them talk, not me, Can I get both?
Innovative and creative meetings; building the capacity to build in change – if I had a blank slate how could I do this differently?
Culture is not emulating what I am espousing, projection – I put roles on others
I am flexible in roles, identity elasticity, when do I stop turning the other cheek; it takes the limits off me.
Denial if you think there is one organizational culture.
It is co-created ... a new path means fear, courage, risk ... how do I? I am enough

The culture is not serving the purpose of the time.
If I am not going to be bold and honest about conversations and values, I cannot be scared of losing membership of the group due to disagreement and resistance to change.
I am vulnerable when turning the other cheek in the hope that we could meet in the middle to create something anew.

I see things I want to see; how do I look at things I fear seeing ... look for this and I can see alternatives.
The one thing is not the only thing ... reframing – what do I do with narratives turning it, reframing as a container that will not be too anxiety provoking or demeaning
I want to be me and allow the space for you to be you, so that we can meet somewhere in the middle

Alan Florence

Florence's Explanation: This is in the context of the integration between two departments in a university.

I have been tasked with project managing this integration and several other projects. What kept me in the doldrums was that I have been acting unofficially in this role and when the job was advertised, I was not shortlisted and given an opportunity to serve in this position even though I am doing so already.

After being asked to attend these meetings, as usual, I went into fast-forward mode: my words were tumbling out of my mouth and I felt that I had no control. I found myself saying things that I did not want to, and I thought I was going to choke ... I took a deep breath, I began consciously to speak slower, to pause every now and then, to slow down my thoughts, to look at the people in the room – I even looked into some of their eyes! I felt in control, I became aware of the room, of the individuals, there was an energy in the room that I had not noticed before, people were smiling. These were friendly faces, not threatening ones. My words were clearer, I hardly stumbled, I was saying what I wanted to say. A sense of freedom I felt at that moment that I am enough. I am not defined by my surroundings but by my actions, and how I respond.

I learnt not to sit in judgement of other people's actions – the right way is usually from one's perspective. Armed with this realisation I am no longer able to be critical of other people's actions and this makes me vulnerable. Working with change management in an organization, I find myself thinking holistically and tend to possess a cyclical view that assumes constant fluctuations and being dexterous in those situations.

6.2 HEROES

The prevalence of people that can identify hero figures that they look up to, as well as the variety of hero figures in society is indicative of its psychological significance to humans. Additionally, the evolution of the hero image from a chiselled male body that depicted physical strength, with a sword in hand to portray protection from physical harm to a more gender-neutral image that is representative of resistance towards external pressures, and admiration of an uncompromising stance on moral values despite risks of repercussions for the hero suggests the continued relevance of heroes to the world today. Yet, unlike admired leaders, relatively little is researched about heroes and heroism.[164]

Despite the vastness of the concept of leaders, the concept of heroism differentiates from that of leadership. The Greek word 'heroes', meaning 'protector', laid the foundations for the word in English. As such, heroic actions are still frequently associated with personal risk-taking to rescue others. For example, mythical heroes are often regarded as heroes due to their story about how they risked their lives to bravely slay beasts to save their loved ones and/or community. Thus, heroism is regarded as: "the embodiment of actions that hold us to the highest standard of caring for another, even against great personal costs".[165] While some leadership styles may be synonymous with care towards others, a heroic standard of caring and rescuing others is beyond the norms of leadership.[166]

The concept of heroism conceptually differentiates from other more frequently researched concepts of mentors and role models as well. While children may often mimic their heroes, and aspire to accomplish what adults may regard as unattainable and unrealistic goals in their future self; as adults, people admire their heroes and are inspired by them, yet they do not necessarily present an attainable image of oneself. This forms a fundamental difference between heroes and role models, where role models personify aspirations of what people hope to achieve, or represent their self-sketched image in their future,[167] and mentors assist people in achieving that goal/image.

The relevance of heroes for revealing one's values makes them enablers in providing a purpose to people, without the need to 're-invent the wheel'. Furthermore, heroes are empirically proven to facilitate in providing meaning to people's lives and alleviating boredom.[168]

Our research participant, who decided to stay anonymous, in the poem: *"The untold story"* (6.2.1), shares the story of her aunt, who is presented as the participant's hero. Anonymous describes a visit to the aunt who had been undergoing chemotherapy, and despite the physical hardships of cancer and chemotherapy treatments, the research participant explains: *"What stood out for me was that she was happy, her vibrant personality was still shining through"*. The participant explains the details of the visit that left both the siblings in tears, yet full of positivity. In the poem, the participant uses the line: *"Lurking behind are lessons to be unlocked with the key of vulnerability"*; thus, emphasizing that such memorable, heroic people bear the potential for one to learn from. Our research participant regrets not sharing her story, as heroes deserve a tale to be told about them, so as not to end up as unsung heroes. The sharing of their stories promotes the values they represented, and in the case of our research participant's aunt, these were values of positivity, resilience, and an acceptance of mortality to an extent so as not to fear death or pain and suffering associated with the hardships of cancer and its treatment. As such, our participant shares the potential for heroes as an enabler for learning values from their behaviours and experiences.

Another research participant, Oliver Vergo, in his poem: *"Virgil's compass"* (6.2.2), reflects upon his time spent at a 'community of practice', where groups of men engaged in shared activities of learning, constructed shared meanings, negotiated social relationships, and the processes of shared wounds were undertaken.[169] His participation in the 'New Warrior Training Adventure' revealed to him that the : *"'Hero's Journey' is in many respects about finding one's purpose"*; thus, reiterating the academic literature regarding heroes and their ability to help lead an individual to their own meaning and purpose in life.[170] The development from the previous participant to Vergo's poem is the move from admiration of heroes to the development of heroic qualities within oneself.[171]

Our last research participant in this section, Camaren Peter, in his poem: *"For when all was said and done ..."* (6.2.3), questions the liberation from Apartheid and the emergence of heroes from the struggle. He challenges the heroic stances of emerging heroes in the following lines of his poem: *"They confused their oppression, their brokenness, with struggle. They became heroes to themselves. They convinced themselves of their own suffering and sacrifice, and quickly made currency of it in the new"*. In doing so, he leverages on an important theory regarding status and heroes. Tesser's self-evaluation maintenance (SEM) model,[172] which assumes that people want to main a positive evaluation of themselves in comparison to others, theorized how a status threat can result in distortion of one's perception of one's performance to psychologically elevate oneself as a hero. While an important element is the thorough sifting out of such individuals by critically assessing heroic figures and their actions, such an assessment of heroic figures is deemed insufficient by this theory. The good (e.g., positive attributes, heroic qualities) and the bad (e.g., unethical or cheating tactics, abuse of power) of potential heroes need to be identified by their admirers, and a rational and critical assessment needs to be undertaken in relation to one's psychological reaction(s) to the self-preserved claims by heroes.

An ability to challenge hero figures, whom society places on pedestals, requires an advanced level of psychological growth and having travelled the journey of self-leadership development oneself. It raises the question of whether many heroic figures are eventually destined to fade as one develops heroic qualities within oneself. Additionally, those heroes that continue to be viewed as such may, with psychological growth, be viewed as 'remarkable people' rather than perfect, magical creatures which heroes are often perceived as. Awareness of the limitations of one's psychological projections onto the hero permits the potential embodiment of ideological values and purposes within oneself to transform oneself into a hero.

6.2.1 THE UNTOLD STORY

Running long and deep, in so fine intricate details are the fault lines
Arriving unexpectedly, and demanding a dance
Moving to the rhythm of destruction, pain and turmoil
Trailing this movement is a scar
Which in itself presents imperfection
Lurking behind are lessons
To be unlocked with the key of vulnerability
Behind the closed door is the untold story
Awaiting the voice of courage

Anonymous

Anonymous' Explanation: I thought of fault lines as representing difficult situations. To give a bit of a personal view on why I emphasised these aspects, I will share a personal story.

About eight years ago, my sister and I went to visit our favourite aunt at Christmas, to drop off some goodies. At that time, she had been through a few sessions of chemotherapy treatment. She sat on the couch, wearing a beautiful headscarf, and at this point, she had already lost all her hair. She had her make-up on with her favourite lip gloss and was all dressed up. She had lost a lot of weight because the chemotherapy made it difficult for her to eat anything. What stood out for me was that she was happy, her vibrant personality was still shining through. I looked over to my sister and I knew like me, she was holding back her emotions. We were both feeding off my aunt's positive energy and were able to laugh and chat away. We said our goodbyes and had a pleasant visit. On our way back home, I looked over to my sister and she was in tears. I had to quickly wipe away mine as I was the one driving. A few months later my aunt succumbed to cancer.

Following her passing, we have not told her life story. We do not speak about her vibrant personality, the strong positive person that she was. In the poem, I use the word 'dance' because unforeseen or uncertain difficult situations call for us to improvise and my aunt was the king of improvising. She was the one the family looked for when we faced a difficult situation. She always had a plan B up her sleeve. She was the one that was there for us when my mum was battling depression. The pain that her passing brought was unbearable. She left behind two beautiful children and when they were younger, they would ask about her. They do not ask anymore probably because they picked up that the family found it difficult to talk about their mum.

I used the word 'scar' to symbolise that there is a reminder of the pain and destruction endured. A reminder that we went through this experience. We live in a world that is not perfect; it has fault lines and we learn from these fault lines. And how each person is touched by the difficult experience is different, there is a different story for each person. I used the word 'courage' as opposed to 'brave', to acknowledge that there are challenges in telling a difficult story and making yourself vulnerable.

6.2.2 VIRGIL'S COMPASS

Life passing, without much thought,
Energies flowing, but none of them caught,
Shadows dancing on the wall,
are you prepared to heed the call?

That voice you hear, it is mine,
Telling you, you're out of time,
This shadow world has served its need,
and now your life is yours to lead.

I know a way out of this cave,
a journey too few dare to brave,
through darkness, swamps and pits abound,
where devils lurk, and gold is found.

The road is long with twists and turns,
tricks and traps and cuts and burns,
but here I offer you a guide,
for you to reach the other side.

Your journey starts by going down,
a long descent below the ground
And as the light begins to fade,
shadows tall and dark are made.

These are yours to hold up high,
in front of you, and you'll see why,
as darkness enters all around,
the child in you might make a sound.

And once you finally reach the pit,
where demons lie and monsters sit,
a voice will ask 'what brings you here?'
and that is how you'll meet your fear.

Fear is how you find the path,
To your magician in the South,
His alchemy can bring about,
The change you seek and move all doubt.

The element of the South is air,
which flows in us and takes us where,
we need to go for our transition,
through introspection and intuition.

Turning now to face the East,
we take the path we like the least,
towards the lover through our grief,

Our sadness is what will bring relief.

As we approach the rising sun,
and tears begin to flow and run,
We see that water is the key,
To new beginnings and being free.

I ask you now to face the North,
And walk the path of anger forth,
And in the heat of midday sun,
Find the warrior to get this done.

The passion in the warrior's heart,
Is fuelled by fire which in part,
gives us strength and courage to,
take action in this world anew.

Finally turning to the West,
as the sun begins to set,
walk the path of joy until,
you meet your King whose feet are still.

Grounded on and to the Earth,
Standing firm in truth from birth,
His judgement and wisdom show the way,
out of dark into light of day.

Join me in this sacred space,
with those who risk to take their place,
and dare to speak their truth to all,
those that listened and heard the call.

Only you can walk this road,
take these steps and bear this load,
This guide is yours, and yours alone,
to find what you've always had, but never known.

Oliver Vergo

Vergo's Explanation: I was inspired to write the first draft of this poem when I returned home from an emotionally intense weekend where I was facilitating men's self-development work. The structure of the weekend takes the participants through a 48-hour 'hero's journey'. This involves:

The descent – dropping into their pain, which often stems from childhood trauma/ wounding.

The pit – dealing with the emotions that arise, and facilitating those through psycho-drama.

The return – finding the gift or 'gold' in the wound and turning that into a personal mission.

This work is based on Jungian principles which include the 4 archetypes mentioned, each of which has a direction, an element, and an emotional pathway to access them:

ARCHTYPE		DIRECTION		ELEMENT		EMOTIONAL PATHWAY
Magician	-	*South*	-	*Air*	-	*Fear*
Lover	-	*East*	-	*Water*	-	*Sadness*
Warrior	-	*North*	-	*Fire*	-	*Anger*
King	-	*West*	-	*Earth*	-	*Joy*

While reflecting on the weekend, I realised that this 'Hero's Journey' is in many respects about finding one's purpose. The theory is that every human being has been wounded in some way (through parenting, school, lack of support, too much support, loss, et cetera.) but in the wound lies that person's gift. Whether or not this is the case, it does seem clear that human beings carry wounds and shadows which can drive their behaviour. Being aware of these and working with them can help one live a more authentic life, which is necessary in order to find one's purpose. Therefore, taking this metaphorical journey to deal with one's shadows and access one's emotions can help someone look at themselves more objectively and help promote transformation in order to step into their power, find their purpose, and be their true selves.

6.2.3 FOR WHEN ALL WAS SAID AND DONE …

And yet what was this liberation? For when all was said and done, those who had lurked in the shadows and in the background of affairs, came forward to claim their share.

They had not cast their bodies against barbed wire, they had not faced bricks and bullets at the barricades. They had never seen the inside of a prison or missed a day of school.

They quietly went on, making ordinary of the abnormal, servicing the system that oppressed those around them. They got on with the business of their own progress, while the others broke their backs, lay in pools of blood, and were lain in shallow graves; their lives – and those they loved – shattered under the terror and the jackboot of the system they resisted.

Spare a thought, they would say, for those of us who "don't want any trouble". We are simple people. We just want to get on with our lives. Spare a thought, for those of us who have much to lose, for whom the immediacy of things cannot be broken, not for others, not for the future, not even for the present. You are asking us to interrupt our lives, and for what? What will all this achieve, anyway? Things stay the same, they do not change!

But when freedom was won, they celebrated with us, invited us in to eat with them, and poured praise upon us. "*Heroes*", they called us.

Over time, they revised their histories, laid claim to suffering, and to struggle, and made heroes of themselves, as though they had been the ones on the streets, facing the bullets. More and more they claimed our suffering and made it theirs. They confused their oppression, their brokenness, with struggle.

They became heroes to themselves. They convinced themselves of their own suffering and sacrifice, and quickly made currency of it in the new. After all, their uninterrupted lives – of studies completed, the acquisition of wealth, security and assets their ever-present priority – enabled them to exploit freedom better than those who had languished in the camps and prisons, or had fought on the streets.

And when the spoils of victory were to be awarded, they jostled and wrangled to the front of the queue. Every memory became filled with themselves, and soon; every path, every avenue, was quickly jammed by them. So, in the end, there was nothing left for the others, namely those who had risked and suffered the most.

Yet they claimed more, and consolidated, and re-consolidated, until the new became a vessel for re-birthing and reproducing the old. They colonised the corridors of power, like those who came before them, held on tightly to their gains, and defended them dutifully.

There was no measure, for how restrictive they became about maintaining the status quo, which was to retain the inherited abnormal; a charade, a performance. The language of duplicity replaced the language of hate; 'cosmetic change' it was dubbed. The cosmetics were superfluous, but they spread like a mould in wet climes nonetheless, covering everything in its path, sucking up nutrients, growing into a dense forest that could not be penetrated.

They became the infection that we had once feared, yet their claims were tendered as noble; their virtue beyond reproach. Comfortably ensconced in their neat living rooms, they preached volumes of their own good.

Those who had faded into the background when the struggles were at its height now moved to the front and centre of things. They occupied the centres of power, and strengthened themselves and their own through it, all the while, preening their new hair, proudly announcing their new cars and large houses for all to see; evidence they claimed, of success, of change. The new bourgeoisie, the nouveau riche and the elite became fishers of men and wealth, and they set in their hooks gleefully.

And those who had once suffered were robbed once again, but this time by those who understood the creeping passage of time, by those who effected the "slow effacement" of the breath on the mirror when freedom was won; the promise of a new future. How fragile our dreams of the new proved to be amidst the secure among us, among those who wanted no trouble. What was lost, was not to be regained, and they were the ones who made sure of it.

So, when you ask me to spare a thought for those who have no thought for others, I will spare a thought, but it will be just one. For a single thought is more than they deserve.

Camaren Peter

6.3 PURPOSE

The pursuit of goals that align with one's values can be effective in allowing one to live a purposeful life. However, the pursuit of meaning and purpose in life, that is associated with the self-actualization stage, is a challenge even when one's values or authentic interests are clear. Our research participant, Lise-Marie Maartens in her poem: *"Waarvoor is ek hier"* (6.3.1, translated by Kurt April to: *"What am I here for?"*), addresses the confusion faced by one in the absence of knowing one's purpose. While the motivations in the earlier stages of self-leadership development are evident, where survival is the foundational purpose in the first stage, conforming in the second, and fitting in with peers in the third, post individuation, and in the stage of self-actualization the purpose becomes more illusive as one starts to aspire to connect with the foundational purpose that one was born to fulfil. While values can guide one towards one's purpose, particularly in the sense of which type of vocation and jobs would interest one, the essence of purpose can stay difficult to find. Maartens recognizes her interest in music, thus prescribing to the aesthetic value; however, it does not readily translate into a purpose. As such, there is a journey of growth between knowing one's values and having a purpose in life. The first stumbling block is not being able to crisply identify one's purpose in life which potentially can have emotional and physiological repercussions for one, as described by Maartens: *"maak my siek in my maag [makes me sick in my stomach]"*. Our research participants, to follow, share similar emotions faced in the absence of identification of a purpose at this stage of self-leadership development, and share some stumbling blocks to identifying a purpose and vital enablers that assisted them in their quest to seek out their purpose.

Another of our research participants, Peter Ransom, in his poem: *"The two-snake dream"* (6.3.2), describes how elusive one's purpose can be, and how the unconscious mind can 'speak' or send 'signals' to the conscious mind about it in one's dreams.[173] Ransom questions many aspects regarding seeking a purpose, such as: *"I have to dig deep and work to find it, or much deeper will it sneak"*? Conforming pressures and the fear of exclusion are expressed as stumbling blocks in the lines: *"I feel fine where I am"*, explained as: *"The risk of making a wrong move was too great"*. Ransom's dream depicted this fear as a: *"... poisonous green serpent"*. In the explanation of his poem, Ransom describes the second snake as: *"... a big fat Gaboon viper – a short and fat, slow-moving snake"*, compared to the venomous, and agile green mamba. The earlier reflects the unindividuated path; while, the dangerous mamba is expressed as the quest for finding a purpose, or self-actualizing. Despite the fears, worries, and concerns regarding chasing his purpose, he exhorts: *"... and the only way through was to deal with the Green Mamba – there was no way around it!"*. Thus, he acknowledges that as one grows along the path of psychological development, upon becoming comfortable at any stage, one's driving motivation progresses along the hierarchy,[174] and despite the fears encountered of progressing to the next stage of development, the motivation enables one to find the courage to confront the fears and progress along the stages of self-leadership development.

A few of our research participants share enablers in seeking out one's purpose. For example, Kira Koopman in her poem: *"On finding purpose"* (6.3.3), regards finding a purpose to be a recipe for accomplishments and happiness simultaneously. She refers to finding a purpose in life in her lines as feelings of: *"... warm glow as we climb our mountains ever higher"*. A key differentiator is a distinct preference for eudaimonic happiness that emerges from having a purpose. The relationship between purpose and eudaimonic happiness is so prominent that eudaimonic happiness is defined to arise from experiences of purpose or meaning in life.[175] While there are significant variances in defining leadership and the common attributes of leaders, there is consensus regarding two constructs for values-based leadership – a purpose in life,[176] and the pursuit of eudaimonic happiness.[177] Koopman also shares some enablers that trigger the search for happiness. She refers to them in her lines: *"The hypnotic monotony of his own melancholy"*. As such, a level of unhappiness or discontent from boredom is experienced from monotony and can serve as enablers which trigger a search for meaning in life, and hence the pursuit of one's purpose. However, the challenge of doing so is shared by her in the explanation of the poem in which she states: *"slave is also deeply dependent on his owner"*. She also highlights the fact that while the purpose is fulfilling and rewarding, it is not free from its own challenges and stresses. Thus, she attempts to de-glamorise living by one's purpose in life, which is frequently portrayed as if it is not a part of life itself, but above and beyond it. In doing so, she sketches a realistic image of the integrating stage, that allows one to enjoy eudaimonic happiness, contentment, and ample energy released from engagement at work and in everyday life, yet she does not dismiss the struggles, challenges, hardships that are experienced in all stages of psychological and self-leadership development.

Similar to the poem: *"Silence"* by Kurt April (4.3.3), another of our research participants, Kosheek Sewchurran in his poem that is also titled *"Silence"* (6.3.4) highlights that silence accompanies the enabler of boredom and monotony. Silence is an essential tool during moments of boredom that is reflected upon as a: *"... medium that carries our soul"*. However, Sewchurran metaphorically compares silence to a sandstorm; thus, highlighting the discomfort associated with the gradual chiselling of the façade by silence, but emphasizes that it facilitates exfoliating into one's soul. In the age of ample distractions and entertainment available at the click of a button, boredom is easily alleviated. However, boredom is a trigger for one to search for meaning in one's life.[178] As such, and complementary to boredom, moments of silence can trigger a search for meaning and purpose in life.

The discomfort of silence may entail difficulty for some to thrive in it. As such, Candice Watson in her poem: *"That thing"* (6.3.5), presents an alternative activity during moments of silence that can assist in attaining a higher perspective regarding one's life. In the explanation of the poem, she describes the process as tapping into: *"... a deeper question on unearthing our passion"*. She describes her habit of keeping a journal, and in opportunities of 'silence' or 'stillness', taking the chance to read it. She expresses how her readings reveal a host of 'things' that make-up life, but effectively distracts one from knowing: *"our true calling and purpose"*. As such, reflection through a journal allows one to read in-between the lines that make-up all of the things that formulate one's everyday life into revealing a greater purpose. In other words, journal keeping and finding the time to reflect using the journal can allow for filtering from the noises that one's life is occupied with, to reveal one's purpose in life.

Our research participant, Kurt April in his poem: *"Synchronicity"* (6.3.6), presents another enabler to discovering one's purpose. April expresses how most people do not notice many forces and events operational in their lives. He suggests becoming more actively conscious of coincidences in life. In the explanation of the poem, April shares his belief in coincidences to be as: *"... meaningful connecting engagements, or connected moments"* that are difficult explain using realism, but he regards coincidences as a 'nudge' towards one's purpose by God or a power greater than people.

While most of our participants reflect on the struggles of identifying a purpose, as well as the courage to seek it out in life, Angel Myeza in her poem: *"Restlessness"* (6.3.7), expresses how vividly clear her purpose in life exists. The search and the restlessness described in her poem is about finding avenues and means to live her purpose rather than to identify it or turn her life in the direction of its pursuit. The traumas (5.2) experienced by her and her community, based on racial bias, have led her to a clear purpose and direction in life. In doing so, she links trauma as a source of revealing one's meaning to life and one's purpose.

6.3.1 WAARVOOR IS EK HIER [WHAT AM I HERE FOR?]

Waarvoor is ek hier, om wat te maak?	What am I here for, to do what?
Is ek 'n kunstennaar, of tokkel ek kitaar?	Am I an artist, or do I just play guitar?
Waarvoor is ek hier, waste opsies is gewaar?	What am I here for, what options were considered?
Moet ek op 'n reisboot klim om die wereld vol te vaar?	Do I have to get on a cruise ship to travel through the world?
Waarvoor is ek hier, maak dit selfs saak?	What am I here for, does it even matter?
Klim ek verder op my leer al los dit my naak?	Do I continue to climb the ladder even if it leaves me naked?
Waarvoor is ek hier, wat moet ek maak?!	What am I here for, what should I do?
Dat ek nie kan se nie maak my siek in my maag.	That I cannot say makes me sick in the stomach

Lise-Mari Maartens

6.3.2 THE TWO-SNAKE DREAM

My purpose is eluding me
Though I sense it close and near
A poisonous green serpent
Its nearness makes me fear

Though I tell myself I search for it
I really feel fine where I am at

I'd rather not search too closely
And let it hide under the mat

I looked around and didn't see it
Though I know its underneath
I have to dig and work to find it
Or much deeper will it sneak?

Shall I cast my gaze above the ground
And walk along my merry way?
And pretend there is no danger
While I whistle or while I pray?

Shall I change my course and destiny
To avoid the fear and pain?
Shall I turn back and run away
And make my journey vain?

No! I must confront that serpent
That hides betwixt my way
And dig and turn things over
Till I find where the serpent lay
And grab the foe behind the head
As it thrashes all the way

And cast the sly and lurking threat
Far from my journey path
And enter the door that lies ahead
And find my life at last

The path to purpose is a hard one
And fraught with deep dark fears
But what is life if not to grow
I'll find my purpose here!

Peter Ransom

Ransom's Explanation: Finding and identifying my purpose and being able to articulate it has been a pressing goal for me at the moment. As I thought about purpose continuously over the past couple of months, I woke up one morning with a vivid dream. I don't recall where I was – only that I was high up on a narrow passageway above the trees. I was leading a few people and I had a snake stick in my hand. As we neared the doorway that I was leading everyone toward, I came upon a big fat Gaboon viper – a short and fat, slow-moving snake. With practiced skill, I picked the snake up by the tail and used my stick to toss the snake off the passageway into the trees. As I was doing this, I was keenly aware that just a few paces ahead of me, there was a Green Mamba hiding under the doormat of the passageway. I knew it was under there but was not sure how to safely proceed. I was fearful of going close to the doormat because I knew how potent and fast a Green Mamba's strike is. The risk of making a wrong move was too great. I had the impression that I had come a long way up to come through this door, and the only way through was to deal with the Green Mamba – there was no way around it!

At this stage in the dream I awoke – not out of a general fear of snakes, but out of being immobilized by fear on how to proceed in this specific situation – I didn't know the solution to my predicament or what it meant. I read up on the Internet about snakes in dreams, but nothing seemed to click and I didn't find anything insightful. I talked about the dream a lot over the next couple of weeks with my wife, and I was puzzled – I couldn't make sense of it.

During one of our lectures in Advanced Leadership, I asked Kurt to describe what it feels like to find your purpose – how does it look and feel, what does it taste like? His response was indirect, but very insightful. He mentioned that sometimes when we find our purpose it can be so strong that it takes control of us and the battle no longer is about working toward purpose but how to balance for health and our life as our purpose drives us along with great force. This concept really clicked for me, and I stewed on it for a couple of days.

A few days later, as I prepared a poem for our Leadership class poetry breakfast, clear and powerful meaning of the dream materialized in the poem. An interpretation of the two-snake dream emerged clearly as I wrote. The poem only took about 15 minutes to write – it was as though the content and connections were there, and just needed to be written down.

My purpose was behind the door guarded by the Green Mamba and could only be found by dealing with the snake – something I was hesitant to do, and was fearful of. The dream and poem have become a powerful metaphor of the point I am at in my purpose journey. I have come a long way and grown and prepared for this transition through the door of my purpose, yet, now as I stand with purpose pulling at me, I am paralyzed with fear. I have the tools to deal with what stands in the way (handling the first snake), but the Mamba still stands in the way. I have begun to see what I am afraid of – and many of these fears are fears that I have never had or been aware of before – the fear of failing, the fear of discomfort, and the fear of feeling alone. The door to our purpose wouldn't have much meaning if it wasn't guarded by our deepest fears, and our purpose wouldn't have much power if we didn't have to journey and conquer ourselves to find it and live it.

6.3.3 ON FINDING PURPOSE

In a moment of clarity, we scan the broad oceans,
lost and uneasy
Knowing always, that it is there,
Across the bay
We peer, longingly, hoping to escape
the sweet venom of the serpents,
the hypnotic monotony of his
owner's melody.

But still we toil,
Until the next time we're reminded
that there always is more

And when our gaze finally breaks
through the mist,
the sun rises to shine brilliantly
on our faces
The search is over.

Now, we bask in the light
feeling the warm glow
as we climb our mountains
Ever higher.

Kira Koopman

Koopman's Explanation: I've used the metaphor of a slave, toiling away for someone else, because it often feels as if working in a job that is unfulfilling for people whose values are misaligned to your own, is unrewarding and that you're not able to be independent, even though this is the desire – "peer, longingly". Tension and comfortability, a calling as it were, every so often causes us to look up, and seek out meaning.

Despite this, the slave is also deeply dependent on his owner, as indicated by the word "sweet" to describe his venom. He is also fully entrenched in the system and the call of this work and way of life is deeply familiar – generations before him toiled at the same system – symbolic of the owner and its reference to families born into slavery – even though he is unhappy.

When he eventually 'sees the light' and accepts it, he is able to move closer towards his purpose. He is lighter, more driven, and motivated. He basks in the confidence of knowing he is no longer trapped. But this is just the beginning of the journey – as he climbs the mountains, he moves both towards a higher purpose and closer towards the sun (a reference to Icarus here, too). There's danger in this as well, in that this new journey, now providing a deeper sense of fulfilment because it is purpose-driven, poses its own challenges which the individual needs to navigate.

I was inspired to write this poem because I experienced this similar awakening of slave myself when I moved out of an organization and industry that was deeply frustrating and unfulfilling, towards starting my own business in the learning industry, bringing me great meaning and gratification, notwithstanding its own challenges and stress.

6.3.4 SILENCE (II)

We yearn for silence and emptiness.
We work with silent dedication, you and I
buffeted by a sand storm discomfort.
We persevere despite the sting, the bruising.
We bruise in this sandy medium.
Stoically staying true to an inner calling.
Guided by this wiser inner voice…
we yearn for its consoling acknowledgment that it's a good
fight…
we yearn, we toil, we grimace, we cry, we yearn
for the solace of stillness, we never rejoice.
This is the medium that carries our souls.
We show up with silent dedication…
when we smile, we warm the earth,
we silence the storm…
we long to smile… and we do smile.

Kosheek Sewchurran

6.3.5 THAT THING

Have you ever wanted time to run along so that it creates distance
between you and that thing?

That thing that torments and taints your progress
That thing that you thought you would never recover from

That thing that still lingers on long past its date of inception
That thing that is tiring your tired

At its inception, this thing received all sorts of attention
But as time passes those who said they would always be there have
left

Left you, and this thing

And as people left, you realize, that everybody has their thing
What is this thing, this moment, this matter, these things that
so easily beset us?
These things that leave us feeling desperate, hopeless, helpless…

I hear a single mother crying for her son with no male role
model
A daughter wondering why her father did not love her enough
to stay
The unemployed graduate wondering which job application will
be successful
The first-time manager anxiously rolling up her sleeves to deliver her
objectives

And then in between these things,
Are the everyday things of life,
The dinners, the lunches, the bills,
These things that make the wheel of life turn

In the midst of all these things
There is one thing that fans the flame of your passion
The thing that makes you get up one more time
That thing that whispers in your soul and says
"You are mine, and I am yours"

In the end, it will be the account of what you did with that one
thing
That will determine your place in history

Find that thing and pursue that thing only.

Candice Watson

153

Watson's Explanation: From an early age I was introduced to the practice of journaling. As I started exploring the pages of my recent journal, I came across some of these words I used in this poem. These words are very personal to me, but I do believe they reflect the journey of many of us walking through life whilst we have so many things to juggle.

From womanhood, motherhood, and building a career, there are some things in life that will forever change the trajectory of your life experience. These things could be a divorce; the death of a loved one; or everyday challenges with raising children and managing careers and finances.

It is important for me to share my experience of these things with everyone who might feel alone with whatever 'thing' they are wrestling with. Through sharing this poem, it brings healing to my soul as I reflect on the things I thought, in the past, I would not overcome and upon reflecting over my journey, I realized that indeed I have overcome them.

I have come to realize that life has been designed in such a way that you will not escape some 'things', but it is in the moments of wrestling and working through it that our strength of character is shaped and we discover the beauty of life through seasons of joy or seasons of pain.

These things have the potential to distract us from our true calling and purpose. Therefore, the poem ends with redirecting our attention to the not-so-obvious things, but a deeper question on unearthing our passion. And it is when we find that one thing that drives our purpose that we can boldly proclaim: When it is all said and done, life will know that I was here, and I lived my life to its fullest expression!

6.3.6 SYNCHRONICITY

Many forces
Some seen, some not
Interlaced
Pushing towards an outcome
Presents the happening
Appearing as a whole
Some notice, some not

Individual wishes
Through conscious purposing
Engaged will

Hoping for an outcome
Oblivious to the unseen
Some aware, some not

Hindered by other purposing
Others
Separate
Some aligned, some not
Compromised outcome
No-one has willed
Some happy, some not

Kurt April

April's Explanation: This poem speaks to the many, meaningful so-called coincidences one encounters throughout life, which, in my experience, occur most often when one is open to "hearing" and "seeing them". Even though one's superficial understanding is that it is mere coincidence, they are experienced, for me anyway, as meaningful connecting engagements, or connected moments. It is hard to explain with ordinary cognitive resources. The hand of God, a governing dynamic, or something larger than my own consciousness or purposeful/causal action, seems to intervene in simple ways to unearth a thread which could not previously be seen – a "pushing", nudging towards one's purpose, a universal wholeness, one's ultimate reason for being on the earth. Synchronicity offers us an opportunity to test our personal choices in the realms of imagination versus reality, and whether we are walking the path that gives us the most energy.

6.3.7 RESTLESSNESS

I am restless
I am searching
I am mad!
I am irked

Surprised by my impromptu activism
This injustice irks me
I must do something
I have to do *something*
I *need* to do something!
It *must* be stopped!

I am restless!

They seem to walk around so aimlessly
So oblivious
It makes me want to scream!!
Can't you see it?
I want to shout "Something is wrong!! This is wrong! It's *all*
wrong!!"
But they won't get it

I am restless!!
Its lonely – this journey, this insight
Its maddening!
I feel awake while the world sleeps

I am restless!!!
I am irked
I can't ignore it
I CANNOT

"Ahhhhhhhhhhhhhhhhhhhhh….!!!!!!!!!!!!!"

Angel Myeza

Myeza's Explanation: Restless is about my frustration at the status quo of continued racial bias and racial injustice in South Africa. It's about my growing awareness, activism, and rebellion against these injustices. As my awareness grows and I continue to observe how as black people we are in an emotional and psychological prison, I become even more occupied by thoughts of how to bring the same awareness to everyone else – hence in paragraph 3, I mention that there seems to be general obliviousness to our plight in most of our people. This paragraph is by no means intended to imply that people are intentionally ignorant but is intended to point out that, as a people, we have become so accustomed to the status quo, that we have started to believe that this is the way things are supposed to be. We have accepted it as normal. So, in my frustration – I want to shout and grab the attention of every black person around me and say – "No!! this is not the way it should be – let's come together and do something about it!"

Paragraph 4 is intended to explain how I sometimes feel lonely in my awareness and in my journey or search to find solutions to what I believe to be an unacceptable way of life for the black person. It's lonely because I am very passionate about it. My passion and my constant preoccupation with endless questions and thoughts, can lead to withdrawal from people who I believe won't get it. The reverse is also true – when one is passionate about something it is always on your mind and tongue and it engulfs everything – conversations with friends, family, and colleagues, and when they are not of the same opinion, it can be a tiring conversation and it can make them withdraw from you as well.

With each paragraph that starts with 'I am restless' you will notice that the number of exclamation marks grow, and this is intentional because as I am having this conversation and sharing my thoughts and feelings, my frustration grows exponentially. I feel more and more unsettled, and it starts to spill over to a point where I can no longer contain it and, in my last line, I eventually let it out in one loud scream.

This poem is meant to be a brief glimpse into some of my daily thoughts and feelings as a young, professional, black woman. The more experiences I have in the workplace with friends and in general, the more agitated I become with the seeming comfort of how black people are perceived and treated. Society has been indoctrinated into believing that this subtle hierarchical society is the way it should be, and even worse, black people have themselves started to believe that indeed, they have something to be ashamed of, that they are second-class citizens, that we should be grateful for the handful of 'opportunities' and 'progressive changes' in our society and that indeed the country has come a long way when it comes to racial bias. This in fact is not true in my personal experience.

6.4 THE INTEGRATED LEADER

Having uncovered one's core values, its application in everyday life in most cases entails aligning one's values and purpose with the work one does. The integration of one's values and purpose with one's work bears the secret to unravelling work engagement.[179] Characteristics of work engagement are high levels of vigour,[180] dedication,[181] as well as absorption[182] at work. These constructs, operating within the work engagement, effectively capture a vital facet of happiness at work[183] which allows for enhanced performance,[184] along with a higher propensity to achieve leadership positions.

From a leadership perspective, the difference between self-actualizing and integrating is that: "The integrator/inspirer is a self-actualized individual who has discovered their sense of purpose. They build a personal vision and mission and a vision and mission for the organization that inspires employees, customers, investors, and society. They promote a shared set of values and demonstrate congruent behaviours that guide decision-making throughout the organization. They demonstrate integrity and are living examples of values-based leadership".[185]

Gandhi, quoted earlier in the individuating stage (4.7), corroborated the perspective that imperfections are a vital aspect of all leaders. If there exists an aspect that can be deemed

157

perfect about the leader, it would be the leader's impenetrable values. He identified truth and non-violence as his core values that supported his leadership. He expresses this in his self-reflective quote:

"When I think of my littleness and my limitations on the one hand and of the expectations raised about me on the other, I become dazed for the moment, but I come to myself as soon as I realize that these expectations are a tribute not to me, a curious mixture of Jekyll and Hyde, but to the incarnation, however imperfect but comparatively great in me, of the two priceless qualities of truth and non-violence".[186]

Our last research participant for this chapter, Kurt April in his poem: *"Leading from values"* (6.4.1), brings together several of the above perspectives of self-leading based on an array of values. Starting with *"truth"*, April emphasizes the theoretical value and states it to be *"gold"*. Thereafter, *"moral character"* is defined as being the *"biggest prize"*, as such, highlighting social values as vital for selflessness and moral leadership that embodies a concern for others' welfare. This is emphasized in the lines: *"Allowing for a serving. The common good, A coming together"*. The regard for values-based leadership as sustainable in times of challenges and other forms of personhood in leadership positions that do not embrace values (e.g., inauthenticity, tyranny, injustice, immorality, and deceit) place it at the highest amongst the self-leadership development goals.

6.4.1 LEADING FROM VALUES

What of truth? It is gold
What of moral character? It is the biggest prize
Values though. Enables truth
Brings light to the dark. Enables the genuine,
The enduring, true voice inside … among the multiple voices that could be
Whispers true all day long. The voice speaks inside
In its domain we wander. Awake to it, or asleep. Refusing it or accepting it,
It is up to you.

No parent, partner, teacher, wise person, mentor can hear your voice,
Nor choose for you. Your values base is yours to choose
Chipped and honed over time. Aspires. Staying true north
As we grow, so shall we lead,
Delivering authentic spaces. Authentic engagement. Encouraging
vulnerable responses
Softening the space
Allowing for a serving. The common good,
A coming together.

When the winds of justice grow,
The despot turns. Tyrants fall. Falsehood blows
The immoral crumbles. The inauthentic shirk
Liars and lies ultimately defeated
The values-based pillar lasts. A pillar of truth. Of triumphant strength
Of purpose. Of hope. Of heart. Its place,
Transcends the limits of the carnal. Weathers the worst.
Stands. Your values base.

Kurt April

April's Explanation: Values-based leadership is the idea that leaders draw on their own, conscientized, positive motivation, and direction. That direction and motivation emanate from being able to identify and move with the 'sound of the genuine' among the many competing voices in both our minds and hearts throughout our lives. As toddlers and young people, many of us came to unconsciously assume and take on the values prescribed to us by those who parented us, who cared for us, and taught us, as well as the cultures and environments in which we found ourselves – the self we created to fit in, to get along and generally to do what we have been told. But this does not suffice as we grow into adulthood. At some point, we have to choose conscious living, purposefully considering the many possibilities of values and values directions that are possible, and then choosing how we wish to live, act, be thought of, and be remembered. To quote Howard Thurman in his 1980 commencement address at Spelman College in Atlanta:

"There is something in every one of you that waits, listens for the sound of the genuine in yourself and if you cannot hear it, you will never find whatever it is for which you are searching and if you hear it and then do not follow it, it was better that you had never been born ... You are the only you that has ever lived; your idiom is the only idiom of its kind in all of existence and if you cannot hear the sound of the genuine in you, you will all of your life spend your days on the ends of strings that somebody else pulls... There is in you something that waits and listens for the sound of the genuine in yourself and sometimes there is so much traffic going on in your minds, so many different kinds of signals, so many vast impulses floating through your organism that go back thousands of generations, long before you were even a thought in the mind of creation, and you are buffeted by these, and in the midst of all of this you have got to find out what your name is. Who are you? How does the sound of the genuine come through to you ...."?

It demands a knowing of who we are in every moment and in every space/ environment in which we find ourselves – and requires patient self-reflection and

159

an unpacking of our own, personal narratives. It is not something someone else can know for you. It can only be discovered and chosen by ourselves. Some get to know this early on in their lives – and the ease within which they exist in their own skins and selves are both visible and tangible – while others, most of us in fact, need patience to seek it out over our lifetimes, to question, to bump our heads and hearts along the way, to test, to resist, to challenge and to eventually come into becoming who we were meant to be. Sadly, some never get to bring congruence between their espoused values and their enacted values – what they believe to guide their best selves, and how they choose to behave and live. If we are open to it, if we are willing to deconstruct our lived experiences, to examine our doubts, and able to mindfully observe ourselves as we live in the present moment, we have the chance to 'hear that genuine voice' and respond in conscious choosing to walk towards and act in accordance with our true north. Often 'unlearning' needs to take place – a personal transformation of courage paradoxically mixed with necessary self-compassion – whereby we interrogate the assumptions and deep beliefs we carry about others, the world and, most importantly, about ourselves, before we can relearn to be a different way. We have to understand that there is a deeper meaning to our lives – the talents we have, the unique gifts we possess, the stories we embody, and the generational knowledge we pass on after adding our own authentic threads. There is a fulfilment, a deep satisfaction, an ease that comes with being thoroughly understood, with being able to live and express the values that we deeply espouse and long to live out. When we are genuine, we help others to be the same, to flourish in life and at work.

7 SERVING

A prominent conviction for social value amongst Spranger's[187] six fundamental values lead one to a believe in community and collectivism. Associated with the belief is that a person's purpose is larger than one's self and the immediate family. Instead, such a value system aligns one's purpose to that of the community or the society, and motivates one to make a contribution to society as a whole. Similarly, a central aspect of the religious value allows for nurturing of a desire to go beyond one's self-interest, and to aspire to make a difference in creating a more meaningful world.[188]

Our research participant, using the pseudonym Gingin in the poem: *"To risk and dare"* (7.1.1), expresses a natural desire to: *"... help others and me"*, even if it requires taking risks and daring to take initiatives for the well-being of others. In the lines of the poem, several aspirations of helping others are described, such as: *"... turn tears to smile ... calm anger down"* and to: *"... soothe the tension"*. The research participant describes that the purpose of doing so is to make life happier; thus, aiming to serve others.

While our research participant above regards the above motivation as a natural tendency, some of our research participants share foundational facets as well as enablers to nurture one's social and religious values so as to develop a purpose that is focused on serving others. For example, our research participant, Bruce Isdale, in his poem: *"Charting the course"* (7.1.2), expresses his purpose in life in the line: *"My Purpose is to help"*. He expresses an enabler for his acute social value in the line: *"A loving family behind me puts wind in my sails"*. As such, a well-nurtured childhood facilitates progression as an adult to the serving stage of self-leadership development. Additionally, in the explanation of the poem, he describes another enabler that supports his externally focused purpose. In addition to family support, he states that living by the sea is an effective enabler to block out noises that may disperse one's focus, or steer one away from one's purpose of helping others. Similarly, another research participant, in the poem: *"Nature vs. nurture"* (7.1.3), expresses how a pastoral setting enables Anonymous to: *"... calm my natural fight-or-flight instincts and nurture new growth"*; thus, confirming the influence of the environment on one's personal growth, particularly in respect of serving others. It can be expected that the solace and calm that emerges from proximity to the sea allows for Isdale to be contemplative, or be more mindful, and therefore allows him to be in a state of Zen, that makes him more observant as well as receptive towards those around him who may need his help. He confirms this by stating: *"I am often asked for help by others (even people I don't know), and that people find me easy to talk to/confide in. I believe this to be an affirmation that my purpose is to help others"*; thus, describing how his 'Zenful energy' is radiated to and picked up by others, and is acknowledged by others in their actions through approaching him for help that they may need. This enhanced approachability affirms his purpose by others' actions towards him.

Our research participants, Belisa Rodrigues and Roshan Bhurtha in their poem: "Queenie" (7.1.4), share how such serving personalities can occupy a central position in communities; and thus serve a leadership role. They reminisce about Queenie who has passed away, whom they describe as being: *"... a larger than life, lady"*. The attributes that make her 'larger than life' are explained as her: *"... warm smile and open arms"* that exuded kindness to all, irrespective of personal differences. In the explanation of the poem, they regard her as an example for all to follow. While such demeanour of having a warm smile and open arms may appear easy to follow, it is the genuineness of the 'warmth' that is radiated from one's social and religious values that makes it authentic. The intense authenticity of her smile and her openness make her deeply missed by the community upon her passing. They made her kindness, openness, pleasant demeanour, and inclusivity worthy of remembrance in poetry by our research participants.

Contrary to the above research participants that present subtle enablers to nurture the social value within oneself, the concept of ego dissolution is argued to be an event of self-surrendering that facilitates a transition from self-centredness to serving-centredness. Neuroscientific studies[189] of such experiences argue it to present a chemically-facilitated opportunity into a heightened sense of self-awareness that leads to self-dissolution. Some indigenous cultures practice such transitions as a part of the initiation ceremonies[190] that are devised to transition the tribe's youth into adulthood. For example, the initiation ceremony followed by the Matis tribe of Brazil includes injecting frog poison, called Kampo, amongst other agonizing rituals to mark the transition from boyhood to manhood. The chemicals in the poison, in addition to physiological reactions such as an intensely laxative effect, have profound psychological effects too. They permit reminiscence of harm done to oneself by others, and the harm inflicted onto others, triggering one to forgive others, as well as an elevated desire for seeking forgiveness from others. Kampo is medically known to include a chemical that facilitates a psychological transition, or crossing of an edge,[191] that leads to a significant difference in one's psychological 'being'. The process forms a vital part of the initiation ceremony, marking the role transition of a boy to a man who is meant to go hunting in the forest and provide food for the fellow tribe members.[192]

While Kampo is not hallucinogenic, our research participant, Alexa Mehos in her poem: *"One"* (7.1.5), shares her experience of psychedelic plant medicine 'Ayahuasca' in Peru. She shares how the chemicals in the pant induced hallucinations that made her re-live traumatic experiences of her life. She describes the immense intensity of these, which are so overwhelming that she states that they left her with: *"... no choice but to let go"* (ego dissolution). Additionally, she summarizes the learning of the experience in the line: *"... to be happy in this life is to learn how to be a mother"*. In the explanation of the poem, she describes what this line entails: *"... to love myself in the way that only a mother can do, and that embodying this kind of compassion is the only thing that can stop the cycle of violence and suffering in the world"*. As such, she not only presents a chemically-induced enabler for a psychological shift in oneself that supports caring for others, but also links self-care as an enabler for it.

Our last research participant, Mary Liu, in her poem: *"Just breathe"* (7.1.6), also expresses the need for self-care, but she regards it as an enabler for progressing along all stages of self-leadership development. She conveys her wisdom of the fact that irrespective of personal growth, successes, accomplishments, failures, or heartbreak, self-compassion must dictate. Self-compassion entitles you to breathe. In the explanation of the poem, she states: *"... nothing worthy comes with ease"*, however, while one is faced with such unease, one still must breathe.

7.1.1 TO RISK AND DARE

When I put down on paper
All the things that for me matter
I think about joy and energy,
That I expect myself to carry,
And share with the most natural way
To the people that don't seem okay.
If I can turn tears into smile
And let it last for a while,
If I can calm anger down
By being some sort of a clown,
If I can soothe a tension
By showing love and passion,
If I can bring people together
When they don't want to talk to each other,
Then I feel fulfilled and satisfied
And ready to go for another ride.
I know that my "pinky sight"
Might sometimes not be right,
But if it can help both others and me
To erase pain temporarily
Then I am willing to risk and dare
To foolish myself somewhere.
At least I will have tried
To make life happier, and provide
My dearest friends and family
With a hint of glitter and beauty.

Gingin

7.1.2 CHARTING THE COURSE

The page that stares at me is blank;
A future still to be written.

The palette of skills acquired, ready to be mixed and applied;
Outline sketches still taking shape.

Strangers often ask me directions;
Family and friends, advice.

My Purpose is to help.

The endless breakers rolling outside reminiscent of life's
challenges;
Or are they waves to be surfed?

Positivity is key.

A loving family behind me puts wind in my sails;
And keeps me on even keel.

This leg of the journey's nearly done;
Looking forward to the next!

Bruce Isdale

Isdale's Explanation: This poem is an expression of my journey this year, from the perspective of the present, loosely using travel metaphors.

It started with a blank page, which caused me to reflect on the fact that I have almost limitless options, and a future which is still to unfold. This is also representative of my lack of direction coming into this year, and open approach to learning and experiencing what the MBA has to offer.

I've learnt a lot but as yet don't have clarity around how those skills and learnings are going to combine, but I do have some options which are currently taking shape.

I've observed that I am often asked for help by others (even people I don't know), and that people find me easy to talk to/confide in. I believe this to be an affirmation that my purpose is to help others.

Two key aspects of my life this year have also featured: Living by the sea (which I have used here as a reminder to myself to stay positive); and last (but certainly not least) the support of my family, which keeps me grounded, and feeling supported.

7.1.3 NATURE VS. NURTURE

steady
one foot passes the other
listen and watch
restrain

eyes fixed on the rooster
seeds were planted in
hard earth to
defy an unforgiving habitat

nurturing the contents of the
fragile soil
resisting the instinct to
move to more fertile fields

cultivating change
pale green will emerge
offering a faint flash of progress
persisting

Anonymous

Anonymous' Explanation: Early in my career, a perceptive colleague congratulated me on demonstrating my ability to navigate a storm but cautioned that my greatest challenge would come from learning to sail through periods of calm. During my EMBA experience, I acknowledged his insightful observation of what would be my greatest leadership challenge: impatience. The shadow of my responsive and motivational leadership style, impatience, has come at a cost, and only by tempering my haste will I be able to appreciate meaningful progress.

Borrowing from the kintsugi practice of adding fortitude and beauty to the broken or cast-aside, my poem reflects upon my professional attempts to rebuild something forgotten or disregarded by others. Having recently moved out of the city, I have embraced the speed of country life, with languid cattle, joggers, and river-wet dogs the sole cause of morning traffic jams. Perhaps due to my pastoral surroundings, I chose the image of the sturdy farmer as a representation of quiet endurance. In the farmer's image, I am able to calm my natural fight-or-flight instincts and nurture new growth in unlikely environments.

7.1.4 QUEENIE

I did not see you, like every other day

Your open-hearted open door
Pumping life from within its coloured walls

Suddenly, I got back to myself

You lived a life so full
And infected the streets with your presence
From across the road, I saw something was not right
And then the fence around your heart
Squeezed us out and we knew

Queenie is gone
Never to return

You reigned Queen on these streets
One door down from Queen Street
Memories of the respect you commanded
Memories of the love you gave, even to those you reprimanded

I went back inside to clear my mind
Only to find murk inside

Not many knew that your living on John
An act of resistance for 25 years

Who knew?

Queenie? Yes, I know her.
Yes, I am proud I knew her.

Belisa Rodrigues and Roshan Bhurtha

Rodrigues and Bhurtha's Explanation:

Note 1 – Message in this poem

This poem is about Queenie, a larger-than-life, lady that lived on John Street, Mowbray [Cape Town]. She passed away recently and has been a proud resident of Mowbray for 25 years.

She always greeted anyone with a warm smile and open arms. She transcended boundaries of race and culture, always making everyone feel welcome in the area. Leading by example, she did not let any bigotry get in the way. She is an example of all to follow. An example of leadership in our new [South African] democracy and our struggle to overcome inequality with kindness.

Note 2 – How this poem was created

This 'tapestry' poem was co-written by Belisa Rodrigues and Roshan Bhurtha, both neighbours on John Street in Mowbray.

Two independent streams of consciousness on a topic dear to both their hearts was interwoven together to create the final poem. The co-creation process served as both a healing and an honouring of the loss of a valuable member of this tight community. During the tapestry process, one has to 'let go' some preconceived notions and incorporate new ideas, thereby disrupting the flow of one's own logic, much like the processing of 'death' or 'loss'.

"Queenie" is our honouring of an ever-present soul, who touched our lives, that it moved us to poetry.

7.1.5 ONE

I lay on my back, deep in the jungles of Peru, staring up at an incredible clear night sky. All around me, the frogs chirped as I lay panting in the darkness, my face sticky with the heavy humid air and my own sweat. I didn't want to close my eyes again, because I knew the visions would come. I had just spent hours in violent hallucinations, reliving some of the most traumatic moments of my childhood and life to that point, but I knew I that I had no choice but to let go.

A bird hooted in the darkness, pulling me under. I struggled for a while with an octopus that I felt was trying to pull me down into the depths of the ocean, until I became exhausted and let her take me. In that moment of surrender, I felt the most incredible release, like all the suffering of my life was lifted, and I suddenly felt my mind and body dissolve into the ocean.

In that moment, I wasn't sure what self was anymore. I felt that I was all the salt in the ocean, all the minerals, and I realized that all the elements that form the earth and the oceans came from space when Earth was formed. I was stardust, I was the water, the sand and the rocks that the sand used to be all at the same time because time didn't exist. I was the plankton floating by those who were afraid of the octopus, and I felt tremendous compassion for all the beings on earth that feel terror; the cow wild-eyed and confused in the slaughterhouse, the refugee fighting for the life of her child, the injured child within myself.

When I came back to consciousness, the fear was replaced with a deep feeling of peace knowing that all I need to be happy in this life is to learn how to be a mother to that child, to love myself in the way that only a mother can do, and that embodying this kind of compassion is the only thing that can stop the cycle of violence and suffering in the world. I know deeply now that nothing is separate from myself – that violence in words or actions against other people, against animals, against the environment, is violence against myself. I also feel a joyful responsibility to stay and do something useful with this extraordinary and strange gift of life.

In my experience with Ayahuasca, I was forced to confront the things my ego tries to protect me from. The same applies in real life, and is what I use in my practice of meditation every day. In meditation, you allow difficult thoughts to come, greet them, and let them float away down the river of consciousness. The same practice can be done in every moment of every day. By finding the spaciousness between thoughts, it is possible to think before reacting out of ego, and to welcome stressful and difficult situations as opportunities for self-examination and growth.

In this way, over time, my thoughts and emotions have become less scary, they've lost their power over me. Every day, I practice making my mind my greatest friend, even when it tells me stories about fear, shame, judging, despair, about not being enough.

And some days, the more I practice sitting in meditation,
all I can hear is my breath, and it sounds like the bottom of the
ocean
And night-time in the jungle
Self and no self
One.

Alexa Mehos

Mehos' Explanation: I spent some time living in a Buddhist monastery a few years ago, and one of my teachers there often said something that has been deeply meaningful in my life: "The mind, untrained, can be your greatest friend. The mind, untrained, can also be your greatest enemy."

I was faced with the reality of the threat posed by my own mind as a young child growing up in a family deeply affected by mental illness. I learnt from a very early age that my dad's mother committed suicide when she was a teenager, which instilled in me a deep fear of my own mind and almost an irrational expectation that I would not survive myself past the age of 20.

Survive I did, although in my early twenties, I was grappling deeply with the existential questions that we all face in some way at some point, some people to different degrees. What is 'the self'? Why do we suffer, and what is the point of it all? Do we stay, or do we go?

I first heard about the psychedelic plant medicine Ayahuasca when I was living in Peru about five years ago. Ayahuasca is a root that grows in the jungles of the Amazon that has been used by shamans for millennia as part of spiritual ceremonies. When administered under the supervision of an elder or a trained guide, it can have a more profound healing effect than years of psychotherapy in a single trip, which was very appealing to me at that stage in my life.

In my experience with Ayahuasca I describe below, I travelled through space, gave birth to myself, and communed with all of my female ancestors and future descendants. While these teachings were all profound, as I have continued to look deeply into my mind in a journey of self-healing through mindfulness in the years following, I've found that one of the most therapeutic effects of these practices is the experience of ego dissolution. In the mind, states elicited by plant medicine and meditation practices, the ego seems to be diminished, leading to a feeling of "oneness".

The questions that haunted me in my childhood remain the essence of my spiritual path. However, my practice has taught me to embrace the whole range of human experience, happiness and suffering, light and dark, as opportunities to wake up to the gift of the present moment. It has also taught me the possibility of transcending the self. I hope that the piece I've written provides a useful snapshot into my experience with this concept of ego dissolution that has, for me, led to the emergence of a more compassionate and joyful way of being.

7.1.6 JUST BREATHE

Just breathe, you may not be perfect, but you need to breathe.
You have not made it yet, but you still deserve to breathe.
You can't always be satisfied but at least you can breathe.
Your anxiety voice screams: why can't it be simpler? smoother?
Why is the path to tomorrow always misty with fear?

Look ahead and breathe.
Somewhere through the mist I long to see the golden thread
that leads me into a formidable future.
But, where are you?
In the centre of my palm?
At the bottom of my heart?
In the depths of my footprints?
For I am not the protagonist of my own life but the author,
I write my own life stories, experiences and ambitions.
Life is never one straight cobble-stoned path, life is a journey.

Mary Liu

Liu's Explanation: As I approach the end of my MBA year, I begin to feel anxious about the uncertainty that the future holds. I want a clearer direction but am not sure where to find the answer. I am inspired by the vulnerability spoken about by the guest speaker on the Advanced Leadership elective, who said that we are the authors who write our own life story. I decided to write my own life story, because I am in control of my life no matter how difficult it is. I have come to the realization that nothing worthy comes with ease. It is all part of a journey, and that I have to go on to learn and grow.

7.2 THE SERVANT LEADER

Our research participant, Donovan du Plooy in his poem: *"Same words, but many ideas"* (7.2.1), raises a concern regarding the diversity of values at the integrating stage of self-leadership development. Acknowledging the significance of teamwork in organizations for achieving goals, he provides an example of his experiences in the military. In the explanation of the poem, he sketches a similarity between the military and corporate organizations: *"... recruitment in modern business works in the same way"*. He claims that in order to achieve an effective organizational culture, employees and new recruits must: *"... not only adhere to this culture, but enthusiastically embrace it"*. However, unlike the military where: *"... initial training that the individual is forced to leave behind, whatever came before, to make a place for the military life which is methodically installed in the minds of everyone"*, in the corporate world: *"... painstakingly sifts through large numbers of applicants to find someone who already demonstrates the "cultural" aspects of the existing organizational culture, thereby ensuring that uniformity of culture is created, maintained and protected"*. As such, our research participant causes us to pause and to (re)consider modern day business challenges in relation to integrating with others with whom our values align and our purpose resonates – asking us to really think about 'true diversity' and effectiveness. While 'superficial diversity' can be ensured in respect of race, gender, colour, ethnicity, and other social categories, our research participant questions whether this is representative of 'true diversity' if the organization seeks out like-valued individuals. If "the primary leadership development goals at the integrating stage of psychological development [include] connect[ing] with other like-minded individuals to make a difference in the world",[193] it rightfully makes it questionable whether it leaves room for value diversity. Particularly since it is said that such leaders: "... create mutually beneficial partnerships and strategic alliances with other individuals or groups who share the same vision and embrace similar values".[194]

Du Plooy, by challenging integrating with those like-minded, highlights the significance of diversity and listening to other perspectives that challenge one's values systems, to be open to modification of value stances, in order to continually refine our values and our mental models.[195] This echoes our research participant, Afzal Dalwai's lines in his poem: *"Purposefully"* (2.1.1), in which he states: *"Never does a moment pass when my values are unknown, but never do I believe my values are complete"*.

In addition to the above, two additional fundamentals are presented for the integrating stage: "(a) release any fears you have about forming unconditional loving relationships, and (b) develop your empathy and social intelligence skills".[196] However, these fundamentals of unconditional love, empathy, and social intelligence that ensure respect and appreciation for diversity by leaders are, arguably, better associated with the serving stage of self-leadership development. For example, the attributes of a servant leader, "Queenie" (7.1.4) are explained as her: "... *warm smile and open arms*" that exuded kindness to all, irrespective of personal differences. Thus, linking inclusive leadership with servant leadership.

Leaders that have grown to the stage of serving, termed 'servant leaders'[197] behave in a radically different manner in their capacities as leaders. The concept of the servant leader is founded on the principle that leaders act as servants to their followers, in that they prescribe to addressing their members' needs rather than their own. This is achieved by de-emphasizing their self-interests, which makes them more readily focused on the moral responsibility that comes with being a leader towards the well-being of the followers, as well as the organization, and the other stakeholders such as suppliers, customers, the community, and the environment. As such, by seeking first to serve their stakeholders, they eventually emerge as leaders.

Our research participant, Kurt April in his poem: *"How blessed are we"* (7.2.2), points out the difficulty with, and resistance to, the term and the concept of a 'servant leader' in the South African context, where the hierarchy between people was founded on race[198] and, today still, many households have 'maids'/'domestics'/'home assistants' being from the majority black population while the home owners are from the white, Coloured/Camissa, Indian/Asian minority populations. As such, dominance and mastery on one hand, and subservience and servanthood on the other are, and were, assigned along the lines of race during Apartheid and which still persists today. However, South Africa gave birth to the thinking and orientations of some of the most famous servant leaders in the world, such as Nelson Mandela and Mahatma Gandhi. Gandhi famously stated: *"I have no hate in me for a single Englishman. I am not*

171

interested in driving him out of India. I am interested in converting him into a servant of India, instead of his being and believing himself to be a ruler or a member of the ruling race".[199] Nelson Mandela declared that "it is better *to lead from behind and to put others in front, especially when you celebrate victory when nice things occur. You take the front line when there is danger. Then people will appreciate your leadership*".

As described by Gandhi, the inclusion of varied values does not entail sacrificing one's purpose, which for Gandhi remained embedded in serving India; however, to align the purpose pursued rather than individual values. Inclusive leadership ensures that, despite the uniqueness of individual employees, a sense of belongingness to the team or organization is ensured to encourage group members to contribute their uniqueness to achieving a collective positive purpose of the organization. As such, the role of an integrated leader, similar to an inclusive leader, is to: "… help individuals fully provide their unique perspectives, and abilities to the work of the group".[200]

Since many iconic leaders have embodied a servant leadership style, such as Christian leadership[201] including Jesus Christ and many Saints, servant leadership as a concept can appear ideological, rather than aspirational. Our research participant, Kathy Harvey in her poem: "Stone circles" (7.2.3), states: *"I aspire to the concept of the Servant Leader but find it is just that, an aspiration just out of reach"*. As such, she suggests 'light touches', using the metaphor of a smooth, rounded stone that is thrown skilfully to allow it to bounce of the surface of water for impactful leadership. She contrasts it with a large, heavy, stone that is pushed into the water, which may make a splash but the impact is lost to the depths of the water to be akin to lecturing where wisdom is more likely to fall on 'deaf ears'. However, 'kindness', which is noted as a significant core element of servant leadership is a vital attribute (observed even in leaders within the primates). Thus, leadership, from an evolutionary perspective, embraces the concept of a kind and helpful leader[202] as it lends a hand in the survival of the individuals within a species, hence for the species itself. "Servant leadership is characterised by empathy, humility, sense of community, awareness of ethics, and a willingness to take on work that involves sacrifice for others",[203] which are vital leadership attributes for any living creature that is communal, since such attributes ensure the survival of the community. While servant leadership may appear to be a supremely high level of humanity, its achievement is not beyond the scope of leaders in many species.

Undoubtedly, the role of a servant leader in humans extends beyond the expectations from other creatures, for example, "Servant leadership focuses on developing and creating success for the members",[204] or by facilitating the members' growth along the stages of self-leadership development. It only requires one to read through the poem: *"Queenie"* (7.1.4) to actively acknowledge the existence of such leaders in one's respective community, and recognize what a vital role they play for the individuals within that community, and for the community as a whole.

7.2.1 SAME WORDS, BUT MANY IDEAS

When we can use the same words
But still fashion many ideas
When we can even know what the other is thinking in silence
And can anticipate what the other is even feeling
Then we can find each other
Even when the noise of the world is deafening
This is how we can do great things together
That each of us alone can only dream about

Donovan du Plooy

du Plooy's Explanation: It has been used so often that the saying "teamwork makes the dream work" has lost most of its meaning by now. However, there is almost nothing that can be done that has any historical significance that is not required to be done in teams. The dreams that humanity shares, which are made even more difficult in a dynamic and complex world, can only be accomplished by highly effective and motivated teams. But how do we choose the individuals that make up these teams? And how do the new requirements of how teams should be constituted affect the effectiveness of these teams?

In trying to write my poem above, I thought about my experience as an Officer in the South African military. I wondered how the military is able to bring so many individuals, from so many races and socio-economic backgrounds, together in such a way that they can function effectively in teams. The military does not do anything outside of teams, hence the tremendous focus on leadership recruitment and development. But buried deep in the military is the all-pervasive initial military socialisation that everyone has to go through in the form of Basic Training. It is through this initial training that the individual is forced to leave behind whatever came before to make a place for the military life which is methodically installed in the minds of everyone. Here, a new language of sorts is learnt, and new interactions with others are inculcated in everyone. This process has been honed over the many centuries of the existence of the professional military discipline in society and is extremely effective, to say the least.

This may be an unpopular viewpoint, but I believe that recruitment in modern business works in the same way. In the overwhelming focus on the development of an effective organizational culture, it has become even more important to ensure that any new members recruited not only adhere to this culture, but enthusiastically embraces it. In this way, the modern business does not inculcate a new member into their culture as such, but painstakingly sifts through large numbers of applicants to find someone who already demonstrates the "cultural" aspects of the existing organizational culture, thereby ensuring that uniformity of culture is created, maintained and protected.

In this way, the question can be asked as to how much diversity actually exists in business today, even when there are people from a myriad of races, genders, and socio-economic backgrounds employed at a business? For example, when everyone comes from private schools, has undergone university education at a major university, and holds the same political and ideological stances and beliefs, is there really diversity in an organization? Everyone, in a way, "speaks the same language" (uses the same words), and can somewhat anticipate each other's thoughts and feelings. In the military definition of a team, this would constitute an effective, but more importantly, a robust team capable of accomplishing its objectives even when the din of the world rises to a pitch that can make many shy away from their responsibilities. When the socialisation of teams is not confused with the homogenisation of individuals, a kind of team is created that is able to find an internal rhythm and integrity that is greater than the sum of its parts by orders of magnitude. These are the teams that are able to manifest our common dreams as a human race through their endeavours.

7.2.2 HOW BLESSED WE ARE

How blessed we are
For men and women
Brown and Yellow
Black and White
Who had patient hearts
Who acted on our behalf
Who moved with cautious respect
With tentative dialogue
With slight compromise

How blessed we are
That they acted on our behalf
Putting family at risk
Scarring their own relationships
Entering a loneliness only they could know
But hopeful of the possibilities

How blessed we are
That they chose to remove their steely breastplates at
appropriate moments

In order to reveal themselves
Their deep humanity
And inviting in the humanity of others
To seed a coming together
For all

Pain and humour, vulnerability and steadfastness
Openness and secretiveness, iron-fistedness and compassion
Anger and love
They held it all comfortably and uncomfortably
Engaging the pain and criticism
But continuously extending themselves
Into their better natures, opening their souls
So that we could be human
So that we could, someday, be soulful and whole

Kurt April

April's Explanation: The word 'servant' has negative connotations for some people, especially those who have previously been oppressed in South Africa. However, if one thinks of a servant as a 'nurturer of the human spirit', 'investor in others' or 'inspirer', it conveys a much more positive tone. According to Webster's New World Dictionary, the word 'inspire' means 'to breathe life into'. It also means 'to cause, communicate or motivate as by divine influence' – drawing attention to a spiritual element to the philosophy, as pointed out by many of its theorists. It is a powerful word that paints a picture of someone or something beyond ourselves, infusing us with a purpose or a mission, and calling us to action. The modern world has stifled much of the creativity of its leaders, by concentrating on a rational, analytical, and transactional approach to leadership. This has tended to suppress the spontaneous, inspired, and good-intentioned nature of many of our leaders. The idea of the leader as a servant first (as popularized by Greenleaf in the 1970s), focusing on the needs of others first and supporting them, provides a sense of release by giving us permission to serve and grow others – harkening to our personal purposes. John Gardiner muses about how the world would be different if the principle of assisting or serving others was viewed equally with that of gaining for one's own – then service above self could lead to the changes that would bring about true global renewal.

Towards the end of the Apartheid years, and at the start of South Africa's democratic years, men and women of all persuasions chose to do the hard work of trying to unite a quite divided country at the time. It required that they put aside the pursuit of only their selfish views and perspectives, and meet those often considered the enemy and opposition, halfway with compromise and engagement in order that the nation could be formed and move forward peacefully. For many, it meant time away from families, long hours around negotiating tables, and spending time with the very people who wanted to get rid of them (and even wanted them killed) just months and years before. What we notice from their extraordinary actions and orientations was a leaning toward servanthood – a servant leader orientation, the seeds of which were self-sacrifice and the common good. Their former suffering and pain did not make them hard and unable to engage others; instead, it offered them profound gains and advantages as humans – beyond that which the ordinary citizen was able or inclined to do.

Scholars of positive psychology have acknowledged the constructive role of suffering in relation to the development of healthy character strengths – servant leaders often are born from suffering, from overcoming past scars, stress and challenges, difficult childhoods and marginalized upbringings, and able to turn that into positive adjustment and positive adaptation. According to Prof. Scott Allison of the University of Richmond: "The redemptive development of hope, wisdom, and resilience as a result of suffering is said to have contributed to the leadership excellence of [notable global] figures …". The leaders referred to in the poem had to know how to reframe how they expressed themselves, and had to find ways to constructively resolve their conflicts, with sharp focusing of their consciousness in order to ensure quality outcomes from the debates and dialogues so that the new nation could be served. It required a vulnerability in how they expressed their feelings and their needs, while it also required strength to fight for a 'different way', a 'different future', and a more 'inclusive system' (the heart of a servant). As described in Shakespeare's Henry V, after defeating the French and meeting with Princess Katharine, there comes a time when one has to stop fighting, take off the armour, take off the breastplates, and even one's intellectual armour – the new dawn required a different stance from South Africa's leaders, to appreciate the Kairos, to be good listeners, to offer and accept respect and feedback, to change their speech from fighting- to reconciliatory language, to be maturely vulnerable and to move from an enemy to a potential friend. They had to hold and make sense of the necessary tension in the conversations, in themselves, and those with whom they were engaging (all admirable leadership qualities) in order to ensure political- and social union. We are grateful and blessed for whom they chose to be at that juncture of our history.

7.2.3 STONE CIRCLES

Right by the shore
Beside the sea
The pebbles shone

Next to the waves,
Astride the rock
She skimmed and watched the stone.

It splashed and bounced
It made its mark
Circles of glistening light across the dark

Kathy Harvey

Harvey's Explanation: I have often observed that good leaders and good teachers make an impact with a light touch. The manager who can't delegate gets nowhere, and the leader who lectures finds his or her wisdom falls on deaf ears. I have struggled to demonstrate rather than explain, to "show, not tell" others what it means to make a difference, to lead and to care for the people who work with you. I aspire to the concept of the Servant Leader but find it is just that, an aspiration just out of reach. For me, the metaphor of the stone, which is skimmed lightly, but with skill, across the surface of the water, is a good reminder that a light touch creates more impact than a forceful plunge into the depths. The poem is my attempt to capture this wisdom in an image.

CONCLUSIONS

Our research participant, Malepe's poem: *"Self-care"* presented in the introduction to the book, sets the basis for applying the framework of a staged development theory of self-leadership. However, **how accurately do our data support the framework of a stage theory of self-leadership development?** This theoretical framework is explicitly supported by many of our research participants by either reminiscing about previous stages of their own psychological growth, or by actively seeking out facets associated with their aspirations to advance to the next stage of self-leadership development. Those of our research participants who did not explicitly conform to the framework of a staged development theory of self-leadership addressed topics in their poems and explanations that prescribed to a stage of development, which assisted to place them within the framework. As such, our data corroborated a staged development of self-leadership.

Our research participant, who has stayed anonymous in the poem: *"Connection"*, presents an overall view of embarking on this journey of personal growth. However, unlike a physical journey, Anonymous challenges the notion of the journey of one's psychological growth to resemble a physical journey undertaken in the suitability of the use of measurements of speed, distance, and time. In doing so, the participant highlights the importance of recognizing that while the references to age may facilitate comprehension of the theory, one's age, as a measure, is not decisive in compartmentalizing and identifying one's placement along the journey. Instead, the journey of growth is said to be a continuum, of becoming the: *"... full spectrum"*. For example, while one may have progressed to higher stages of psychological growth, the survival instincts, such as a fight-, flight-, or freeze response, continue to remain vital elements that cannot just be abandoned. Similarly, belonging needs to a family or social group remains a psychological necessity for those who may be individuated or self-actualized.

CONNECTION

Speed, growth, distance, time
progress in continuum
myself full spectrum

Relativity
rage, joy, fear, anxiety
Speed, growth, wisdom, time

Laughter strikes at last
Leaders high, in perception
Ebb and flow unstuck

Anonymous

Anonymous' Explanation: The structure of this poem consists of three verses: awareness, experience, and success. Each verse is a Haiku – a form of Japanese poem of 17 syllables, in three lines of 5, 7, and 5 syllables. Haikus traditionally portray images of the natural world. In the context of this poem, the natural world exists within.

Awareness: We find ourselves running around, physically, and inside our heads. We learn our imperfections, and our strengths–full spectrum, and pursue our ideal selves continuously.

Experience: Our emotions – often stumbling blocks – sway our perception of time. Our experience of personal growth, wisdom, and achievements (speed to reach them) is relative, based on our emotions.

Success: Also, relative, determined in accordance with our inner world. Perception of self and others. A continuous journey of rising and falling, we do not know when success will occur. And when deep laughter is felt and shared, we know we have succeeded.

This is how we connect: past, present, future, followers.

Instead of speed, distance and time, the participant regards emotions as 'measurements' for the journey, including: *"... rage, joy, fear, anxiety"*. In the explanation of the poem, the participant states that these emotions can prevent one's progression along the stages. As such, Anonymous highlights the fact that one's journey of self-leadership development is signalled to one's conscious mind through one's emotions.

So, **which stage of self-leadership development is one to aspire to?** The participant also regards this journey to be full of highs and lows, with the possibility of stumbling upon success and happiness at each corner. While a stage development approach may be seen as a hierarchy, where 'serving' aligns with having satisfied one's own needs to such a degree that the motivations shift to serving others; thus, ranking it at the top and ranking 'surviving' at the bottom of the pyramid, it is argued that its presentation as a hierarchy is an inaccurate representation. While one psychologically develops along the stages, successes and happiness exist at various points along the journey and do not exclusively belong to any stage.

Examples of happiness along the stages are shared by our research participants. Childhood is largely associated with care-free living with little responsibilities and happiness. This is evident in our research participant Meena's explanation of her poem: *"Dear Orchid"* (1.2.3), in which she expresses the loss of joy in growing up, and: *"... losing the joys and safety of youth and the parent-child relationship"*. Similarly, another research participant, Regis Mukumbuzi in explaining his poem: *"You are human"* (3.3.2), states: *"I thoroughly enjoyed my childhood, even more so being a toddler"*. The above participants highlight facets of happiness during the early stage of psychological development. As such, happiness is not an aspiration for progressing along the stages of self-leadership development.

So, if there is no stage to aspire to, then **why bother progressing along the stages?** Lauren Williams in her poem: "Longing *to belong*" (4.2.2), uses the line: *"Self-indulge and inhale contentment of self"* in which she presents an example of the nature of happiness associated with earlier stages of self-leadership development, and contrasts it with happiness at later stages of development in her statement: *"My actions are based on these values and this sense of contentment"*, where values-based living becomes the recipe for one's happiness. As such, in her statement: *"Face your fears, choose problems you enjoy, overcoming them is what gives you joy"*, she suggests that happiness exists in progressing along the stages of self-leadership development, where stagnation, fixation, or becoming trapped at a stage leads to experiences of negative affect, and upon conquering of the stage, the experience of successful 'crossing of an edge'[205] at each stage is awarded with positive affect.

Additionally, our research participant, Namuziya Sikatali in the explanation of her poem: *"Positive lucid dreamer"* (3.2.4), states: *"... something that makes us happy ... is to manage oneself well by creating a balance"*. As such, sharing her perspective that earlier stages of development are potentially more emotionally volatile. While these allow for the high intensity of happiness, such as ecstasy and exhilaration, progressing along the journey of growth entails lower fluctuating emotions in the latter stages, representing a greater balance of emotions, where the recipe for happiness changes to one of seeking to be content and comfortable with who one is, which is a more stable and less fluctuating type of happiness.

While each stage may satisfy individuals, as it presents them with happiness and successes, it raises the question as to **which stage is most useful from a collective or societal perspective?** A 4000-year-old poem listed the attributes of a successful city. Cities are regarded as birthplaces of civilisation, and are still considered to be the places where the aspirations for civilisation find their most concrete expressions.[206]

The warehouses are well-provisioned,
and the houses within the city are well-built.
Those who bathe before the holidays rejoice in the courtyards,
and foreigners flock to and fro like exotic birds.

The old women are full of good advice,
the old men are full of good counsel.
The young women are full of dancing spirit,
the young men are full of fighting spirit,
and the little ones are full of the spirit of joy.
The people are happy!

Unknown[207]

Diversity of different psychological maturity, at different levels of leadership within a society, helps to make it a civilization. As such, the argument prescribes a notion that no stage of self-leadership development effectively ranks above another. Our research participant, Babar Dharani in his poem: "*Soldierly*" (2.3.1), suggests the suitability of those in the conforming stages of psychological growth to family businesses and corporates, where agency relationships dictate – the latter is shared by Lauren in her poem: "*Leadership Claustrophobia*" (3.3.1). As such, leadership emanating from specific stages of psychological development may allow for a better alignment with the leadership needs in different scenarios. For example, "*the young men are full of fighting spirit*" are potentially better led by peers in a similar stage of psychological development in combat scenarios. However, they may be better led by "*The old women*" and "*the old men*" who are full of "*good advice*" and "*good counsel*" in scenarios not pertaining to combat, but to scenarios where counsel and advice are sought by others. It is the diversity of leaders emanating from varying stages of psychological development that supports a community to become a civilisation.

So, if progressing along the stages is a need arising from psychological and emotional maturation, **which transitions between the stages are the easiest and the hardest to accomplish?** While no transition between any stages is identified as being more difficult than another, arguably birth may be regarded as the most seismic transition of them all. "As birth itself seems a kind of gigantic, systemic wound, so the exigencies of everyday life bring other wounds, the wounds of too muchness and not-enoughness, engulfment or abandonment".[208]

Since our research participants have shared ample examples of what has stopped them from progressing along the stages (stumbling blocks), as well as what has facilitated them to cross the edges between the stages (enablers), it emerges that fixations, or traps, at each stage of psychological development, are more specific to the respective stages than the enablers. The reason why enablers emerge to be in common along the journey from one stage to the other is founded on the fact that transitioning from one stage to another emerges – similar to 'crossing an edge'.[209] Each transition requires courage to face fears associated with leaving one stage and progressing on to another. As such, common enablers that facilitate the journey along the stages of self-leadership development are bravery and the ability to cope with anxiety.

However, in addition to generalised enablers for progressing along the stages of self-leadership development, the specificity of 'traps' or 'fixations' at each stage entails that 'stumbling blocks' can be unique to the stages that halt one's continued progression on the path of self-leadership development. To overcome these specific stumbling blocks, certain enablers emerge as conducive for transitioning from one stage to another and which are specific to the stage in question. So, **what are the enablers associated with each stage of transition?**

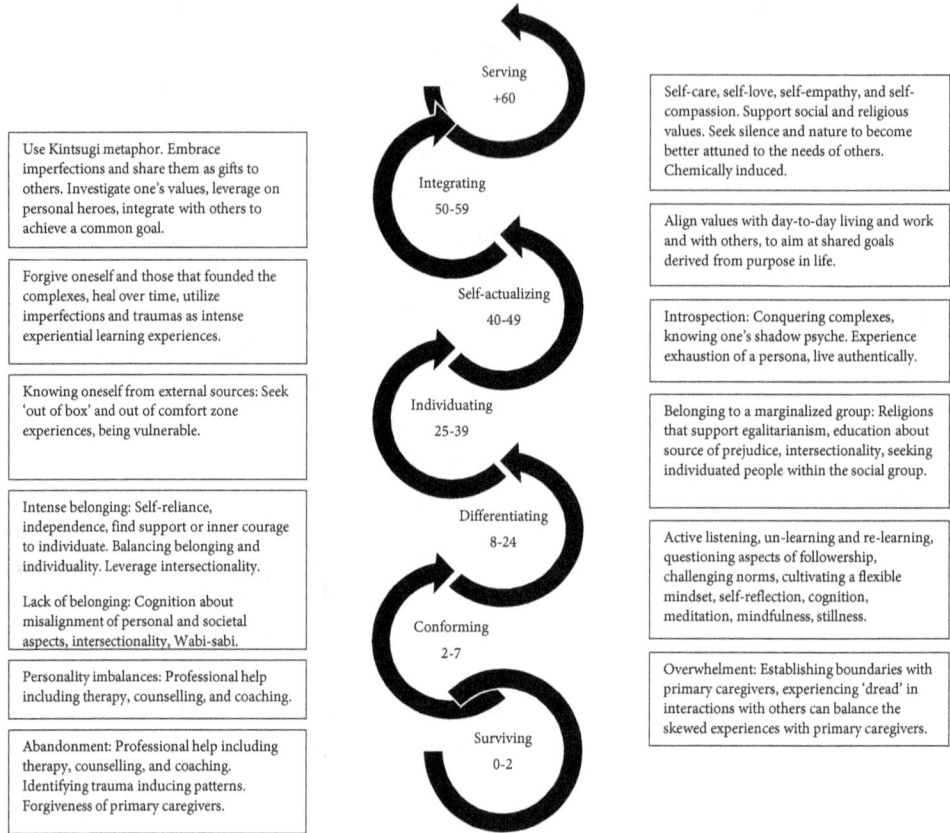

Use Kintsugi metaphor. Embrace imperfections and share them as gifts to others. Investigate one's values, leverage on personal heroes, integrate with others to achieve a common goal.

Self-care, self-love, self-empathy, and self-compassion. Support social and religious values. Seek silence and nature to become better attuned to the needs of others. Chemically induced.

Forgive oneself and those that founded the complexes, heal over time, utilize imperfections and traumas as intense experiential learning experiences.

Align values with day-to-day living and work and with others, to aim at shared goals derived from purpose in life.

Knowing oneself from external sources: Seek 'out of box' and out of comfort zone experiences, being vulnerable.

Introspection: Conquering complexes, knowing one's shadow psyche. Experience exhaustion of a persona, live authentically.

Intense belonging: Self-reliance, independence, find support or inner courage to individuate. Balancing belonging and individuality. Leverage intersectionality.

Belonging to a marginalized group: Religions that support egalitarianism, education about source of prejudice, intersectionality, seeking individuated people within the social group.

Lack of belonging: Cognition about misalignment of personal and societal aspects, intersectionality, Wabi-sabi.

Active listening, un-learning and re-learning, questioning aspects of followership, challenging norms, cultivating a flexible mindset, self-reflection, cognition, meditation, mindfulness, stillness.

Personality imbalances: Professional help including therapy, counselling, and coaching.

Abandonment: Professional help including therapy, counselling, and coaching. Identifying trauma inducing patterns. Forgiveness of primary caregivers.

Overwhelment: Establishing boundaries with primary caregivers, experiencing 'dread' in interactions with others can balance the skewed experiences with primary caregivers.

Figure 1: *Stages of psychological development and typical ages associated with the age. Mapping self-leadership development onto the stages reveals the prominent enablers for progression along the stages.*

SURVIVING

A prime cause of fixation at the survival stage of self-leadership development is the feeling of abandonment during the early years of childhood (1.2). Such existential threats, embedded in the psyche, present the most foundational psychological work for transitioning to the next stage of psychological development. If unattended, they heighten the risk of repeated encounters by unconsciously seeking similar traumas in life, wearing a mask or a persona as a defence mechanism,[210] defining oneself by the roles one performs, evaluating one's self-worth from one's achievements, and most importantly, expecting a change in behaviour from the primary caregivers who are the source of one's psychological scars to remedy the situation – this can become a life-long quest for the individual. Such psychological under-development presents a serious stumbling block for self-leadership development. While it may appear surprising that one consciously or unconsciously repeats the psychological scarring of the stage in later years of life, it is explained by the fact that irrespective of the hardships experienced, since these represented one's 'home' and ensured survival for the child to grow older, it is deemed 'suitable' for one's survival. It is said that: "The attachment between infant and caregiver must be solidified in order for the infant to survive".[211] However, even in the case of physical or psychological harm during these ages, an 'attachment' or a feeling of 'home' for the child during adulthood can form between the harm or trauma-inducing aspects of childhood, which fixates the psyche to search for the same later in life. As such, fixation at the survival stage of psychological growth entails that the same hardships are sought out during adulthood. This leads to self-harming patterns of behaviour or choices, and actually breaking away from the pattern(s) can enable one to progress to further stages of personal psychological growth.

For the survival stage of self-leadership development, our research participants emphasise an inability of unaided cognitive measures to assist (1.1.1). Instead, professional counselling, therapy, and coaching are suggested by our research participants to tackle a fixation at the survival stage of self-leadership development. This suggests that the psychological scars are deep-seated and require professional assistance for one to emerge out of living a life that is founded on ensuring one's survival or the survival of one's family. Therapy, counselling, and coaching can lend a helping hand to either recollection or acknowledgement of traumas experienced, and in segregating the positive aspects of one's childhood that need to be sought in life from those that need to be relinquished from repetition. Thus, professional help can assist in extracting learning from embracing prior traumas and one's imperfect childhood homes, and to use them as tools for reflective learning and development past the survival stage of psychological growth. A key enabler for doing so is the development of self-empathy, self-love, and self-care (1.2.1) to transition one from the survival stage to the stages beyond; thus, launching one on the self-leadership development journey.

CONFORMING

While the survival stage of psychological development is dominated by feelings of abandonment by the primary caregivers, the contrary is a sense of overwhelment or engulfment by them that can facilitate one to move to the conforming stage of psychological development. While sufficient care during the first stage of infancy can enable a transition from survival to the conforming stage, such intense caregiving in the conforming stage has the potential to rob the child of independence. Subsequently, this can trap or fixate one in this second stage of self-leadership development. One stumbling block arising from overwhelment is a disregard for survival needs by the child as an adult, such an inclination to trust everyone. An effective enabler for balancing the imbalance of care by the primary caregivers is to distance oneself from the primary caregivers so as to allow for experiential learning (1.2.3). Such experiential learning includes experiences of traumas from others. Our research participants share the significance of experiencing 'dread',[212] for example, when one's over-trusting behaviour towards others leads to being 'let-down' (1.2.2). Such traumas present useful experiences to balance one's imbalance experienced during formative years.

In addition to the imbalance between abandonment and overwhelment,[213] that is shared by many participants, is one's fundamental psychological traits such as self-esteem[214] and locus of control[215] – these can also develop so as to be skewed towards the polar extremes. In the case of control, while a perception of a lack of self-control over oneself and one's surroundings is regarded as a shortcoming for self-leadership development and corroborated by our participants, the notion of excessive control and its shortcomings are also shared (2.2.1).[216]

Enablers for balancing personality imbalances were contested by the participants. Similar to fixation at the survival stage of psychological development, that is deemed unresolvable by cognitive measures, some of our participants regarded the same for psychological traits (2.2.1); thus, suggesting the need for therapy, counselling, and coaching to address such imbalances. However, in listing enablers for challenging the fundamentals of the conforming stage, which involve obedience and adherence to the family's values and status-quos, cognitive measures are shared as effective enablers. As such, we conclude that imbalances in personality development during the stage of conforming may also require professional assistance. While milder personality imbalance problems may be resolvable through introspection, the fundamental traps associated with the stage of conforming are founded on followership of the family's status-quo. Our research participants share the possibility of effectively challenging these by cognitive thought processes. As such, active listening, unlearning and re-learning, and a flexible mindset (2.1.4) can enable one to transition from this stage of psychological growth.

Additionally, along with cognitive measures, the significance of self-reflection through thought processes and journaling, stillness of the mind through contemplative tools such as mindfulness and meditation (2.1.5), and other tools of cognitive measures start to emerge as enablers at the conforming stage. Since the earlier stages of psychological development are explained using evolutionary psychology and behaviourism, that are founded on a link between the stimuli in the external environment and the responses of humans to it, human behavioural responses appear to support hard-determinism[217] that rejects the notion of free-will. However, our research suggests that free-will appears as a distinctly significant lever for progressing along the stages of self-leadership development. Firstly, by exercising free-will to succumb to parental pressures in the conforming stage, thereafter peer-pressure in the differentiating stage of development, and free-will to support an increasingly authentic self emerges as the essence of the journey along the next few stages of self-leadership development. Threats appear out of nowhere, such as depression and mid-life crises, but our research participants suggest that threats associated with psychological growth cannot be effectively addressed through 'noise' and 'busy-ness', but rather through purposeful cognition. As such, a lack of cognition can lead to trapping at any subsequent stage of self-leadership development.

DIFFERENTIATING

Similar to the risk of an imbalance between abandonment and overwhelment in the earlier stages, in the differentiating stage of psychological development, a fixation can arise from an imbalance of either an inability to find a group to belong to or an overindulgence in belonging to a group. Both act as a stumbling block for individuation. Thoroughly belonging to a social group can lead to such 'comfort' and a feeling of 'home' that peeling one away is seen as a threat to one's well-being. Similarly, a lack of belonging leaves the desire to belong to a group unsatisfied, as such fixating one to strive to belong to a group which involves the adoption of behavioural aspects of the group in order to 'fit-in'.[218] Such a compulsion, that leads to mimicking a group, acts as a stumbling block for individuating (3.2.2). As such, a balance that is achievable by maintaining a sense of belonging to a group while retaining one's individuality permits an optimal level of attachment to the group while supporting one's uniqueness, thereby enabling individuation.[219] Additionally, our research participants share enablers that, specifically in reference to the differentiating stage, facilitated a transitioning into the individuation stage of self-leadership development. These include an awareness that one needs to stop searching for a 'home' in others, but to seek the feeling within oneself (3.2.5). Similarly, it also re-emerges in love relationships, where the dependence on a magical other[220] for personal happiness and for making one 'whole' are deemed to be a youthful view of love relationships that needs to develop into self-reliance for completing oneself.

The context for many of our research participants' lived experiences was Southern Africa. As such, founded on race relations that have historically divided countries, a novel perspective emerges from the struggles associated with a significant, societal presumption of negative attributes towards black people (3.2.2). Firstly, the societal divide pulls one's identity to be founded on race. However, the negative connotations associated with certain races, and aspirations for self-betterment in contrast to the societal views or for escaping societal prejudices, can push one's identity away from the social group. Our participants share the challenge of the above, and present enablers that have facilitated their psychological growth from this trap. For example, a belief in God and followership of religion that supports egalitarianism enables one to belong to one's respective race while denouncing inequality (3.2.3). A cognitive understanding of prejudice and where it stems from enables one to reject societal notions (3.2.2). Our research participants also suggest leveraging alternative identities within oneself to enable one to differentiate oneself from the social group one belongs to (3.2.1), thus prescribing to the theory of intersectionality.[221] Knowing that one's identity is intersectional, and is derived from more social categories than one's race facilitates the balance of belonging yet differentiating oneself from a group. Lastly, finding people who belong to the social category that exhibits traits of individuation (3.2.4) can assist one in collectively challenging the pigeonholing, stereotyping, and prejudices associated with the social group.

INDIVIDUATING

As with all stages, a stumbling block for progressing from the differentiating stage to the individuating stage is fear. In the progression from the differentiating stage to the individuating stage, this fear of differentiating oneself from the social group that one belongs to can be confronted with the assistance of feelings of guilt as an enabler. Guilt is felt for not aspiring to individuate and fulfil one's full potential (4.2). Other stumbling blocks include one's daily routine (4.3.1), which does not allow for sufficient time, change in one's activities, or times of silence (4.3.3) for better knowing oneself (4.3.2). Enablers to individuation are shared as freeing oneself by experiencing new things, stepping out of one's comfort zone, and one's routine (4.3.1). Leveraging on Jung's[222] concept of individuation, psychological enablers for knowing oneself are enabled through exploring one's unconscious mind (complexes (4.4) and the shadow psyche (4.6.2)). By exploring one's unconscious psyche, one can become wholly oneself. While theories prescribe the recipe of conquering complexes by linking them to the traumas that seeded them, and giving them time for healing, our research participants share how the process can be facilitated or sped-up through forgiveness (of both oneself and others who caused the trauma) to enable one to escape fixation (4.3.4).

Upon exploring oneself fully, and denouncing the uncritical followership of family and societal predestination, one confronts one's imperfections in the eyes of the family or the society that one belongs to. A novel contribution to the individuation stage of self-leadership development by our research participants is the introduction of the Japanese philosophy of Wabi-sabi (4.5) that requires one to embrace one's perceived imperfections in the eyes of oneself, one's family, or one's social group. This concept provides philosophical foundations for the psychological concept of ego-dissolution.[223] By shifting one's aim not to attend to one's ego, but to incorporate one's unconscious parts of the psyche, one can strive towards being authentic. Enablers that support one to accept one's weaknesses and imperfections range from exhaustion felt due to the energy required to maintain a persona, or in keeping up appearances, or in hiding one's imperfections (4.5.3), or learning to live with one's vulnerabilities and embracing them (4.6.1).

SELF-ACTUALIZING

The role of traumas in life emerges as a significant enabler for self-actualization, as these represent opportunities for accelerated, experiential learning from which substantial psychological growth emerges. The utilization of traumas/struggles for self-leadership development is founded on the principles of Wabi-sabi, but requires one to metaphorically incorporate the Japanese art-practice of kintsugi (5.1). Adopting the metaphor of kintsugi practice, we notice that the individuated self has an extremely high level of authenticity in its clear celebration that the original, inauthentic self cannot be retained. This metaphor allows one to not only accept one's imperfections, but to embrace the overcoming and mending of them so that one is stronger, and beautify them with 'gold strands' that emerged during challenges/struggles (e.g., the personal resilience that emerged during struggle, strategies for working around poverty, and so on) so that they become one's assets/gifts that need not be hidden but, as in Plato's *The Republic*, be compassionately presented to the world to serve the common good and humanity (using one's gift to help release others from their own chains/scars/challenges). Essentially, without the possibility of scars over time, there can be no beauty, no gift. This orientation requires a radical philosophical shift from feeling ashamed of one's imperfections, traumas, brokenness and vulnerabilities, to seeing them through fresh, constructive eyes. Founded on an ability to view one's scars as an asset can leverage one to the heights of achievement associated with the stage of self-actualization. As such, traumas become vital enablers for, and healing integral and not something to disguise during, self-actualization – in many ways, a celebration of the irreversible nature of Self.

INTEGRATING

A key outcome of self-actualization is the cognition of one's values. Upon becoming knowledgeable of one's values, an alignment of one's values with one's everyday life is naturally sought. An affect-related enabler experienced as a shift from enjoyment in predominantly hedonic to a preference towards eudaimonic happiness[224] emerges (6.3.3). Such alignment during the integrating stage gives one meaning and purpose in life. To facilitate in the uncovering of one's values, the significance of self-reflection through thought processes and journaling (6.3.5), stillness of the mind through contemplative tools such as mindfulness and meditation (2.1.5, 4.3.3, 6.3.4) even if these lead to experiences of boredom,[225] emerge as tools that enable and facilitate in this transition.

Additionally, heroes serve a vital purpose in assisting people to know their values in life. To follow heroes is to follow the values they represent or represented. By integrating with those who share the same visions; hence, the same heroes, one can align one's values with others and with organizations of work. Nonetheless, the perspective on heroes shifts during one's psychological progression along the stages, from unattainable goals that are set for oneself during childhood, to greater scrutiny of heroes and their intentions in the latter stages of self-leadership development. This is facilitated by becoming more deeply acquainted with one's values and values-motivations, incorporating them in one's life, and hence developing the ability to challenge the embodiment of those values by societal heroes (6.2.3).

Additionally, a novel enabler for finding one's purpose in life is shared by our research participants which most people regard as coincidences (6.3.6). Our research participants that have a religious inclination share how the universe or powerful force in an individual's life guides them to their purpose or calling through a natural unfolding of their life, and the enabler is helped by cognition of such an intervention or opportunities that they may come across.

SERVING

A challenge of the integrating stage is shared by our research participants: aligning one's values with one's everyday life and work bears the risk of engaging with like-minded people. As such, a lack of 'value-diversity' around people and in organizations can emerge for the intention of achieving a shared purpose (7.2.1). An enabler for overcoming such a risk is a greater emphasis or priority towards the social and religious values.[226] These encourage one to progress towards the serving stage (7.1.2), where love and care for all humans is the key foundational element. Such care in organizational settings promotes the growth of subordinates and followers of such leaders. A leader who has not matured through the stages of self-leadership development will find it difficult to not only facilitate, but even allow others to individuate and become mature themselves.[227] Such a leaders' "... actions are geared toward improvement. Not just improvement for yourself, but for all stakeholders".[228]

Several enablers are shared by our research participants to facilitate progression to this stage; however, a foundational element of care for others is said to start with due care for oneself. As such, self-care, self-love, self-compassion, and self-empathy emerge as being fundamental for the serving stage of psychological development (7.1.6). Additionally, the impact of one's surrounding environment where one spends time or lives, is a significant enabler. A connection with nature, such as living by the sea or in a rural community, that is 'noise-free' allows one to be more attuned with nature, which nurtures looking through the perspectives and addressing the needs of other people (7.1.3). As such, silence and tools associated with facilitating moments of being present continue to emerge as enablers up to this last stage of self-leadership development.

A more dramatic mind-shift towards heightened care for others can also be achieved through chemically induced methods (7.1.5). These are often associated with indigenous, initiation ceremonies of transitioning from youth to adulthood, where selfishness associated with earlier stages of psychological development needs to be transformed for care for the entire tribe or society for the survival of the group. Such servitude is facilitated by certain rituals during which natural chemicals from plants and animals trigger the reliving of traumas, some through hallucinations, so as to force one to confront and address them.

CONCLUSION

Though we conclude that a lack of hierarchy between the stages of psychological development, and desirability of different leaderships emanating from various stages of self-leadership development to be suited to different scenarios, maturation dictates that progression along the stages becomes necessary upon psychological saturation within the stage, which dampens positive affect and triggers negative affect and demands crossing of an edge to progress to the next stage of psychological development for one's own well-being. In doing so, such progression presents novel opportunities for leadership and serving for the collective or communities.

Nonetheless, the journey across the stages is brim-full with stumbling blocks and traps to fixate one at any stage of psychological development. Though specific enablers are shared for each transitioning between the stages of development, certain shared enablers emerge as helpful tools for progression along several stages of the journey. Since these enablers have emerged from our research as common when transitioning from one stage to the next, these can be regarded as 'generalized enablers' for the journey to self-leadership. With the possible exceptions of fixation at the survival stage of psychological development and addressing significant personality imbalances, self-awareness and cognition developed either through tools that facilitate introspection or engagement in varied people, activities, and environments present vital learning opportunities for the journey along the stages of self-leadership development.

While imbalances consistently emerge as stumbling blocks, thus representing 'generalized stumbling blocks' for progression along the self-leadership journey, a vital element that was commonly shared was negative experiences, or traumas, that with the philosophical shifts in one's mindset bear the potential for exponential learning and growth through healing. This conclusion supports the need for a philosophical shift from aspiring for perfectionism in earlier stages to nurturing Wabi-sabi philosophical principles for successful progression along the journey of self-leadership. This conclusion goes hand-in-hand with empirical research that has confirmed the decrease of perfectionism tendencies with age,[229] which suggests that maturation requires an acceptance of one's imperfections[230]. However, for self-leadership, our research concludes the need to go beyond abandonment of striving for perfection and acceptance of one's imperfections. For self-leadership, the need for a cognitive shift to regard one's imperfections, particularly traumatic psychological experiences, as personal assets and as potential gifts to society presents a vital engine for a heroic journey[231] through the stages of self-leadership.

REFERENCE LIST

Ahmed, S. (2010). *The promise of happiness*. Durham: Duke University Press.

Allison, S. T., & Goethals, G. R. (2013). *Heroic leadership*. London: Routledge.

Anderson, C. R., & Schneier, C. E. (1978). Locus of control, leader behavior and leader performance among management students. *Academy of Management Journal, 21*(4), 690–698. https://doi.org/10.2307/255709

April, K. A., Dharani, B., & April, A. (2022 in press). *Lived experiences of exclusion: The psychological and behavioural effects*. Bingley: Emerald Publishing.

April, K. A., Dharani, B., & Peters, K. (2011). Leader career success and locus of control expectancy. *Academy of Taiwan Business Management Review, 7*(3), 28–40.

April, K. A., Dharani, B., & Peters, K. (2012). Impact of locus of control expectancy on level of well-being. *Review of European Studies, 4*(2), 124–137. https://doi.org/10.5539/res.v4n2p124

Bakker, A. B., & Demerouti, E. (2008). Towards a model of work engagement. *Career Development International, 13*(3), 209–223. https://doi.org/10.1108/13620430810870476

Bakker, A. B., Schaufeli, W. B., Leiter, M. P., & Taris, T. W. (2008). Work engagement: An emerging concept in occupational health psychology. *Work & Stress, 22*(3), 187–200. https://doi.org/10.1080/02678370802393649

Baltaci, A., & Balcı, A. (2017). Complexity leadership: A theorical perspective. *International Journal of Educational Leadership and Management, 5*(1), 30–58. https://doi.org/10.17583/ijelm.2017.2435

Barrett, R. (2016). *A new psychology of human well-being: An exploration of the influence of ego-soul dynamics on mental and physical health*. London: Richard Barrett Fulfilling Books.

Baumeister, R., Dale, K., & Sommer, K. (1998). Freudian defense mechanisms and empirical findings in modern social psychology: Reaction formation, projection, displacement, undoing, isolation, sublimation, and denial. *Journal of Personality, 66*(6), 1081–1124. https://doi.org/Doi 10.1111/1467-6494.00043

Boyd, R., & Richerson, P. J. (2009). Culture and the evolution of human cooperation. *Philosophical Transactions of the Royal Society B: Biological Sciences, 364*(1533), 3281–3288. https://doi.org/10.1098/rstb.2009.0134

Braslow, M. D., Guerrettaz, J., Arkin, R. M., & Oleson, K. C. (2012). Self-doubt. *Social and Personality Psychology Compass, 6*(6), 470–482. https://doi.org/10.1111/j.1751-9004.2012.00441.x

Bretz, R. D., & Judge, T. A. (1994). Person–organization fit and the theory of work adjustment: Implications for satisfaction, tenure, and career success. *Journal of Vocational Behavior, 44*(1), 32–54. https://doi.org/10.1006/jvbe.1994.1003

Bricheno, P., & Thornton, M. (2007). Role model, hero or champion? Children's views concerning role models. *Educational Research, 49*(4), 383–396. https://doi.org/10.1080/00131880701717230

Brons, L. (2015). Othering, an analysis. *Transcience, A Journal of Global Studies, 6*(1), 69–90. https://doi.org/http://dx.doi.org/10.17613/M6V968

Buckingham, W., Burnham, D., Hill, C., King, P. J., Marenbon, J., & Weeks, M. (2011). *The philosophy book: The big ideas simply explained*. London: Dorling Kindersley.

Buetow, S., & Wallis, K. (2019). The beauty in perfect imperfection. *Journal of Medical Humanities, 40*(3), 389–394. https://doi.org/10.1007/s10912-017-9500-2

Burrow, T. (1917). The theories of Freud, Jung and Adler: II. *The Journal of Abnormal Psychology, 12*(3), 161–167. https://doi.org/10.1037/h0070901

Clark, K. B., & Clark, M. P. (1950). Emotional factors in racial identification and preference in negro children. *The Journal of Negro Education, 19*(3), 341–350. https://doi.org/10.2307/2966491

Cook-Greuter, S. R. (2000). Mature ego development: A gateway to ego transcendence? *Journal of Adult Development, 7*(4), 227–240. https://doi.org/10.1023/A:1009511411421

Corlett, J., & Pearson, C. (2003). *Mapping the organizational psyche: A Jungian theory of organizational dynamics and change*. Gainesville: Centre of Application of Psychological Type.

Coughlan, G., Igou, E. R., van Tilburg, W. A. P., Kinsella, E. L., & Ritchie, T. D. (2019). On boredom and perceptions of heroes: A meaning-regulation approach to heroism. *Journal of Humanistic Psychology, 59*(4), 455–473. https://doi.org/10.1177/0022167817705281

Crenshaw, K. (1991). Mapping the margins: Intersectionality, identity politics, and violence against women of color. *Stanford Law Review, 43*(6), 1241–1299. https://doi.org/10.2307/1229039

Csikszentmihalyi, M. (1990). *Flow: The psychology of optimal experience*. New York: Harper and Row.

Damiani, J., Haywood Rolling Jr, J., & Wieczorek, D. (2017). Rethinking leadership education: Narrative inquiry and leadership stories. *Reflective Practice, 18*(5), 673–687. https://doi.org/10.1080/146239 43.2017.1307726

Darwin, C. (1859). *On the origin of species*. London: John Murray.

Derrick, W., Smith, J., Brandon, M., Searle, G., Clay, J., Robinson, S., & Johnston, G. (2005). *Tribe*. UK: BBC Worldwide Ltd./Discovery Channel Corporation.

Dharani, B. (2019). *Organizational lifecycle and happiness at work: Investigating best-fit for employees based on their locus of control expectancy* (Unpublished Doctoral thesis, Graduate School of Business, University of Cape Town).

Dharani, B., Giannaros, M., & April, K. (2021). Alleviating state boredom through search for meaning and affirmation of workplace heroes. *Management Research Review, 44*(9), 1298-1319. https://doi.org/10.1108/MRR-08-2020-0490

Dharani, B., Vergo, O., & April, K. (2020). An intersectional approach to hegemonic masculinity and internal hegemony: A thematic analysis in South African men. *Journal of Gender Studies, 30*(3), 329–343. https://doi.org/10.1080/09589236.2020.1852918

Diener, E., Emmons, R. A., Larsen, R. J., & Griffin, S. (1985). The satisfaction with life scale. *Journal of Personality Assessment, 49*(1), 71–75. https://doi.org/10.1207/s15327752jpa4901_13

Duguid, M. M., & Thomas-Hunt, M. C. (2015). Condoning stereotyping? How awareness of stereotyping prevalence impacts expression of stereotypes. *Journal of Applied Psychology, 100*(2), 343–359. https://doi.org/10.1037/a0037908

Edwards, J. (1991). Person-job fit: A conceptual integration, literature review, and methodological critique. In *International Review of Industrial and Organizational Psychology* (Vol. 6, pp. 283–357). London: Wiley.

Ein-Dor, T. (2015). Attachment dispositions and human defensive behavior. *Personality and Individual Differences, 81*(1), 112–116. https://doi.org/10.1016/j.paid.2014.09.033

Eisenhardt, K. M. (1989). Agency theory: An assessment and review. *Academy of Management Review, 14*(1), 57–74. https://doi.org/10.5465/amr.1989.4279003

Fahlman, S. A., Mercer, K. B., Gaskovski, P., Eastwood, A. E., & Eastwood, J. D. (2009). Does a lack of life meaning cause boredom? Results from psychometric, longitudinal, and experimental analyses. *Journal of Social and Clinical Psychology, 28*(3), 307–340. https://doi.org/10.1521/jscp.2009.28.3.307

Fisher, C. D. (2014). Conceptualizing and measuring wellbeing at work. In P. Y. Chen & C. L. Cooper (Eds.), *Wellbeing: A complete reference guide, Work and wellbeing* (Vol. 3, pp. 9–33). New York: Wiley Blackwell. https://doi.org/10.1002/9781118539415.wbwell018

Franco, Z. E., & Efthimiou, O. (2018). Heroism and the human experience: Foreword to the special issue. *Journal of Humanistic Psychology, 58*(4), 371–381. https://doi.org/10.1177/0022167818772201

Frankl, V. E. (1984). *Man's search for meaning* (Rev.). New York: Washington Square Press/Pocket Books.

Glaeser, L., & Glendon, S. (1998). Incentives, predestination and free will. *Economic Inquiry, 36*(3), 429–443. https://doi.org/10.1111/j.1465-7295.1998.tb01724.x

Goethals, G. R., & Allison, S. T. (2012). Making heroes: The construction of courage, competence and virtue. In J. Olson & M. Zanna (Eds.), *Advances in experimental social sychology* (1st ed., Vol. 46, pp. 183–235). San Diego: Academic Press.

Greenleaf, R. (2007). The servant as leader. In W. C. Zimmerli, K. Richter, & M. Holzinger (Eds.), *Corporate ethics and corporate governance* (pp. 79–85). Berlin: Springer-Verlag.

Greenleaf, R. (2002). *Servant leadership: A journey into the nature of legitimate power and greatness* (25th anniversary ed.). New Jersey: Paulist Press.

Greenleaf, R. K. (1995). Servant leadership. In J. T. Wren (Ed.), *The leader's companion: Insights on leadership through the ages* (pp. 18–23). New York, NY: The Free Press. https://doi.org/10.1016/j.jada.2010.04.021

Grey, N., & Holmes, E. A. (2008). "Hotspots" in trauma memories in the treatment of post-traumatic stress disorder: A replication. *Memory, 16*(7), 788–796. https://doi.org/10.1080/09658210802266446

Grisham, T. (2006). Metaphor, poetry, storytelling and cross-cultural leadership. *Management Decision, 44*(4), 486-503. https://doi.org/10.1108/00251740610663027

Guerin, D. W., Oliver, P. H., Gottfried, A. W., Gottfried, A. E., Reichard, R. J., & Riggio, R. E. (2011). Childhood and adolescent antecedents of social skills and leadership potential in adulthood: Temperamental approach/withdrawal and extraversion. *The Leadership Quarterly, 22*(3), pp. 482–494. https://doi.org/10.1016/j.leaqua.2011.04.006

Gusmano, B. (2018). The kintsugi art of care: Unraveling consent in ethical non-monogamies. *Sociological Research Online, 24*(4), 661–679. https://doi.org/10.1177/1360780418816103

Hamilton, W. D. (1970). Selfish and spiteful behaviour in an evolutionary model. *Nature, 228*(5277), 1218–1220. https://doi.org/10.1038/2281218a0

Hansemark, O. C. (1998). The effects of an entrepreneurship programme on need for achievement and locus of control of reinforcement. *International Journal of Entrepreneurial Behaviour & Research, 4*(1), 28–50. https://doi.org/10.1108/13552559810203957

Hjelle, L., & Ziegler, D. (1976). *Personality theories: Basic assumption, research and applications.* New York: McGraw-Hill.

Hodgetts, D., & Rua, M. (2010). What does it mean to be a man today? Bloke culture and the media. *American Journal of Community Psychology, 45*(1–2), 155–168. https://doi.org/10.1007/s10464-009-9287-z

Hollis, J. (1998). *The Eden project: In search of the magical other.* Toronto: Inner City Books.

Holmes, O. W., Bourdieu, P., & Wacquant, L. J. D. (1994). An invitation to reflexive sociology. *The American Historical Review, 99*(5), 1644–1645. https://doi.org/10.2307/2168398

Hsiao, C., Lee, Y.-H., & Chen, H.-H. (2016). The effects of internal locus of control on entrepreneurship: The mediating mechanisms of social capital and human capital. *The International Journal of Human Resource Management, 27*(11), 1158–1172. https://doi.org/10.1080/09585192.2015.1060511

Huta, V. (2015). The complementary roles of eudaimonia and hedonia and how they can be pursued in practice. In S. Joseph (Ed.), *Positive psychology in practice: Promoting human flourishing in work, health, education, and everday life* (2nd ed., pp. 159–182). Hoboken, NJ: John Wiley & Sons. https://doi.org/10.1002/9781118996874.ch10

Huxley, A. (1932). *Brave new world*. London: Chatto & Windus.

Iilling, H. A. (1963). Memories, dreams, reflections. *American Journal of Psychiatry, 120*(6), 616–616. https://doi.org/10.1176/ajp.120.6.616

James, W. (2014). The dilemma of determinism. In W. James, *The will to believe and other essays in popular philosophy* (Vol. 13, pp. 145–183). Cambridge: Cambridge University Press.

Janis, I. L. (1972). Victims of groupthink: A psychological study of foreign-policy decisions and fiascoes. Boston: Houghton Mifflin.

Jones, A., & Crandall, R. (1986). Validation of a short index of self-actualization. *Personality and Social Psychology Bulletin, 12*(1), 63–73. https://doi.org/10.1177/0146167286121007

Jones, P. (2018). Mindfulness-based heroism: Creating enlightened heroes. *Journal of Humanistic Psychology, 58*(5), 501–524. https://doi.org/10.1177/0022167817711303

Jung, C. G. (1921). *"Psychological types". Collected works of C.G. Jung.* Princeton: Princeton University Press.

Jung, C. G. (1985). *Modern man in search of a soul* (1st ed.). London: Routledge. https://doi.org/10.4324/9780203991701

Kahn, W. A. (1990). Psychological conditions of personal engagement and disengagement at work. *Academy of Management Journal, 33*(4), 692–724. https://doi.org/10.2307/256287

Kaufmann, P., Welsh, D., & Bushmarin, N. (1995). Locus of control and entrepreneurship in the Russian Republic. *Entrepreneurship: Theory & Practice, 20*(1), 43–56. https://doi.org/10.1017/CBO9781107415324.004

Kenneth, C. (1943). *The nature of explanation*. Cambridge: Cambridge University Press.

Keulemans, G. (2016). The geo-cultural conditions of kintsugi. *Journal of Modern Craft, 9*(1), 15–34. https://doi.org/10.1080/17496772.2016.1183946

Kierkegaard, S. (2017). From the concept of dread. In N. Langiulli (Ed.), *European existentialism*. New York: Routledge.

King, M. (1999). *Mahatma Gandhi and Martin Luther King Jr.: The power of nonviolent action.* Paris: UNESCO Publishing.

Kinsella, E. L., Ritchie, T. D., & Igou, E. R. (2015). Zeroing in on heroes: A prototype analysis of hero features. *Journal of Personality and Social Psychology, 108*(1), 114–127. https://doi.org/10.1037/a0038463

Kirby, T. (2010). *Ancient worlds*. UK: BBC Worldwide Ltd.

Kroeck, K., Bullough, A., & Reynolds, P. (2010). Entrepreneurship and differences in locus of control. *Journal of Applied Management and Entrepreneurship, 15*(1), 21–49.

Landa, C. E., & Bybee, J. A. (2007). Adaptive elements of aging: Self-image discrepancy, perfectionism, and eating problems. *Developmental Psychology, 43*(1), 83–93. https://doi.org/10.1037/0012-1649.43.1.83

Letheby, C., & Gerrans, P. (2017). Self unbound: Ego dissolution in psychedelic experience. *Neuroscience of Consciousness, 2017*(1), 1–11. https://doi.org/10.1093/nc/nix016

Levon, E., Milani, T. M., & Kitis, E. D. (2017). The topography of masculine normativities in South Africa. *Critical Discourse Studies, 14*(5), 514–531. https://doi.org/10.1080/17405904.2017.1342678

Lewin, K. (1947). Frontiers in group dynamics. *Human Relations*, *1*(1), 5–41. https://doi. org/10.1177/001872674700100103

Littunen, H., & Storhammar, E. (2000). The indicators of locus of control in the small business context. *Journal of Enterprising Culture*, *8*(4), 343–360. https://doi.org/10.1142/S0218495800000188

Luyt, R. (2012). Constructing hegemonic masculinities in South Africa: The discourse and rhetoric of heteronormativity. *Gender and Language*, *6*(1), 47–78. https://doi.org/10.1558/genl.v6i1.47

Luyt, R. (2015). Beyond traditional understanding of gender measurement: The gender (re)presentation approach. *Journal of Gender Studies*, *24*(2), 207–226. https://doi.org/10.1080/09589236.2013.824 378

Manz, C. C. (2015). Taking the self-leadership high road: Smooth surface or potholes ahead? *Academy of Management Perspectives*, *29*(1), 132–151. https://doi.org/10.5465/amp.2013.0060

Marques, J. (2013). Understanding the strength of gentleness: Soft-skilled leadership on the rise. *Journal of Business Ethics*, *116*(1), 163–171. https://doi.org/10.1007/s10551-012-1471-7

Marques, J. (2020). *The Routledge companion to happiness at work* (J. Marques, Ed.). New York: Routledge.

Marques, J., & Dhiman, S. (1998). *Leadership today: Practices for personal and professional performance* (J. Marques & S. Dhiman, Eds.). London: Macmillan Education UK.

Marques, J., & Dhiman, S. (Eds.) (2018). *Engaged leadership: Transforming through future-oriented design thinking*. Cham, Switzerland: Springer International Publishing. https://doi.org/10.1007/978-3- 319-72221-4

Maslow, A. H. (1943). A theory of human motivation. *Psychological Review*, *50*(4), 370–396. https://doi. org/10.1037/h0054346

McCullough, P. M., Ashbridge, D., & Pegg, R. (1994). The effect of self-esteem, family structure, locus of control, and career goals on adolescent leadership behavior. *Adolescence*, *29*(115), 605–611. https://doi.org/Available at: http://www.ncbi.nlm.nih.gov/pubmed/7832024

Messner, M. A. (1998). The limits of "the male sex role." *Gender & Society*, *12*(3), 255–276. https://doi. org/10.1177/0891243298012003002

Miles, R. (2010). *Ancient worlds: The search for the origins of western civilization*. London: Allen Lane.

Miller, D., & Toulouse, J.-M. (1986). Chief executive personality and corporate strategy and structure in small firms. *Management Science*, *32*(11), 1389–1409. https://doi.org/10.1287/mnsc.32.11.1389

Mindell, A. (1995). *Sitting in the fire: Large group transformation using conflict and diversity*. Portland: Lao Tse Press.

Moolman, B. (2017). Negotiating masculinities and authority through intersecting discourses of tradition and modernity in South Africa. *NORMA: International Journal for Masculinity Studies*, *12*(1), 38–47. https://doi.org/10.1080/18902138.2017.1293398

Cheng, J. T., Tracy, J. L., & Anderson, C. (Eds.) (2014). *The psychology of social status*. New York: Springer-Verlag.

Mumford, M. D., Watts, L. L., & Partlow, P. J. (2015). Leader cognition: Approaches and findings. *The Leadership Quarterly*, *26*(3), 301–306. https://doi.org/10.1016/j.leaqua.2015.03.005

Neck, C. P., & Milliman, J. F. (1994). Thought self☒leadership. *Journal of Managerial Psychology*, *9*(6), 9–16. https://doi.org/10.1108/02683949410070151

Neff, K. D., Kirkpatrick, K. L., & Rude, S. S. (2007). Self-compassion and adaptive psychological functioning. *Journal of Research in Personality*, *41*(1), 139–154. https://doi.org/10.1016/j. jrp.2006.03.004

Neisser, U. (1967). *Cognitive psychology*. London: Meredith Publishing Company.

Nelson, D. L., & Cooper, C. L. (2007). *Positive organizational behavior*. London: SAGE Publications Ltd.

Nienaber, H., & Martins, N. (2014). An employee engagement instrument and framework building on existing research. *Mediterranean Journal of Social Sciences, 5*(20), 485–496. https://doi.org/10.5901/mjss.2014.v5n20p485

Oles, P. K., & Hermans, H. J. M. (2010). Allport-Vernon study of values. In *The corsini encyclopedia of psychology* (pp. 67-68). New Jersey: John Wiley & Sons, Inc. https://doi.org/10.1002/9780470479216.corpsy0038

Patton, L. D., Shahjahan, R. A., & Osei-Kofi, N. (2010). Introduction to the emergent approaches to diversity and social justice in higher education special issue. *Equity and Excellence in Education, 43*(3), 265–278. https://doi.org/10.1080/10665684.2010.496692

Racine, W. P. (2015). Social identity development and the situation of scientists and engineers as new leaders. *Journal of Leadership Studies, 9*(3), 23–41. https://doi.org/10.1002/jls

Randel, A. E., Galvin, B. M., Shore, L. M., Ehrhart, K. H., Chung, B. G., Dean, M. A., & Kedharnath, U. (2018). Inclusive leadership: Realizing positive outcomes through belongingness and being valued for uniqueness. *Human Resource Management Review, 28*(2), 190–203. https://doi.org/10.1016/j.hrmr.2017.07.002

Rojas, M., & Veenhoven, R. (2013). Contentment and affect in the estimation of happiness. *Social Indicators Research, 110*(2), 415–431. https://doi.org/10.1007/s11205-011-9952-0

Roszak, T., Gomes, M. E., & Kanner, A. D. (1995). *Ecopsychology: Restoring the earth, healing the mind*. San Francisco: Sierra Club Books.

Rotter, J. B. (1966). Generalized expectancies for internal versus external control of reinforcement. *Psychological Monographs: General and Applied, 80*(1), 1–30. https://doi.org/10.1017/CBO9781107415324.004

Rowan, J. (2015). Self-actualization and individuation. *Self & Society, 43*(3), 231–236. https://doi.org/10.1080/03060497.2015.1092332

Ryff, C. D. (2014). Self-realisation and meaning making in the face of adversity: A eudaimonic approach to human resilience. *Journal of Psychology in Africa, 24*(1), 1–12. https://doi.org/10.1080/14330237.2014.904098

Salinas, C. J., & Beatty, C. (2013). Constructing our own definition of masculinity: An intersectionality approach. *Men and Masulinities, ACPA Annual Convention*, 24–29. Las Vegas.

Sansone, C., & Harackiewicz, J. M. (2000). *Intrinsic and extrinsic motivation: The search for optimal motivation and performance* (D. P. Gary, Ed.). San Diego: Academic Press.

Schaufeli, W. B., & Salanova, M. (2014). Burnout, boredom and engagement in the workplace. In M. C. W. Peeters, J. de Jonge, & T. Taris (Eds.), *An introduction to contemporary work psychology* (pp. 293–318). New York: John Wiley & Sons.

Schraw, G. (1998). Promoting general metacognitive awareness. *Instructional Science, 26*(1–2), 113–125. https://doi.org/10.1007/978-94-017-2243-8_1

Seligman, M. E. P. (1972). Learned helplessness. *Annual Review of Medicine, 23*(1), 407–412. https://doi.org/10.1146/annurev.me.23.020172.002203

Seligman, M. E. P. (1975). *Helplessness: On depression, development, and death*. San Francisco: W.H. Freeman.

Shirom, A. (2010). Feeling energetic at work: On vigor's antecedents, in A. B. Bakker, & M. P. Leiter, *Work engagement: A handbook of essential theory and research* (pp. 69-84). Hove, East Sussex: Psychology Press.

Shuck, B., & Reio, T. G. (2014). Employee engagement and well-being: A moderation model and implications for practice. *Journal of Leadership & Organizational Studies, 21*(1), 43–58. https://doi.org/10.1177/1548051813494240

Skinner, B. (2009). About behaviorism (1974). In *Foundations of psychological thought: A history of psychology* (pp. 261–278). Thousand Oaks: Sage.

Smit, H. (2014). *The depth facilitatator's handbook: Transforming group dynamics.* Cape Town: Moonshine Media.

Spranger, E. (1928). *Types of men: The psychology and ethics of personality.* Halle: Max Niemeyer Verlag.

Stoeber, J., & Stoeber, F. S. (2009). Domains of perfectionism: Prevalence and relationships with perfectionism, gender, age, and satisfaction with life. *Personality and Individual Differences, 46*(4), 530–535. https://doi.org/10.1016/j.paid.2008.12.006

Thomas, J. C., & Segal, D. L. (2006). *Comprehensive handbook of personality and psychopathology: Personality and everyday functioning* (Vol. 2). New Jersey: John Wiley & Sons, Inc.

Toit, D., Veldsman, T., & Van Zyl, D. (2016, July). The testing and validation of a model for leadership maturity based on Jung's concept of individuation. *7th European Conference on Management Leadership and Governance*, Nice.

Torun, E., & April, K. A. (2006). Rethinking individual control: Implications for business managers. *Journal for Convergence, 7*(1), 16–19.

van Tilburg, W. A. P., & Igou, E. R. (2017). Can boredom help? Increased prosocial intentions in response to boredom. *Self and Identity, 16*(1), 82–96. https://doi.org/10.1080/15298868.2016.1218925

Waterman, A. S. (1999). Identity, the identity statuses, and identity status development: A contemporary statement. *Developmental Review, 19*(4), 591–621. https://doi.org/10.1006/drev.1999.0493

Wijbenga, F. H., & van Witteloostuijn, A. (2007). Entrepreneurial locus of control and competitive strategies – The moderating effect of environmental dynamism. *Journal of Economic Psychology, 28*(5), 566–589. https://doi.org/10.1016/j.joep.2007.04.003

Wilson, B. D. M., Harper, G. W., Hidalgo, M. A., Jamil, O. B., Torres, R. S., & Fernandez, M. I. (2010). Negotiating dominant masculinity ideology: Strategies used by gay, bisexual and questioning male adolescents. *American Journal of Community Psychology, 45*(1), 169–185. https://doi.org/10.1007/s10464-009-9291-3

Wilson, E. O. (1978). What is sociobiology? *Society, 15*(6), 10–14. https://doi.org/10.1007/BF02697770

World Bank. (2017). GINI index (World Bank estimate) – Country Ranking. https://www.indexmundi.com/facts/indicators/SI.POV.GINI/rankings

ENDNOTES

1 Throughout the book, where appropriate, we have used 'he/she/they', 'his/her/their', 'him/her/them', etc., to acknowledge the gender spectrum which different people identify with. Referring exclusively to only the male gender (as is the case in many management and leadership articles and books) when writing or talking about organizational life, is not really acceptable for us as authors. We have, however, kept the ascribed gender, when individual poets have used gendered language/terms in their own poems and/or in the explanations of their poems (to preserve the integrity of their 'voice' and 'choice').
2 Grisham, 2006, p. 487.
3 Barrett's 2016.
4 Marques & Dhiman, 2018, p. 53.
5 Hamilton, 1970.
6 Hjelle & Ziegler, 1976.
7 Lewin, 1947.
8 Waterman, 1999.
9 Jung, 2014.
10 Buckingham et al., 2011, p. 255 citing Martin Heidegger.
11 Damiani, Haywood Rolling Jr, & Wieczorek, 2017.
12 Thomas & Segal 2006, p. 115.
13 Darwin, 1859.
14 E. O. Wilson, 1978.
15 Guerin et al., 2011.
16 Marques & Dhiman, 2018, p. 54.
17 Hollis, 1998.
18 Marques & Dhiman, 2018, p. 55.
19 Insert footnote reference
20 Corlett & Pearson, 2003.
21 Hamilton, 1970.
22 Jung, 1921.
23 Hollis, 1998.
24 Kierkegaard, 2017.
25 Satre cited by Buckingham et al., 2011.
26 Throughout the book, where appropriate, we have used 'he/she/they', 'his/her/their', 'him/her/them', etc., to acknowledge the gender spectrum which different people identify with. Referring exclusively to only the male gender (as is the case in many management and leadership articles and books) when writing or talking about organizational life, is not really acceptable for us as authors. We have, however, kept the ascribed gender, when individual poets have used gendered language/terms in their own poems and/or in the explanations of their poems (to preserve the integrity of their 'voice' and 'choice').
27 Marques & Dhiman, 2018, pp. 54–55.
28 Edwards, 1991.
29 Marques, 2020.
30 Toit, Veldsman, & Zyl, 2016.
31 P. Jones, 2018.
32 Marques & Dhiman, 2018, p. 54.
33 Skinner, 2009.
34 Rotter, 1966.

35   Anderson & Schneier, 1978; Hansemark, 1998; Hsiao, Lee, & Chen, 2016; Kaufmann, Welsh, & Bushmarin, 1995; Kroeck, Bullough, & Reynolds, 2010; Littunen & Storhammar, 2000; Miller & Toulouse, 1986.

36   April, Dharani, & Peters, 2011; Torun & April, 2006.

37   Sansone & Harackiewicz, 2000, p. 43.

38   Neisser, 1967.

39   Burrow, 1917.

40   Seligman, 1972.

41   Wijbenga & van Witteloostuijn, 2007.

42   April, Dharani, & Peters, 2012.

43   Torun & April, 2006.

44   April et al., 2012.

45   Dharani, 2019.

46   April et al., 2012.

47   Bretz & Judge, 1994.

48   Randel et al., 2018.

49   Eisenhardt, 1989.

50   Marques & Dhiman, 2018, p. 55.

51   Braslow, Guerrettaz, Arkin, & Oleson, 2012, p. 471.

52   Clark & Clark, 1950.

53   Ein-Dor, 2015.

54   Boyd & Richerson, 2009.

55   Brons, 2015.

56   Racine, 2015.

57   World Bank, 2017.

58   Crenshaw, 1991.

59   Salinas & Beatty, 2013.

60   Patton, Shahjahan, & Osei-Kofi, 2010, p. 270.

61   Clarks 1950.

62   Marques & Dhiman, 2018, p. 57.

63   Maslow, 1943.

64   Randel et al., 2018.

65   Eisenhardt, 1989.

66   Levon, Milani, & Kitis, 2017; Luyt, 2012; Messner, 1998.

67   B. D. M. Wilson et al., 2010.

68   Cheng, Tracy, & Anderson, 2014, p. 243.

69   Luyt, 2015, p. 212.

70   Luyt, 2015.

71   Duguid & Thomas-Hunt, 2015.

72   Crenshaw, 1991.

73   Marques & Dhiman, 2018, p. 57.

74   Marques & Dhiman, 1998, p. 63.

75   Thomas & Segal, 2006, p. 197.

76   Mindell, 1995.

77   Marques & Dhiman, 2018, p. 57.

78   Baltaci & Balcı, 2017.

79   Huxley, 1932.

80   Glaeser & Glendon, 1998, p. 429.

81   Ahmed, 2010.

82   Manz, 2015.

83   Marques & Dhiman, 2018, p. 57.

84   Mumford, Watts, & Partlow, 2015.

85   Roszak, Gomes, & Kanner, 1995.

86   Smit, 2014.

87   cited by Iilling, 1963.

88   cited by Hollis, 1998.

89   Holmes, Bourdieu, & Wacquant, 1994.

90   Corlett & Pearson, 2003.

91   Burrow, 1917.

92   Rowan, 2015, pp. 233–234 citing Singer, 1972, p. 12.

93   Hollis, 1998.

94   Grey & Holmes, 2008, p. 788.

95   Grey & Holmes, 2008, p. 788.

96   Hollis, 1998, p. 82.

97   Toit et al., 2016.

98   Cook-Greuter, 2000; Neff, Kirkpatrick, & Rude, 2007.

99   Toit et al., 2016.

100 Frankl, 1984; Kierkegaard, 2017.

101 Thomas & Segal, 2006, p. 192.

102 van den Bosch & Taris, 2014.

103 Rowan, 2015, p. 232.

104 Rowan, 2015, p. 232.

105 Marques & Dhiman, 1998.

106 Thomas & Segal, 2006, p. 120.

107 Jung, 1960.

108 Thomas & Segal, 2006, p. 120.

109 Thomas & Segal, 2006, p. 120.

110 Marques, 2020.

111 Marques & Dhiman, 2018, p. 57.

112 Thomas & Segal, 2006, p. 193.

113 Thomas & Segal, 2006, p. 120.

114 Toit et al., 2016.

115 Marques & Dhiman, 1998.

116 King, 1999, p. 207.

117 Toit et al., 2016.

118 Randel et al., 2018, p. 95.

119 Maslow, 1943.

120 Marques & Dhiman, 2018, p. 89.

121 April, Dharani, & April, in press.

122 Diener, Emmons, Larsen, & Griffin, 1985.

123 Rojas & Veenhoven, 2013.

124 Huta, 2015.

125 Marques, 2020, p. 131.

126 Maslow, 1943.

127 A. Jones & Crandall, 1986.

128 Huta, 2015, p. 175.

129   Marques & Dhiman, 2018, p. 58.
130   Marques & Dhiman, 1998, p. 63.
131   Buetow & Wallis, 2019, p. 392.
132   Keulemans, 2016, p. 15.
133   Buetow & Wallis, 2019, p. 392.
134   Buetow & Wallis, 2019, p. 389.
135   Marques & Dhiman, 2018, p. 59.
136   Grey & Holmes, 2008.
137   Thomas & Segal, 2006, p. 71.
138   Smit, 2014.
139   Marques & Dhiman, 1998.
140   Thomas & Segal, 2006.
141   Seligman, 1975.
142   cited by King, 1999.
143   Smit, 2014.
144   Baumeister, Dale, & Sommer, 1998.
145   Schraw, 1998.
146   Hollis, 1998.
147   Gusmano, 2018.
148   Cheng, Tracy, & Anderson, 2014.
149   Marques & Dhiman, 2018.
150   Maslow 1943.
151   Thomas & Segal, 2006, p. 198.
152   Kahn, 1990.
153   Jones & Crandall, 1986.
154   Marques, 2013.
155   Hjelle & Ziegler, 1976, p. 311.
156   Spranger 1928.
157   Ibid.
158   Ibid.
159   Ibid.
160   Allport cited by Oles & Hermans, 2010.
161   Spranger 1928.
162   Bakker, Schaufeli, Leiter, & Taris, 2008.
163   Schaufeli & Salanova, 2014.
164   Kinsella, Ritchie, & Igou, 2015.
165   Franco & Efthimiou, 2018, p. 372.
166   Kinsella et al., 2015.
167   Bricheno & Thornton, 2007.
168   Coughlan, Igou, van Tilburg, Kinsella, & Ritchie, 2019.
169   Hodgetts & Rua, 2010.
170   Coughlan et al., 2019.
171   Goethals & Allison, 2012.
172   cited by Cheng, Tracy, & Anderson, 2014.
173   Iilling, 1963.
174   Maslow, 1943.
175   Fisher, 2014.
176   Nelson & Cooper, 2007.

177 Ryff, 2014.
178 Coughlan et al., 2019; Fahlman, Mercer, Gaskovski, Eastwood, & Eastwood, 2009; van Tilburg & Igou, 2017.
179 Kahn, 1990.
180 Shirom, 2010.
181 Bakker & Demerouti, 2008.
182 Csikszentmihalyi, 1990.
183 Shuck & Reio, 2014.
184 Nienaber & Martins, 2014.
185 Marques & Dhiman, 1998, p. 70.
186 King, 1999, p. 207.
187 Spranger 1928.
188 Neck & Milliman, 1994.
189 Letheby & Gerrans, 2017.
190 Moolman, 2017.
191 Mindell, 1995.
192 Derrick et al., 2005.
193 Marques & Dhiman, 2018, p. 60.
194 Marques & Dhiman, 1998, p. 70.
195 Kenneth, 1943.
196 Marques & Dhiman, 2018, p. 60.
197 Greenleaf, 2007; Greenleaf, 1995.
198 Babar, Vergo, & April, 2020.
199 King, 1999, p. 241.
200 Randel et al., 2018, p. 196.
201 Marques & Dhiman, 2018.
202 Allison & Goethals, 2013.
203 Kinsella et al., 2015, p. 30.
204 Randel et al., 2018, p. 196.
205 Mindell, 1995.
206 Miles, 2010.
207 cited by Kirby, 2010.
208 Hollis, 1998, p. 20.
209 Mindell, 1995.
210 Jung, 1921.
211 Thomas & Segal, 2006, p. 118.
212 Kierkegaard, 2017.
213 Hollis, 1998.
214 McCullough, Ashbridge, & Pegg, 1994.
215 Rotter, 1966.
216 April et al., 2012.
217 James, 2014.
218 Janis, 1972.
219 Randel et al., 2018.
220 Hollis, 1998.
221 Crenshaw, 1991.
222 Jung's 1921.
223 Letheby & Gerrans, 2017.

224 Huta, 2015.
225 Coughlan et al., 2019.
226 Spranger, 1928.
227 Toit et al., 2016.
228 Marques & Dhiman, 2018, p. 9.
229 Landa & Bybee, 2007.
230 Stoeber & Stoeber, 2009.
231 Dharani, Giannaros, & April, 2021.

www.ingramcontent.com/pod-product-compliance
Lightning Source LLC
Chambersburg PA
CBHW080609270326
41928CB00016B/2980